"It gives me great pleasure to  important and useful book, *The Tru[*] for Healing.* Among his many imp[ ] makes the important connection b[e] depression. Written for both a lay and clinical professional audi- ence, this book will be of great value to readers because it clearly lays out the parameters of the various types of depression—as well as its treatment. It also documents the relationship between child abuse of all kinds and the later possibility of lifetime depression and other serious psychological illness. Although psy- chology and psychiatry have been addressing the reality of trauma in childhood as a major cause of mental illness, before Whitfield's book this strong evidence was spread throughout the clinical and scientific literature. It has not been condensed in one volume until now. *The Truth About Depression* is an essential, clearly written explanation of one of the most common illnesses that strikes humankind."

—Paul Jay Fink, M.D.
past president, American Psychiatric Association
professor of psychiatry, Temple University
School of Medicine

"Important and useful. From his extensive experience with adult survivors of childhood trauma, Charles Whitfield, M.D., challenges conventional views about the cause and treatment of depression. Clear and well-documented, this book shows us that depression is usually best understood not as a mental illness, but rather as a *normal* response to abnormal life experiences (trau- mas), most of which go unrecognized because of their conceal- ment by shame, social nicety and taboo. Integrating current developments in neurobiology, Dr. Whitfield helps us appreciate the important distinction between experiential cause and neuro- chemical mechanism in depression. Physicians, other clinicians, patients and families will find this a helpful book about the cause and treatment of depression. Highly recommended."

—Vincent J. Felitti, M.D.
California Institutes of Preventive Medicine

THE TRUTH
about
DEPRESSION

CHOICES FOR HEALING

Charles L. Whitfield, M.D.
Bestselling author of *Healing the Child Within*

Health Communications, Inc.
Deerfield Beach, Florida

www.hci-online.com

Library of Congress Cataloging-in-Publication Data

Whitfield, Charles L.
    The truth about depression : choices in healing / Charles L. Whitfield.
        p.   cm.
    Includes bibliographical references and index.
    ISBN 0-7573-0037-5
    1. Depression, Mental—Treatment.   I. Title.

RC537.W445 2003
616.85'2706—dc21   2002032939

Publisher: Health Communications, Inc.
                3201 S.W. 15th Street
                Deerfield Beach, FL 33442-8190

Cover design by Lawna Patterson Oldfield
Inside book design by Lawna Patterson Oldfield
Cover photo ©Digital Vision

Contents

Tables

Figures

To my wife Barbara

Acknowledgments

A special acknowledgment and thanks to Barbara Whitfield for her untiring support and assistance in completing this book. Also to those who have contributed in diverse and important ways. These include Rob Anda, M.D.; Vincent Felitti, M.D.; Josh Kendall; J. Douglas Bremner, M.D.; Doreen DuPont, M.D.; Steve Gold, Ph.D.; Paul J. Fink, M.D.; Michael De Bellis, M.D.; C. Bruce Greyson, M.D.; John Kab and Robynne Moran; David Healy, M.D., and Charles Medawar. I also acknowledge everyone at Health Communications who contributed, including Christine Belleris, Allison Janse, Kathy Grant, Lawna Oldfield, Mary Ellen Hettinger, Erica Orloff, Bob Land and Peter Vegso.

I thank all of my patients who over the decades have inspired and informed me with their truth and their courage.

I am grateful for all the recent research studies by hundreds of dedicated clinical and basic scientists who continue to validate the truth about the link between trauma and illness.

And last, but certainly not least, I thank my daughter and my grandchildren, who continually give me hope for our species to finally evolve into a safe and healthy society.

Statement of Intent

This book is not intended to replace the counsel of a licensed therapist in sorting out individual concerns and healing from depression. Each person's case is unique and deserves special attention. The references in the back of this book may assist the reader with the further exploration and explanation of this important information. This information is not the final word on the subject and may represent only the tip of the iceberg of the many dimensions of depression and trauma. For a more complete account of other mental disorders, the reader may refer to my companion book, *The Truth About Mental Illness,* which will be available in September 2003.

Introduction

Throughout history we have looked for the cause of depression and other mental illness, and we still don't know it. The two major theories have long been and remain: nature (genes, biology) versus nurture (environment, family).

Our mistake has been to focus on only one or the other. In fact, based on our current knowledge, it appears that both nature and nurture are active factors in most people with mental disorders. These afflictions include:

Depression and suicidality
Anxiety disorders
Alcohol and other drug problems
Personality disorders
Attention deficit disorder (ADD) and violence
Eating disorders
Schizophrenia
Dissociative disorders

In 1999 I began writing notes for my own use that summarized what I understood about depression and other so-called mental disorders based on what I had observed in my private practice and what I was reading in the clinical scientific literature. After I wrote half of it as these "notes to myself," I realized that this information was too important not to share it. Sixteen years ago I wrote *Healing the Child Within* in a similar vein. I wrote it as educational material for my private patients, and not for public distribution. Eventually it was published by Health Communications and has sold about 1.5 million copies. Its usefulness was spread mostly by word of mouth from readers.

Since then the principles I described there have not changed. They are still valid. But the literature to back it up has expanded to such an extent that I believe that it is now worth sharing with you. Its main problem is that this valuable and validating literature is scattered over numerous journals and books, many of them unknown to most people, published both in this country and around the world—mostly over the last twenty years.

In this book I take a new look at the common problem of depression. In the second and companion volume, *The Truth About Mental Illness,* I take a similar fresh look at other common mental illness. While many helping professionals and consumers have made the connection between childhood and later trauma and the onset of mental disorders, many have not. Some may be partially aware but don't know how strong the trauma-mental disorder link is. This book will:

1. Show the strong and perhaps even causal relationship between trauma and depression;
2. Show the risks, side effects, marginal efficacy, and high cost of antidepressant and other drugs commonly used today;

3. Provide an alternative treatment and recovery program for people who have depression and a history of childhood and other traumas.

Mental illness is common. It may affect up to 40 percent of the United States population during their lifetime. Since about 1960 psychiatry has gradually been building a biological base for the mental illness that it treats. While some have criticized it, its evolving *American Psychiatric Association Diagnostic and Statistical Manual (DSM)* has helped clarify a number of ways that psychiatrists and other clinicians have come to view some of the more painful aspects of the human condition. During this time, countless articles and books were published to support their growing idea that most mental illness is due to a genetically transmitted brain problem. With the help of the drug industry, this theory spread throughout medicine and the helping professions, and eventually into the public belief system.

In 1974, the United States Congress passed the *Child Abuse Prevention and Treatment Act,* which supported the child abuse prevention and treatment movement. Although there had been sporadic papers and reports describing the effects of childhood trauma since 1896 (e.g., written by Freud, Janet, Brauer, Ferenzci and Horney), clinical and basic researchers began to report their findings on these effects, especially from the mid-1980s.

It may be timely now to promote the role of the helping professions in the treatment of traumatized children and adults, as well as the personal power of trauma survivors to help themselves heal. This is because the documented evidence in the clinical scientific literature has increased since 1980 to show a strong link between trauma and depression and other mental disorders.

In this book and the next, I describe this evidence for each of the most common illnesses. The most studied and commonly reported disorder linked with a history of childhood trauma is *depression,* which I cover in this book. I also present principles of trauma, its effects, and its treatment and recovery. In the second volume I then review the next most reported and trauma-linked disorders. These are: *addictions,* including alcohol and other drug problems, *eating disorders, nicotine dependence, post-traumatic stress disorder, anxiety disorders, dissociative disorders, personality disorders, psychosis, behavior problems* and *violence.* These two volumes will interact and support one another periodically in their text.

The data found in the nearly 300 scientific reports that I summarize and cite raises potentially important questions and concerns for all child, adolescent and adult victims of trauma and the clinicians who assist them. How can we improve our awareness of and our approach to people who have experienced childhood and later trauma? Given this new knowledge, how can mental health services best be improved? And how can survivors of trauma recognize its effects on themselves and then find effective recovery aids, including knowledgeable and experienced health professionals? While assistance from clinicians may provide an important way for trauma survivors to help identify the causal factors for their pain and help them discover how best to handle it, it is ultimately up to affected individuals to become aware of the link between their pain and numbness and their past trauma.

In my research over the years I am sure that I have missed some important articles, chapters and books that support the numerous findings that I cite here in this book. I hope that the authors of studies I may have missed will tell me of their work so that I can add it to this already massive collection of important but overlooked data proving my observations.

I also ask that the reader bear with me when the reading may be dry. By translating this wealth of otherwise dense and complex information into a more reader friendly and useful format, this may be the first time that anyone has gathered and explained the truth about depression and other mental illness and our choices to heal from them.

We can step out of the box of our conservative and sometimes limited beliefs about the nature and cause of mental illness. I ask the reader to consider opening your mind to the possibility that trauma from childhood could be contributing to or even causing some mental illness. And perhaps with this new information you will understand an important alternative to healing it. Armed with this understanding, people with depression and other so-called mental illnesses can now consider more possibilities and choices as they heal. At the same time, some of their family may now be able to support these alternative forms of healing. This book offers state-of-the-art information that I hope will allow affected people and their families, their clinicians and other important people in their lives, to expand their understanding of the mystery of depression and other mental illness.

Charles L. Whitfield, M.D.
Atlanta, Georgia
January 2003

1 THE TRUTH ABOUT DEPRESSION

The truth about depression is that it is not as advertised. It is not what some special-interest groups tell us. It is not the single, simple disorder that drug companies and some mental health groups may claim. It is not simply a genetically transmitted disorder of brain chemistry. It is not a brain serotonin problem.[339, 769] And it does not reliably respond to antidepressant drugs. And these drugs are not the only available recovery aid.[339]

These special-interest groups may have misled us.

Their special interest is in large part about money, power and influence in the diagnosis and treatment of common mental health problems. Much of what they tell us about depression and other mental illness is actually in their own best interest. It is not always in the interest of the people who experience the pain.

At the top of the list of these groups is the drug industry. While drug companies have produced some effective pharmaceutical agents, such as antibiotics, insulin and others, they fall short when it comes to mental illness. But to help market and sell their drugs, they have often resorted to making up a limited theory about the cause of mental illness. This theory is that depression and other common mental disorders are caused by genetic and other biological defects that are somehow inherent in our makeup. In other words, they claim that we are born with faulty genes and brains—which their chemical will fix. A problem is that after a century of looking for a cause, and since 1960 looking for a "magic bullet" drug, we still do not know what causes depression and other mental illness, and our drug treatments for them do not work very well.

Influenced and often financially supported by the drug industry, and probably for other reasons, health insurance companies, including those who call themselves "managed care," some academics, professional organizations, some mental health advocacy groups and government agencies have bought this unproven theory. These groups, which some call a major part of the "mental health industry," have used this limited theory as a basic principle in diagnosing and treating people hurting with what they call "mental illness." On the surface, they espouse the more accurate and balanced *bio-psycho-social* theory of mental illness. But they focus primarily on the biological aspects of these disorders and commonly ignore or even neglect the physical, psychological and social traumas in the person's past and current history.

Though it is in their name, managed care companies don't really appear to care. They are pure business. They are *managed money*. Some have called them "managed greed." Their goal appears to be to make as much money as they can without getting into legal trouble. For starters, just look at the salaries of their CEOs. Forget helping sick people in need. Most do everything they can to delay or disapprove coverage and not pay clinicians appropriately for their services. Some, such as the nonprofit HMO Kaiser-Permanente, are exceptions to the rule.

In my thirty-seven years as a physician, and for the last twenty-five years of that time as a psychotherapist, I have seen and assisted countless patients with a wide variety of mental and physical illnesses. Whether their problem was depression, an addiction or some other illness, in most of them I have not seen convincing evidence that the cause of their disorders was solely a genetic or another biological defect. In fact, I regularly saw evidence for another equally, if not more important, factor: a history of repeated childhood trauma. Among all of these people, I have rarely seen one who had a major psychological or psychiatric illness who grew up in a healthy family.

Over the past century, numerous observers have looked at trauma and how it affects us. But since 1980, there has been an outpouring of nearly 300 clinical scientific studies that have shown a strong link between repeated childhood trauma and the development of subsequent mental illness—often decades later. In most of these investigations, the authors have controlled for other potential associations with mental symptoms and disorders (called "modulating" or "confounding" variables in the research trade), and they have usually found them to play a less important role than did the trauma itself. These findings have major implications for the prevention and treatment of mental illness, which I will address throughout this and the next book.

THE ACE STUDY

As an example, one of those studies conducted on perhaps the largest sample of people was the "ACE" (adverse childhood experiences) study.[254] The information that it has provided us is not just helpful—it is astounding. Internist and researcher Vincent Felitti and epidemiologist Rob Anda and their colleagues looked at 9,508 middle-class, middle-aged people in Southern California. All were members of a health maintenance organization (HMO), who were medically evaluated, and then each completed a sixty-eight-question survey about seven categories of childhood trauma and subsequent illness. The authors also had the medical records of each patient with which to verify and correlate any of these findings. They found that a large percentage of this general medical clinic population reported the following traumatic experiences from their childhoods.

1. Lived with problem drinker,
   alcoholic or street-drug user 25.6%
2. Were sexually abused (overt abuse only) 22.0%
3. Lived with mentally ill person 18.8%
4. Saw mother treated violently 12.5%
5. Were emotionally abused 11.1%
6. Were physically abused 10.8%
7. A household member went to prison 3.4%

One or more ACEs occurred in 59 percent of these 9,508 people. Thus, childhood trauma may be more common than we thought.

For those people who had *four or more* adverse childhood experiences, the following disease conditions and the risk factors for each were found to be substantially more common when compared to those persons with no ACEs (see table, next page).

These serious and life-threatening medical conditions and disorders were clearly more common (by the affixed numbers) than they are known to exist in the general population. Note that these

Disorders Associated with a History of Unresolved Childhood Trauma & Their Risk Factors

(data from ACE study, reference 254)

Disorder	Risk Factor	Disorder	Risk Factor
Cigarette smokers to **2+** times those with no ACEs		Had a sexually transmitted disease	2.5
Severe obesity	1.6	Coronary heart disease	2.2
No leisure time physical activity	1.3	Cancer	1.9
Depressed 2 weeks or more past year	4.6	Stroke	2.4
Suicide attempt	12.2	Chronic obstructive pulmonary disease	3.9
Alcoholic	7.4	Diabetes	1.6
Illegal drug use	4.7	Broken bones	1.6
Injected drugs	10.3	Hepatitis/jaundice	2.4
50+ intercourse partners	3.2	Fair/poor health	2.2

numbers (in epidemiology called "odds ratios" or "risk factors") each represent multiples of 100 percent, so that a risk factor of 2 means that a person's chance for having that particular illness was 200 percent greater, or happened twice as often as in people with no repeated childhood trauma (ACEs). As an example, smoking cigarettes is well-known to double a person's risk of having a heart attack. Epidemiologists consider such a *doubling* of an odds ratio to represent a *strong* or *substantial* degree of risk, and they believe an odds ratio of 3 to be extremely high. The ACE study revealed five disorders or illnesses to have an odds ratio of from 1.3 to 1.9, six were from 2.2 to 2.5, and the remaining seven were from 3.2 to an astounding risk of 12.2 times that for those who had no identified childhood trauma. When compared to most risk factors that both researchers and the public are used to seeing, these figures are staggering.

Thus, these are not the small numbers that they may initially appear to be. Don't let the above numbers and figures confuse you. Their results are telling us about how dangerous it is not to recognize and treat repeated childhood trauma. This message is true for people with illness that occurs decades after their experience of the repeated trauma.

Depression

Using the example of depression, the study found that those people with four or more ACEs reported 4.6 times more experiences of having been depressed for at least two weeks over the past year. Furthermore, the more ACEs a person had experienced, the more likely they were to have been depressed, as shown in Figure 1.1. This illustrates a dramatic *graded increase* of the relationship between the trauma-effect (depression) link. In epidemiology, this magnitude of an increasing relationship, called a "dose-response effect," is also considered to be extremely high. The results show that the more unrecognized, unaddressed and untreated is childhood trauma, the more depression.

While these results are impressive, if other researchers were unable to replicate the ACE study's results, its findings would be invalidated. But the opposite has happened, as I will show throughout this book. Nearly every study that has examined a potential relationship between trauma and depression has found it to occur to a statistically significant degree. These investigations have also found a similar trauma-disorder link for most of the other common or major mental illnesses, which I will describe in the next book.

The truth about depression is that the published clinical scientific evidence overwhelmingly shows the link between having a history of childhood trauma and the development of subsequent depression. The truth is that antidepressant and other psychoactive drugs are not as effective as we would like them to be in ameliorating the symptoms of depression.

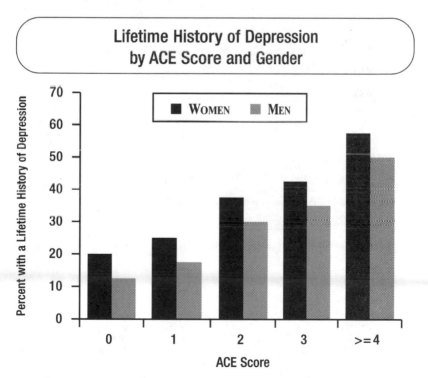

FIGURE 1.1. THE INCREASING GRADED RELATIONSHIP BETWEEN DEPRESSION AND CHILDHOOD TRAUMA

From Anda, R. *Presentation of ACE Study Data,* CDC, Atlanta, GA, March 11, 2002.

The truth is that the very diagnosis of "depression" may be inaccurate and at times even totally invalid for many people so labeled. And the most important truth is that people with depression have several more choices that they can use to heal their pain than using drugs alone.

In this book, I will describe these truths and more.

2 WHAT IS "DEPRESSION"?

The original description in 400 B.C. of the group of symptoms and signs that we now call "depression" was already fairly accurate, as shown in Table 2.1. Called *melancholia* for twenty-three hundred years, it included having an experience of prolonged sadness and fear, with a decreased appetite and insomnia, sometimes with somatic symptoms such as gastrointestinal distress, suicidality, and in extreme cases, a limited or "circumscribed" delusion.[381]

Over two thousand years later, Emil Kraepelin named melancholia "depression," and further described it as having a decrease in thought, feelings and activity. But even over halfway through the twentieth century it was not a popular diagnosis among the helping professionals or the public. In his review, independent London researcher and consumer advocate Charles Medawar said, "In the 1960s, the lack of any defined, mass market for depression inevitably meant that pharmaceutical companies were reluctant to try to develop drugs for it.[523]" There were no good epidemiological studies, but with an eye for opportunities in the early 1960s, Merck Sharp & Dohme sent fifty thousand copies of

Table 2.1. A History of Depression

Time	Description at the Time
400 B.C. to 1500 A.D.	*Melancholia:* Prolonged sadness and fear. Despondent, low appetite, insomnia; irritable, restless, sometimes with GI distress, suicidality & circumscribed or limited delusion.
16th to 17th century	References to: somatic symptoms, guilt & "partial insanity" (delusion). Continuum of severity from hypochondriasis to melancholia to mania.
18th century	Little additional description.
19th century	"Partial insanity" idea dropped, though mono-delusions were still seen.
20th century	Called *depression* by Kraepelin, as decrease in thought, feelings & activity. Vegetative signs & symptoms. Drug co's. support biological psychiatry. Although trauma is a major cause[10, 254, 360, 788] depression is still seen as a mostly biological problem.

*Some part of this now outdated, untrue and even humorous "black bile" theory nevertheless served a useful purpose related to its metaphorical meanings. For example, Galen described melancholia as caused by a black substance, the "black bile," throwing a shadow, wherein a dark vapor rises from it, dimming the light and confusing our mind and vision, leaving gloom and dejection. Combined with a feeling of being "weighed down," this gives images of darkness and heaviness and can offer a beginning understanding of what it may be like to be depressed to those who have not experienced it personally.

(compiled from references 381, 363, 761, 798)

Causal Theory	Treatment Theory
Due to humoral (blood, yellow bile, black bile, phlegm) imbalance (as most mental disorders). Experts of the time thought black bile excess was the cause. This theory persisted through the 17 century.	Decrease black bile by purgatives,* diuretics, or, if severe, bloodletting. Massages, warm baths, pleasant company, encouragement, reassurance and even coitus (for evacuation & calming).
Constriction of soul & animal spirits, chemical problem in brain, with sadness & fear as a result (Willis).	Continued the above, plus diet & exercise (Galen). Divert soul from troubling passions; spa waters, hypnotics (Willis).
Poor circulation of blood, lymph & nerve fluid.	Emerging psychosomatic orientation.
Other causes proposed & explored: heredity, nutritional, cerebral anemia & nerve disorders.	Added tonics & stimulants. Pinel rejected purgatives & bloodletting.
Psychologic & -analytic are examined, though biological theories predominate. Neurotransmitter problems. A group of neuroendocrine-metabolic disorders. Relation to PTSD, trauma & normal grieving (1917–2000) (minority view).	Live elsewhere, with a happy family (mild case) or asylum (if severe), a wholistic "rest cure" (Kraepelin).** Psychoanalysis, various psycho-therapies. ECT (1940s to present). Antidepressant drugs. Trauma psychology approach***.

**Meyer recommended adding a search for what the patient can change, a common-sense psychotherapy (kindly, humanely searching the patient's past and current life history), with the patient as collaborator.
***Since trauma is a common cause of depressive disorders, this approach includes a careful trauma history, physical examination, differential diagnosis and then tailoring the most effective recovery aids from the seventeenth century to the present (see, e.g., refs. 96, 171, 174, 186, 363, 517, 656, 793). Recovery usually takes time and cannot be rushed.

a short book on depression to psychiatrists, internists and family physicians. As a new physician at that time, I received and read this booklet, and remember underlining parts of it.

From the 1960s to 1994, the American Psychiatric Association's *Diagnostic and Statistical Manual of Mental Disorders (DSM)* refined the diagnostic criteria for all of the psychiatric disorders, including depression.[7, 8] While helpful in several ways, it has had some serious drawbacks, including that it has not fully addressed all of the many subtypes of depression, which I discuss below, although it did suggest ruling out organic causes.

DIAGNOSIS

Medawar asked, "If *DSM-IV* were a fishing net . . . what mesh size should be used to catch depressed fish but not others?" He answers, "The mesh has been getting smaller over the years, but is this a good or bad thing?"[523] Since its first edition in 1952, the *DSM* has contributed to helping legitimize a dramatic increase in drug use among so-called "mental health" patients. To diagnose what it calls "major depression," in addition to having a sad or down mood (criterion A1), the *DSM-IV* requires the finding of only *four* of its remaining eight symptoms or signs (criteria A2–9), from decreased appetite to low energy to low self-esteem. These diagnostic criteria include:

A1. Sad or down mood *or* anxiety *or* depressed facial expression *or* body aches and pains
  2. Loss of interest or pleasure
  3. ↓ (decreased) or ↑ (increased) appetite

4. $\downarrow$ or $\uparrow$ sleep
5. $\downarrow$ psychomotor activity
6. Low energy or fatigue
7. Low self-esteem
8. Difficulty concentrating or remembering
9. Suicidal ideation or attempts
B1. Exclusion of other disorders . . . (See full criteria in *DSM-IV*)[8]

If we use these suggested *DSM* diagnostic criteria, how accurate is it? While some have criticized the *DSM* (e.g., Kutchins & Kirk[464]; Caplan[133]), just looking at these proposed criteria may tweak us to wonder how "low self-esteem" or any of these other symptoms or signs alone (with the exception of suicidality) might have been chosen.

A MORE LIKELY CAUSE

Does such a diagnosis of "depression" automatically indicate that people will require the daily ingesting of antidepressant drugs (ADPs) to heal from their condition? Does it mean that they have only one kind of depression—i.e., the "genetically transmitted" variety, and therefore should automatically be prescribed ADPs? When might other treatment aids be indicated? When we find a person with symptoms of depression, how should we proceed with making a differential diagnosis? Several observers have emphasized that "depression" is not a single disorder, but that it has a number of subtypes.[127, 426, 812] These include the two major ones of exogenous (external) and endogenous (internal) origins,

Table 2.2. Major Depressive Disorder Subgroups

(compiled & expanded from refs. 127, 339, 424, 425, 426, 812)

Subgroup	Causes	Incidence (estimate)	Treatment	Prognosis
Exogenous— Secondary, (situational, reactive, bereavement)	Trauma, major loss, chemical dependence, postpartum, corticosteroids, thyroid disease	60–70%	Trauma focused &/or treat medical disorder	Good if treatment is appropriate kind & duration, ± ADP drugs (if support given long term)
Atypical (reversed neurovegetative symptoms)	Trauma common	(part of exogenous above)	Trauma focus if present, ± ADP drugs	
Endogenous Primary, familial, "genetic"	Trauma may occur in family transgenerationally; SAD** (also exogenous)	30–40%*	ADP drugs, plus trauma Tx. focus, if trauma history present	Fair to good, ADP drugs often don't work; may be mistaken for exogenous
Psychotic	Trauma possible (611–613)	Uncommon	ADP drugs ± neuroleptic drugs	Poor-fair

*Based on the data on the depression-trauma link presented in this book, this may be a high estimate; we do not know the exact or even approximate percentage.
**SAD = Seasonal Affective Disorder

with further subtypes under each of these, as shown in Table 2.2. I and others believe that treatment of the whole person would be based on the *origin* of the depressive symptoms, and not on the assumption of a proposed genetically based disorder alone.

For the person with bothersome *endogenous* (internally generated) depression, i.e., a person whose history and other findings have no exogenous (external) causes, perhaps a trial on an ADP would offer this person a chance of lessening their symptoms for a time. In my estimation, at the most, endogenous depression appears to make up no more than 30 to 40 percent of all depression. However, for the person with *exogenous* depression, treatment would include measures that would be appropriate for ameliorating the particular cause(s) or associations.

"Anxiety" (which I usually prefer to call *fear*) is a common part of depression, and "depressed" people often have other co-morbid disorders, including anxiety disorders such as post-traumatic stress disorder (PTSD) (common among trauma survivors), personality disorders, thought disorders (schizophrenia or other psychoses) and addictions. Each of these has a specific treatment approach—and ADPs may or may not be an appropriate part of the regimen. Some clinicians believe that a brain serotonin abnormality has more to do with anxiety than with depression, but since 1990 drug companies have promoted it for depression more than they have for anxiety disorders, so by habit we tend to associate it more with "depression."[339, 759]

Not only does depression occur commonly as a *part* of PTSD, but PTSD can mimic nearly every diagnostic criterion of depression, as shown in Table 2.3. Research psychiatrist J. Douglas Bremner said:

There also is considerable overlap in the actual symptoms listed under the trauma spectrum disorders. For instance, many symptoms of depression are equivalent to symptoms of PTSD. Psychomotor agitation can be rephrased as hyperarousal, and hopelessness as a sense of foreshortened future. Other symptoms that are identical in the criteria for depression and PTSD include decreased sleep, decreased concentration, and feelings of being cut off from others. In fact, the only symptom of depression that is not included in the criteria for PTSD is depressed mood, and on a clinical basis feelings of depression are common in patients with PTSD. The only symptoms of PTSD that are not part of depression are increased startle, feeling on guard, flashbacks, and amnesia. There are also important overlaps between PTSD and other disorders.

What this can mean for any given person is that they may not have a simple biological disorder that clinicians can call "depression." They may also have another, perhaps more important one: PTSD. And PTSD suggests some kind of trauma, for which there is now a *way to heal* from its numerous and varied effects. Thus, making a preliminary diagnosis of depression only opens a door for us. It does not let us see the contents of the room, much less enter into it so that we can explore it further (as shown in Figure 2.1). So it is up to us as patients and clinicians to keep our awareness at a maximum so we can find the real cause of the depressive symptoms and signs. A problem is that people with symptoms of depression may feel so down and have such a low energy that they don't have the full awareness to look for the real cause *without outside help.*

Table 2.3. *DSM-IV* Diagnostic Criteria for Major Depression, as Compared with Associated Symptoms in Trauma Survivors and PTSD

Major Depression (A1 + any 4 of A2–9)	Trauma survivors/PTSD
A1. Sad/down mood, or anxiety, or depressed faces, or body aches and pains	
	Commonly have any
2. Loss of interest or pleasure	or a combination of
3. ↓ or ↑ appetite	these signs or symptoms
4. ↓ or ↑ sleep	*(see Bremner 2002).*[82]
5. ↓ Psychomotor activity	
6. Low energy or fatigue	Monitoring these symptoms
7. Low self-esteem	doesn't fully address
8. Difficulty concentrating or remembering	patient's quality
	of life *(see text).*
9. Suicidal ideation or attempts	

Figure 2.1. Exploring the Door and Room of Depression

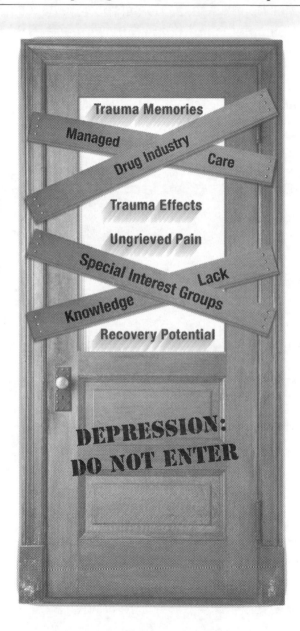

3 A DOUBLE-EDGED SWORD

From 1970 to 1990, three developments came together that resulted in what is now a large business among the helping professions and the drug industry. These included: 1) drug companies' gradual escalation of ADP drug development and marketing, eventually resulting in large financial profits, 2) the emergence of the field of neuroscience; and 3) the transition of modern psychiatry from a then-eclectic field that included psychodynamics, drug treatments and social issues, into one that focused heavily on the biological aspects of human health and disorders, which turned out to mean using drugs almost exclusively. But this now booming business has had the qualities of a double-edged sword.

On the plus side, we have learned much useful information about ourselves, our bodies, and how we respond to stress and various mental disorders. We have delved deeper into the physiology and biochemistry of the brain and nervous system, and in a number of ways have reached a greater understanding of ourselves. We have also improved the ways we treat people with some mental disorders.

MEDICALIZING MENTAL HEALTH

On the downside, we have allowed the health insurance industry, with its managed "care," and the drug industry, with its mass advertising and inflated prices, to distract us often from getting the appropriate assistance that we need to help us heal ourselves. In its need to survive, psychiatry renamed itself psychiatric medicine. It has now mostly dropped using psychotherapy as a primary aid to help people heal, to using, instead, briefer sessions for diagnostic and drug treatment evaluations, as required and enforced by the clinical and money managers of the health insurance industry. This leaves the patients responsible, if they are aware enough to do so, to find and pay for recovery aids that their real self seeks, since most health insurance companies won't pay for this appropriate and deeper kind of care.

Unfortunately, this inner-urging of our true self to heal is usually so subtle that most people living in this loud and stressful world can't hear it for a number of reasons, and instead may join a growing number of drug-dependent consumers. Several factors influence the genesis and maintenance of this insidious social trance, from multibillion-dollar psychoactive drug advertising to countless diversions from the actual underlying causes of many mental and physical disorders.

DRUG MONEY

Another factor is the dependence of academic psychiatry, which trains future psychiatrists, upon the drug industry and U.S. government for much of its financial support. This payment is in the form of grants or other funding from the drug companies that pay substantial parts of the salaries of a large percentage of the psychiatry faculties and staff. But there is a catch here: If faculty members do not produce positive results in favor of the drug being tested, in some cases their income may be in jeopardy and their future grant applications may not be approved. What is more, government grants are usually for biological and sometimes psychosocial research, while mostly excluding studies on the effects of trauma.[613a]

In spite of this bleak picture, over the past twenty years many helpful research reports on the multiple psychological, social and physical effects of trauma have been published in clinical scientific journals. These have given us an early and rich supply of potentially useful information that we can use to help heal ourselves. Unfortunately, these few reports have made up an estimated less than 1 percent of the entire published research reports from psychiatry, psychology and the other helping professions. This is regrettable, because recent data-based reports suggest that a substantially large percentage of common disorders are caused by or associated with having a history of childhood trauma. I will describe and summarize nearly three hundred such important study results throughout this book and the next.

GENERAL MEDICINE

In a similar vein, medicine in general has avoided looking deeper into the recognition and treatment of the effects of trauma that frequently underlie common medical conditions. Most of the concerns described above for psychiatry apply to the field of medicine as a whole, except that medicine has always had a strong biological base and has given almost no attention to the causal and treatment links between physical disorders and childhood trauma.

However, a few researchers and clinicians, with colleagues from other fields, have noticed some of these important connections. For example, Felitti has observed that of the ten most common causes of death, nine result from diseases, disorders or conditions that are commonly caused by or associated with having had a history of childhood trauma. Table 3.1 shows a summary list of these, with the causal behaviors or disorders for each and the risk for having each of them as shown in the landmark ACE study.[254] How could we have gone for all this time without recognizing this possibility, much less not making the connection?

These and numerous other studies show us that we have been overlooking a major causal factor that has practical application in the treatment of many common medical disorders and conditions. Now, clinicians can ask their patients and clients about a history of various traumas. Felitti said:

Most clinicians don't like to think about any form of child abuse, and as a result we know little about it. That self-protective belief and the resulting ignorance that it engenders in us harms patients. It also frustrates us, because it precludes our understanding significant numbers of the most difficult cases in our practices. Child abuse is common. What is rare is its recognition, and so we ask every patient who comes through our office if they have ever been sexually molested [or experienced any other form of child abuse or neglect]. When someone answers, "Yes," our response is, "Tell me how that affected you later in life . . ."

Table 3.1. Ten Leading Causes of Death, with Cause or Association of Disease/Disorder and Risk of Having a History of Childhood Trauma/Adverse Childhood Experience (ACE) *(expanded from refs. 253, 254)*

Cause of Death	Cause/Association of Disease/Disorder	ACE Risk*
Heart disease	Obesity, smoking, unhandled anger (at having been abused)	1.6– 2.2x
Cancer	Smoking, early intercourse	2+x
Stroke	High blood pressure (HBP)	?**
Asthma & emphysema	Smoking *(Felitti & Anda believe most smokers today are trauma survivors)*	2+x
Accidents	High-risk behaviors; unstable gait from obesity/intoxication; drunk driving, etc., from alcohol or drugs	3.2– 7.4x
Pneumonia	Smoking, alcoholism & other drug dependence	2+– 7.4x
Diabetes	Obesity	1.6x
Suicide	Depression	4.6x
AIDS	IV drug use and other high-risk behaviors	10.3x
Liver disease	Alcohol and other drug use	4.7–
Summary of the 10 common diseases and disorders	Listed above: **High-risk behaviors** —7x (including: **alcoholism** & **other drug misuse**—6x, & **smoking**— 4x), **Obesity**—2x, HBP—?x, **Depression**—4.6x ***	10.3x 9,805 patients: 1.6– 10.3x the control population

*Risk factors, from: Felitti et al. [254]

**Cornell cardiologist Samuel Mann, M.D. (1999) has some suggestive data that HBP (high blood pressure) can be associated with past trauma, in his 1999 book *Healing Hypertension.* [513]

***All in *italics* are commonly caused by or associated with having a history of childhood trauma.

*That's a good phrase to remember. It's easy to say, implies seri-
ous interest, and it is non-threatening to the listener. All you need
to do in response is to listen.*[253]

If we look back at Table 2.1 in chapter 2, we can see that the
recommended treatment for depression during the particular historical time was based on the existing theory of what caused it.
Most of these treatments were helpful, and some were not.
Several hundred years ago, Galen prescribed a healthy diet and
exercise, which today remains a useful treatment aid.[381]
Supportive care was often a part of the treatment given, but not
always; for example, today appropriate supportive care is usually
not provided, since most managed "care" will not approve of it
by paying for even a reasonable percentage of its cost.

*   *   *

Currently, the prevailing causal theory of depression is by a
"genetic" transmission that is manifested by a proposed biochemical abnormality of the brain, which translates to "use ADP
drugs," or at worst, electroshock treatment. Yet, this approach,
while safer and more humane-sounding today, may in the future
appear to be not too far removed from the primitive use of
"decreasing black bile by purgatives, diuretics, or, if severe, by
bloodletting," as shown in Table 2.1 earlier.

However, today there remains a constructive holdover from
Meyer, Kraepelin and others who observed that depression is
often caused by or at least associated with having a history of
situational causes, including childhood trauma. Indeed, Meyer

recommended adding a search for what the patient can change*, a commonsense psychotherapy (kindly, humanely searching the patient's past and current life history), with the patient as collaborator. In the early twentieth century, Kraepelin described what today might be called staying away from "toxic" people, even if some of them may be from our own family of origin.[381] Since trauma is a common cause of depressive disorders, this approach includes a careful trauma history, physical examination, differential diagnosis, and then tailoring the most effective recovery aids from the seventeenth century to the present (see, e.g., references 96, 171, 174, 186, 363, 517, 656, 793). Recovery usually takes time and cannot be rushed.

Qualifier for Book

The central thesis of this book is to show the strong link between repeated childhood trauma and subsequent mental illness. However, important parts of the truths about depression and other mental illness involve a complex web of interlocking clinical, financial and political influences.

Prior to the recent biological psychiatry era, which began around the 1960s, health professionals learned about mental illness and its treatment from a combination of reading textbooks and journals, supervision from more experienced clinicians, attending continuing education programs, and their own

---

*The Serenity Prayer, written by Reinhold Niebuhr and adopted by the fellowship of Alcoholics Anonymous, says:
"God grant me the serenity to accept the things I cannot change, the courage to change the things I can, and the wisdom to know the difference."

observations while providing direct patient care. Since then, there has been a gradual but strong encroachment by the drug companies, who have taken on a progressively increasing role of educating health professionals, especially psychiatrists and other physicians, about the nature of mental illness. This situation presents a clear conflict of interest. Over the last few decades and today, the drug makers are calling the majority of the educational shots. They not only make the drugs, but directly or indirectly, and usually subtly, they define the nature of mental disorders to fit their product.

Because of the above, throughout this book, where appropriate, I will point out examples of the reasons that it is not only inappropriate for the drug companies to be educating us to this extent, but that it is also a clear and major conflict of interest that translates to a lack of trust and to a possible toxic monopoly (in the practice of law, this kind of behavior is sometimes called "undue influence"). A recent editorial in the medical journal *The Lancet* said, "[The drug] Industry's ubiquitous influence has corrupted the integrity of medical research and the scientific literature upon which scientific research is built"[470]. It has done so by paying or otherwise manipulating researchers and authors to speak in favor of their drugs. In addition, due to the fact that government agencies such as the FDA and its equivalents in other countries are commonly enmeshed with the drug companies and the academics who research and write about mental illness and its treatment, they are increasingly unable to objectively monitor and when necessary restrict the drug companies or restrain them to protect the public.[47a, 165a, 676] Scientists who conduct the research are too often being unduly influenced by the drug industry, as are some bioethicists (who are supposed to watch and help them be honest).[282, 676] This escalating and precarious situation is similar to the fox guarding the henhouse. Finally, many otherwise reputable professional associations, such as the American Psychiatric Association, are increasingly funded by drug companies, and thereby are possibly losing their objectivity. For the reader who is not interested in this part of the story, feel free to skip these paragraphs or sections throughout this book.

4 THE GENETICS AND BRAIN CHEMISTRY THEORY

What percentage of people with "depression" have a genetic cause? We don't know.

For the past fifteen years or so, the predominant view is that depression and most other mental disorders and diseases are genetically transmitted disorders of brain chemistry. This is in part because of the sometime-finding of suggestive evidence for such an abnormality in mice, rats or other nonhuman animals, and rarely in humans. While most research papers on numerous aspects of the cause of mental illness have made such a conclusion, the actual evidence for it does not appear to be as solid as we have come to believe.[178, 572, 573, 644, 759]

How then can we *prove* the hypothesis of the existence of a purely "genetic" cause for depression (or any other disorder)? Doing so can be complicated.

A FAMILY HISTORY

One way to *suspect* (but not prove) a genetic cause is to show that it runs from generation to generation in the first-degree relatives in the lineage of the same family over time. But 1) we usually have only one generation (i.e., the patient or subject) to examine directly. Since we usually can't directly examine others in the patient's family, all we can do is to ask the subject in front of us to describe their perceptions of the behaviors and moods of their relatives. And 2) most depression researchers don't appear to ask about the childhood trauma histories of their subjects. They also do not consider the fact that 3) living with a depressed parent may also be traumatic in itself for a child.[10, 254]

Most depression researchers don't usually ask about the childhood trauma histories of their subjects, or of their depressed family members. We are then left with these two gaping holes of missing information—a very limited, usually only a one- or at best two-generational history of depressive symptoms, plus no assessment of a possible history of childhood trauma—which would otherwise be crucial in trying to sort out this important question of nature and nurture.

By contrast, numerous peer-reviewed data-based studies on large numbers of people suggest that as many as 60 to 70 percent most likely have their "depressive" symptoms because of or associated with a history of having been abused as children, as suggested and shown in Tables 2.2 and 4.1, and further developed in chapter 5. Many of these trauma survivors in appropriate treatment and recovery, over time, express and grieve the pain that remains with them as part of the effects of their trauma. Doing so helps them lessen their sadness, low energy and other depressive symptoms.[132, 791]

LABORATORY FINDINGS

In addition to looking for a long, multigenerational family history of depression, researchers could methodically seek out specific laboratory tests that might indicate its presence. But there is no laboratory test known today to make or support a diagnosis of depression. In the 1980s an abnormal dexamethasone suppression test (DST—a special measure of hormone function) was thought to be a "biochemical marker" for depression, but it was eventually found to be nonspecific and unreliable.[640a] Later, the abnormal DST results among many depressed people were reported to be due to the decreased caloric content of their diets.[550] An assumed rapid eye movement (REM) sleep abnormality associated with depression was also disproved.[550] Researchers have likewise looked for specific abnormal genes among people with depression, and have not found them.[178] Finally, there is no reliable way to measure or show an abnormal serotonin or any other neurotransmitter level in people with depression.[759]

GENETIC MARKERS

A third and perhaps final way to *suspect* (but not prove) a genetic cause, factor or association with depression is to repeat the same procedure as in *Laboratory Findings* above, but with a *genetic marker* as the laboratory test in question. In my reading to date, I have not seen any of these ways to try to prove a genetic cause, factor or association with depression demonstrated convincingly.

From reviewing the literature, my sense is that since no one has proved a genetic cause, factor or association for depression, the best that we can do is to *suspect* its existence as a possibility. But depression researchers, with their apparently fragmentary data, have gone beyond suspecting. Rather, they have *assumed* that this genetic hypothesis is true, even though they have not yet proven it.[178, 406, 572, 573, 638]

DRUG RESPONSE

A few researchers and clinicians have also used a fourth way to try to prove their genetic hypothesis, but it is not a valid test. The sometimes proposed "test" has been to give people with symptoms of depression drugs that they have deemed to be "antidepressants"—and then observe their response. If the patient has a positive response, i.e., a lessening of their symptoms, they assume that not only do the "antidepressants" work, but—in a kind of sideways or backwards thinking—that this finding also demonstrates that they were indeed "depressed." As I will show below, it appears that despite several decades of research and clinical experience, unfortunately there is no convincing evidence that antidepressants work much better than do placebos. And even if they did help the depression, that would not prove its existence.

GENETIC EVIDENCE FOR MENTAL DISORDERS

Not only are most of the subtypes of depression lacking for convincing evidence that they are caused by genetic transmission, but the same can be said for most other mental disorders. The question remains: Are most psychiatric disorders genetically transmitted abnormalities of brain chemistry? Geneticist Dave

Curtis said, "In spite of an intensive worldwide effort, to date there have been no convincing localizations of any genes influencing susceptibility to functional [i.e., those not caused by physical medical conditions] psychiatric disorders." This is a bold but apparently accurate statement of the facts, made by a widely published, international authority on the genetics of psychiatric disorders, on whether the hypothesis that most psychiatric disorders are genetically transmitted abnormalities of brain chemistry is valid. He adds, "However there seems clear evidence for such genetic influences to exist and it is not unreasonable to hope that over the next few years genes may be found which account for at least a proportion of these diseases".[178] In such absence of direct or hard evidence, lawyers might say that this assumption is, at best, based on a small degree of circumstantial evidence.

What evidence do we have? Most consider the existence of a positive family history to be at least a start in assuming that heritability might be present. But, as I mentioned earlier, *child maltreatment also runs in families,* and childhood trauma is much more common than are genetic defects. Thus, *a positive family history may also indicate* the presence of *childhood trauma,* which could also be a cause of depression and other mental disorders. A problem is embedded in our current state of collective (un)awareness and many helping professionals' lack of treatment skills for assisting trauma survivors, plus pressure from the drug and managed care industries, and from academic psychiatry and medicine. These all bring us to the erroneous conclusion that it may be easier to try to take a shortcut around human suffering by believing the biologic hypothesis, thus taking a "biologic bypass" around addressing the effects of trauma. Thus, we bypass the history of trauma, its probable causal connection to the effects of trauma (i.e., "mental illness") and the ways we can assist people as they heal, and instead focus on their symptoms and/or their assumed brain biochemistry.

Table 4.1 shows an outline of family history and possible genetic associations among selected common psychiatric disorders, with the observed frequency for each of a history of childhood trauma. Of all the psychiatric disorders, it appears that alcoholism shows the most research data to support a genetic hypothesis as one of its possible causes. There are three main bits of evidence that alcoholism is a genetically inherited disorder or that it is at least a familial one, i.e., that it tends to run in families across generations. These include: 1) family studies, 2) twin studies, and 3) adoption studies.[18] Family studies show that children of alcoholics had a three- to fourfold increased risk of becoming alcoholic. Twin studies compared rates of alcoholism among fraternal twins (30 to 39 percent) with identical twins (60 percent). Finally, initial adoption studies show that adopted sons of alcoholic fathers had a four times higher risk of alcoholism, although more follow-up data are needed, and most studies go back only one and at the most two generations. There is also evidence that other kinds of chemical dependence run in families.[532]

More recently, a fourth venue has opened: physiologic and biochemical markers of alcoholism's familial transmission, which appears to be in its infancy. From the many studies over the past two decades on the familial and genetic factors in the causation of alcoholism, we can conclude that these factors do play a role in the occurrence of alcoholism.[18] And so do the various forms of childhood trauma, as shown by the strong evidence that I present in the final volume.

Table 4.1. Family History and Possible Genetic Associations Among Selected Psychiatric Disorders, with Frequency of Childhood Trauma History

(compiled from refs. 18, 178, 572, 612, 613)

Disorder*	Family History**	Genetic Evidence***	Childhood Trauma History
Alcoholism	+ to +++	Twin (30–39% rates among fraternal, 60% in identical), adoption & marker studies	Nearly always
Bipolar	± to +	One study estimated that 10 to 20% may be x linked, but it has not been replicated	Some evidence
Depression	+ to ++	Little, mostly as limited family history, & a small association with bipolar-disordered relatives	Common
Anxiety	± to +	Little to none	Common
Personality	± to ++	Little to none	Common, especially in BPD
Schizophrenia	± to +	Twin, adoption, pedigree & marker studies; 3 studies favor environment	Common
Alzheimer's	?	Some	?

*Tourette's syndrome, a rare disorder, has good evidence for association with a single gene locus. Other than this and those listed in the table above, so far most other functional (i.e., nonorganic) psychiatric disorders show little or no evidence for genetic transmission as a causal factor.[178]
**Family history of disorder, frequency: ± = Low; + = Some (up to 20%), ++ = 25 to 50%, +++ = 50 to 75%
***Genetic determinants may interact with environment as cofactors in the pathogenesis of a disorder.

Bipolar disorder (an early study suggested that 10 to 20 percent may be linked to the x chromosome) and schizophrenia (some twin, adoption, pedigree and marker studies have suggested genetic causal factors) are the next most likely to show evidence of familial and genetic factors, but the evidence is not convincing that these disorders are exclusively or even commonly related to such a cause (e.g., refs. 43, 69a, 572, 573). There is little hard evidence that anxiety disorders and personality disorders are genetic in origin. And as I have shown, there is little such evidence that exists for depression, currently existing mostly as findings of a limited family history, and a small association with bipolar disorder relatives among some first-degree relatives. In all, the "runs-in-families" observation does not prove a genetic cause, since childhood trauma is also intergenerational.[572, 573]

Research-Quality Criteria

Most clinical scientists, including the authors of the sources for Table 4.1, have used several if not most of ten common criteria to help evaluate clinical and scientific research reports. This kind of careful evaluation process can help us to determine the quality of and the causal conclusions or inferences that we can make from research articles on mental and physical health problems. Shown in Table 4.2, these aids assist the reader to determine whether any study may be reliable.

When we employ these ten criteria to evaluate research on whether mental disorders are genetically transmitted, we find strong evidence that familial or intergenerational transmission occurs among many mental disorders. There is also some suggestive evidence that actual genetic transmission may at times be

Table 4.2. Research Quality and
Causal Inferences Criteria

Criterion	Comment/Description
1. Data-based	Specific reproducible methods are used and data are accurately collected, reported, analyzed and critiqued
2. Multiple designs	Studies are conducted across more than one study design, e.g., 1) prospective, 2) retrospective, 3) controlled, 4) case controlled (index) 5) double-blind,
3. Multiple independent researchers find similar results	Studies are conducted by multiple independent observer/researchers and result in similar findings
4. Variety of sample subjects	Studies conducted on a variety of sample subjects, e.g., random samples, clinical, community, forensic, etc.
5. Replicated	Studies are repeated to look for consistency of results across different population samples
6. Meaningful odds ratios	Significant strength of the association with variable assessed
7. Graded response to variable	Cumulative or dose-response relationship to variable
8. Temporal sequence appropriate	Temporal relationship (exposure precedes the outcome)
9. Biologic plausibility	Findings have a plausible biologic explanation
10. Appropriate interpretation of findings	The researcher works, reports and analyzes within the bounds appropriate to their study design and findings

involved, as in the case for the rare Tourette's syndrome, and to some extent for alcoholism, with an even smaller likelihood for bipolar disorder and schizophrenia. However, except for Tourette's syndrome, this evidence is not nearly as strong as what we have found over the past twenty-five years for the relationship of a history of childhood trauma to subsequent mental and some physical illness.

Genetic and Pedigree Research

But what has this research actually shown? According to Alvin Pam, Ph.D., research to try to prove a genetic cause of mental disorders has usually addressed one or more of four main areas of study, as shown in the first column in Table 4.3. Within these four areas, researchers have employed two or three common kinds of study designs, each of which has an estimated potential to produce accurate and reliable results in favor of a genetic cause.[572, 573]

Examining the third column in the table, we can see that the first three methods are inconclusive, mostly because of the corresponding reasons described for each of them in the fourth column. Study design number 4 has a powerful potential, but is not practical, since almost no identical twins have been found who were raised apart where appropriate data could be collected from them and their families. Family tree (consanguinity) and most twin studies can't usually control adequately for environment, which makes them unlikely methods to prove a genetic cause.

For adoption comparisions, study designs number 5 and 6 may be suggestive at best, but the results of such reported studies have been negative or equivocal. No conclusive results have been reported for design 7, although its potential can be powerful. Finally, there is genetic marker research, which, though also potentially powerful, has been neither replicated (design 8) nor reported (design 9).

This summary leaves us with a paucity of supportive evidence for the existence of a predominant genetic cause of mental illness. This lack appears to be the case in spite of a vast psychiatric and psychological literature that acknowledges genetic transmission at almost every turn, in almost every article, editorial and research report, while rarely if ever mentioning the above negative, contradictory or at best equivocal information.[572, 573, 759]

Looking at both sides of the nature/nurture issue, Pam said, ". . . following about a century of effort, a harsh assessment would be that no substantive results have been tendered for the [biological] pathogenesis of any major psychiatric disorder" and ". . . in defense of biological psychiatry . . . the problems studied are complex and it is reasonable to anticipate delays and setbacks before medicine can identify constitutional mechanisms involved in 'mental illness.' The lack of definitive answers does not mean that there will never be answers. . . ."[572]

Table 4.3. Genetic and Pedigree Research: Methods,

Method/Study	Design	Potential Power
Consanguinity ("blood")	1. Genealogy (family tree)	Inconclusive
	2. Concordance rates (compare to others in the family)	Inconclusive
Co-twin controls	3. Identical vs. nonidentical same-gender twins	Inconclusive
	4. Identical twins reared apart	**Powerful,** but **impractical**
Adoption comparisons	5. Compare disorder rates for biological vs. adopted relatives, especially parents	Suggestive
	6. Compare rates for children of index parents v. children of controls	Suggestive
	7. Cross-fostering: index parent children rates vs. control biologic parents & index adoptive parents' children	Powerful
Genetic marker	8. Identifying marker with disorder	Powerful
	9. Prospective-longitudinal: predicting the disorder in adults	Can be conclusive

Potential Evidentiary Power and Results *(expanded from ref. 572)*

Results & Comments

The beginning of the "runs-in-families" search. Complicated by hearsay diagnosis of current, distant or dead relatives, these and related methods do not prove genetic transmission. Also, they do not fulfill Mendelian genetic principles.

Because twins share the same environment, we can't interpret their different percentages affected as proof of a genetic cause. Identical twins elicit similar treatment. No useful data.[404, 407] Regarding #4, almost none found to study, thus numbers are far too small to use.

Most of these several studies produced negative or equivocal results and had one to several methods flaws, described in four critiques (e.g., selective adoptions, delayed placements, poor diagnositic criteria, over- or misinterpretation of data, etc). One suggested environmental factors over genetic. Results remain negative or equivocal.

No conclusive results.

A small number of early anecdotal reports on bipolar disorder and schizophrenia have not been replicated in a larger number of later studies.[69a] Studies on depression continue.

None reported to date

THE CURRENT THEORY

We can now summarize the current theory or hypothesis that has developed over the past two decades or so, with the evidence proposed and the corresponding findings from the trauma literature, as shown in Table 4.4. The theory goes that most mental illness (i.e., that which is not caused by underlying medical diseases) is a genetically transmitted disorder of brain chemistry. The chemicals involved are usually listed as norepinephrine, dopamine, acetylcholine and serotonin, even though there are more than one hundred such neurotransmitters in the brain.[749] The "treatment of choice" for nearly all mental disorders is any one or a combination of drugs that have been developed by various drug companies.[39, 759]

A problem is that not only is this theory unproven for depression and most mental illness, as shown in the second and third columns of Table 4.4 and throughout this and the next book, but it is possibly erroneous in its base and neglects to include a major potential cause, i.e., childhood and other trauma. Unfortunately, its continued repetition seems to have hypnotized our otherwise sophisticated society into believing it. Regarding depression, geneticist Dave Curtis reviewed the world's literature and concluded, "Although there appears to be some genetic contribution to the susceptibility to depression, it is less marked than for bipolar disease [and evidence for bipolar is weak]. The pattern of transmission is unclear, and there is no strong evidence from linkage or association studies to demonstrate which [gene] loci may be involved."[178]

Table 4.4. The Cause of Mental Illness: Evidence for the Current Theory

(Compiled and expanded from refs. 178, 339, 523, 572, 573, 587, 759)

Hypothesis/Theory	Evidence Proposed	Actuality
Genetically transmitted . . .	Little (for most)* to none (for some)	Childhood trauma also tends to "run in families"
Disorder . . .	Categorization of selected observation**	Large percentage also due to trauma
of Brain chemistry:	Mostly assumptions from animal experiments No lab tests in humans	Trauma alters brain chemistry and, at times, anatomy
Proposed Neurotransmitters***	Focuses on four neuro-transmitters	Over 100 NTs in CNS, with a complex physiology (see chapter 7)
Treatment choice: Drugs	Some ($\frac{1}{3}$ to $\frac{2}{3}$) to no Improvement In life quality or overall	At best may help some & may supplement a FRP****
Conclusion: Mostly Biological problem	Some for biological *effects*, not for cause† Uses catchwords	Bio-psycho-social (including trauma)

*Some suggestive evidence for alcoholism/chemical dependence, and weaker evidence for bipolar disorder (an early report) and schizophrenia [698, 572, 573]
**Arrived at by a somewhat primitive process by a consensus of mostly men psychiatrists; some diagnostic categories eventually undergo field trials
***Although there are over one hundred neurotransmitters in the brain, current theory continues to focus on norepinephrine, dopamine, acetylcholine, and serotonin [572, 759]
****Full recovery program for trauma effects recovery
†Common catchwords—e.g., "predisposed to," "genetic predisposition," "biochemically predisposed to," "can be inherited," "runs in families," . . .[572]

5 CHILDHOOD TRAUMA AS A POTENTIAL CAUSE OF DEPRESSION

We can now consider in more detail some of the findings that document childhood trauma as being a potential causal factor for depression and other mental disorders. In the late nineteenth and early twentieth centuries, pioneers such as Jean Charcot, Pierre Janet, Joseph Brauer, Sigmund Freud, Carl Jung, Karen Horney, John Bowlby and others gave us a basis and some concepts and skills to begin working with survivors of childhood trauma. During that time, however, there were no research reports on large populations that documented the relationship of the trauma with subsequent mental illness.

STRONG EVIDENCE FOR TRAUMA

It was not until the last quarter of the past century, perhaps related to our growing awareness of the common occurrence of child abuse and neglect and the need to prevent it, that research on large numbers of people began to be conducted and published.

I am currently aware of 251 such peer-reviewed published reports that examine the relationship of childhood trauma to subsequent depression and other mental illness, which I summarize and discuss throughout this book and the next. These studies were conducted and written by independent authors and nearly all were published in reputable, peer-reviewed journals such as the *American Journal of Psychiatry,* the *Psychological Bulletin,* and *Child Abuse & Neglect.*

I found 209 studies that linked depression with having a history of childhood trauma, as summarized in Table 5.1. Of these, 96 looked at *clinical* populations (i.e., patients or clients in clinics or hospitals), which totaled 29,292 people. These reports found that among those with a history of childhood trauma, depression was from 1.6 to 12.2 times more common than was found among the controls, who said they had no such trauma history, and with whom they were compared. I found an additional 70 published studies from the *community* on 69,724 trauma survivors and controls that showed up to a 10-fold increase in depression. And I found 22 *prospective* studies on 11,009 people followed for up to 20 years that revealed an increase in depression of up to 10-fold. (Prospective studies are sometimes called the "gold standard" of study designs.) I also found 21 *index case* (also called *proband*) studies on 11,415 depressed people and their controls (where available) that concluded that those who were depressed had a significantly increased history of childhood trauma.

These are impressive numbers. By contrast, the studies generally cited to support the genetic theory of depression do not approach this many people or have this strong an association with convincing evidence.[178,572,573] The studies that claim to

Table 5.1. Depression and Childhood Trauma: Summary of 209 Clinical, Community, Prospective & Index Case Reports*

Year/Author	Study Characteristics	Depression/suicide*	Other effects of trauma
Clinical 96 Studies 1942–2003	29,292 patients & controls	Depression 1.6 to 12.2x ↑ to 12x suicidality	Increased & often multiple Co-Morbidity
Community 70 Studies 1985–2002	69,724 trauma survivors & controls	Depression ↑ to 10x Suicidality ↑ to 18x	Increased Co-Morbidity
Prospective 22 Studies 1984–2001	11,009 trauma survivors & controls followed from 1 to 20+ years	Depression/suicide ↑ to 10x	High & multiple Co-Morbidity
Index Case 21 Studies 1975–1998	11,415 depressed subjects	↑ childhood trauma	Miscellaneous findings
All 4 Populations 209 Studies 1974–2001	**121,440 childhood trauma survivors & controls****	**Depression 1.6 to 12.2x, ↑ to 12x Suicidality Common graded relationship to trauma severity**	**High and multiple Co-Morbidity. 2 showed substantial improvement with trauma-focused treatment******

↑ = increased
* All summaries include international population samples from multiple locations.
** CT was mostly sexual abuse, some physical, all likely psychological
*** Of the 209 studies two assessed treatment outcomes.

support the related neurotransmitter theories are rarely conducted on humans.[749] But supporting evidence for the trauma-depression link is derived from a total of 121,440 people. These studies were conducted by over 500 independent researchers and authors on diverse populations from the United States, the United Kingdom, Canada, Australia, New Zealand, Europe, Scandinavia and elsewhere.

Furthermore, while most study subjects are adults, some are children and adolescents (which, along with the fact that some investigators studied college students, would tend to skew the results *away* from a positive relationship between trauma and mental illness). My understanding is that none of these studies was funded by a drug company or a similar special interest group with a hidden agenda. This fact adds even more credibility to their results.

While some of these authors commented that other factors were or may be important, such as other manifestations and dynamics of family dysfunction, few found hard evidence of genetic factors as being a cause of depression, suicidality or almost any of the other mental and some physical disorders that were frequently found (many of the authors were not looking for specific genetic evidence).

The other disorders and conditions frequently found to be associated with childhood trauma included substance abuse, anxiety and anxiety disorders, PTSD, eating disorders, personality disorders (including especially borderline personality disorder and antisocial personality disorder), anger, aggressive behaviors, violence, ADHD and somatization, including: headaches and jaw disorders and pain, chronic pain, fatigue, gynecological problems, PMS, and other somatic symptoms. I address these disorders, illnesses and problems in the next volume.

While these results do not rule out genetic factors, they demonstrate strongly that the effects of repeated childhood trauma, consisting of one or usually a combination of physical abuse, sexual abuse, and/or mental and emotional abuse, often with neglect, are commonly associated with depression, and often with one or more other mental and some physical disorders.

Taken as a whole, these studies and their results fulfill all of the ten research quality criteria summarized in Table 4.2 on page 37. The strong weight of this massive amount of evidence at the least *implies* causality, that is, that repeated childhood trauma causes the subsequent depression in a substantial percentage of people who have it. While many of the authors of these 209 articles suggested causality as a possibility, four of these studies' authors were convinced enough by their results to conclude that the trauma was *causal* of depression and other mental disorders, as shown in Table A.7 of the Appendix (page 224).

Suicide

Serious suicidal ideations, attempts and completion (also called *suicidality* to mean any one or a combination of these) are the dreaded end of the spectrum of the symptoms and signs of depression. They are included as item A-9 in the *DSM-IV* diagnostic criteria for depression (pages 12 and 17). I have never seen a person who attempted suicide who was not acutely or chronically "depressed," nor have several colleagues whom I interviewed.

Because of this near-universal juxtaposition of suicidality with current depression, it is safe to assume that anyone who is seriously suicidal is also depressed. Therefore, it can be useful to look at any additional studies that examine the research variables of suicidality and a history of childhood trauma. While many of the 209 above-cited studies that found a depression-childhood trauma link also found a significant relationship to suicidality, I found an *additional* 29 *reports* that looked at suicide and childhood trauma. These results are summarized in Table 5.2, and in further detail in the Appendix as Tables A.9 and A.10. These included 22 *clinical* studies on 34,911 people and their comparison controls and seven *index case* studies on 787 suicidal people. As was found for depression, these several independent authors reported a strong suicide-childhood trauma connection, including suicide risk factors of up to a massive 74 times more than was found for the controls.[551]

Accepting then that nearly all seriously suicidal people are also depressed, we can then add these results to the already overwhelming evidence for a depression-childhood trauma link, as shown in Table 5.3. The final total that I found will thus be 238 studies (209 + 29) on 157,138 people and their controls that essentially universally reported a significant depression and suicidality-childhood trauma link.

With this massive amount of evidence, we might ask why conventional medicine, psychiatry, psychology, and related clinical and research fields have not recognized its magnitude and importance? For example, I have heard several recent talks by experts on depression and suicide, and not one mentioned childhood trauma as something to consider and address. Instead, their focus was on the need to diagnose these conditions early and to treat them almost exclusively with antidepressant drugs. This observation reminds me of the story of The Emperor's New Clothes.

Table 5.2. Suicide and Childhood Trauma:
29 Clinical & Index Case Reports

Year/Author	Study Characteristics	Depression/suicide	Other effects of trauma
Clinical 22 Studies, 1983–2001 2 Lit. Reviews	34,911 CT People & Controls	↑ to 74x suicidality, including attempts and completions	↑ Co-Morbidity
Index Cases 1989–1995 7 Studies	787 Suicidal People & Controls	↑ CT in 5 of 6 studies	Control bias in 6th study
SUMMARY			
29 Studies 1983–2001	35,698 People & Controls	Strong CT-Suicide Association	↑ Co-Morbidity

KNOWING THE TRUTH ABOUT DEPRESSION

How long is it going to take us to see the truth about depression? Stepping outside of the box of conventional thinking and believing may help us understand the importance of this powerful information. I believe that the totality of the data gives us more than simple evidence: It *establishes* the link as *fact*. This kind of factual evidence may be hard for the health insurance industry and its managed care components to counter. My experience is that, like the tobacco industry, they will do everything legally possible to disallow use of the money *their members have paid them* for appropriate trauma-focused treatment.

Table 5.3. Depression, Suicide and Childhood Trauma: Summary of 238 Clinical, Community, Index Case & Prospective Reports

Year/Author	Study Characteristics	Depression/ suicide	Other effects of trauma
Depression 209 Studies 1974–2003	121,440 childhood trauma survivors & controls	Depression 1.6 to 12.2x ↑ to 12x Suicidality	High and multiple co-morbidity Common graded relationship to trauma severity. 2 showed substantial improvement with trauma-focused treatment
Suicide 29 Studies 1983–2001	35,698 people & controls	Strong CT– Suicide Association	↑ Co-Morbidity
SUMMARY			
238 Studies	**157,138 People & Controls**	**Strong CT–Depression /Suicide Association**	**High and multiple Co-Morbidity**

Because of this long-established behavior pattern, it will be up to the health consumers and their clinicians to tell them and others about this evidence, and to demand that they pay for legitimate trauma-focused treatment. Short of that, the consumer will have to find their own best recovery program, including locating experienced trauma-savvy clinicians, and pay for it out of their own pocket. This does not mean that every depressed person should begin trauma-focused treatment and recovery. But it does mean that where there is a history of repeated childhood trauma, coverage by the insurance company should be approved and provided. By paying for such treatment now, health insurance companies can save us all (them included) money and pain in the long run by helping people heal and thereby preventing future outpatient, emergency room and hospital expenses.

Bipolar Disorder

Also called "manic-depressive" disorder, bipolar disorder is an uncommon variant of depression. The affected person classically has alternating periods of mania (i.e., distinct times of abnormal and persistently elevated expansive or irritable mood lasting at least a week, and grandiosity, disordered speech, thoughts or behavior, and much less need for sleep) and depression. Many people are misdiagnosed as having bipolar disorder, especially among those who are drinking or using drugs heavily, and rarely those with medical conditions such as hyperthyroidism.

People with bipolar disorder may have a frequent history of childhood trauma. I found 13 reports wherein the researchers had looked for it (Table 5.4).

Ten of these looked at index cases of bipolar disorder and all found an increase in childhood trauma among their sample patients. The other three studies examined children with a history of trauma and found an increased association with bipolar disorder. The total number of people from these thirteen studies, all reported over the past 10 years, was 2,655 bipolar or traumatized children or adults and, where appropriate, their controls who had neither bipolar illness nor a history of childhood trauma (Table 5.4).

Table 5.4. Bipolar Disorder and Childhood Trauma: Associations from 13 Reports

Year/Author	Study Characteristics	Childhood Trauma or Bipolar	Other Effects of Trauma
1992 Palmer et al.	36 bipolar women	50% (childhood sexual abuse) CSA	
Carlin & Ward	11 bipolars	46% CSA	
1995 Darves-Bornoz et al.	26 bipolar women	28% CSA	23% revictimized
1997 Bauer et al.	103 BP	↑ CT	
1998 Levitan et al.	653 depressed people, some BP	↑ CT among bipolars	
Ackerman et al.	204 CTs	↑ bipolar	
Read	17 bipolar	↑ CT	
Mueser et al.	275 BP, schiz, other	↑ CT & other trauma	
Kennedy et al.	20 BP, 30 schiz	50% had PTSD	CT may be a factor
1999 Woziak et al.	260 children CT v. controls	↑ CT among bipolars	
2000 Hyun et al.	333 uni/BP depressives	↑ CT among bipolars	
2001 Chang et al.	56 children from 36 BP families	↑ family conflict & dysfunction	54% children had other mental illness; 14% had BP
2002 Leverich et al.	631 BP outpatients	45% CT	CTs = early onset, severity & co-morbidity
SUMMARY			
13 Studies 1992–2002	**2,655 BP/CTs v. Controls**	**↑ CT among bipolars**	**↑ Other co-morbidity**

↑ = increased, CT = childhood trauma, BP = bipolar disorder, schiz = schizophrenia

This amount of evidence suggests childhood trauma as a possible factor in the genesis of bipolar illness. In my clinical experience, although it is anecdotal, I have never seen a person with bipolar disorder who grew up in a healthy family. Evidence for a possible genetic cause of bipolar disorder is scant, and no more than 10 percent of people with the disorder will have a parent who also has it.[43] This leaves us with the unanswered question of what may cause the illness among the other 90 percent.

If one is not a purist, these studies add 13 more to the already overwhelming number of 238 studies that link depression to childhood trauma, for a grand total of 251 studies, with a sample size of 159,793 people. I summarize the numbers of these studies and their table numbers for easy reference in Table 5.5.

Table 5.5. Summary of Data Linking Depression with Childhood Trauma

Type of Study		Number of Studies	Number of People Studied	Table/Page for Reference	
Clinical		96	29,292	A.3	(page 201)
Community		70	69,724	A.4	(211)
Prospective		22	11,009	A.5	(218)
Index Case		21	11,415	A.6	(222)
	Total	209	121,440	5.1	(47)
Suicidality		22	34,911	A.9	(227)
Index Case		7	787	A.10	(229)
	Total	238	157,138	5.3	(52)
Bipolar Disorder		13	2,655	5.4	(54)
	Grand Total	251	159,793	5.5	(55)

Other Methods and Results

Some researchers have looked at many of these studies in the form of literature reviews and have also found a positive link.[50, 52, 263, 288a, 289a, 293, 421] Still others have used a study design called *meta-analysis,* wherein the data from several previously reported studies are reanalyzed together using special statistical methods.[408, 560, 574] As an example, research psychologist Elizabeth Paolucci and her colleagues did a meta-analysis on the effects of childhood sexual abuse (CSA) reported among 37 studies, most of which are listed in this book. They found a medium to high link between the CSA and depression and suicidality. More remarkable, however, they also did a special "file drawer" analysis which indicated that 277 studies that showed no or a negative link between CSA and depression/suicide would be required to negate the positive results of these 37 studies.[574] In my research for this book I found only two such negative studies.[279, 280] In addition, I made a simple proportional calculation for a theoretical file drawer analysis on all 251 positive study results cited in this chapter, which indicated that 1,886 negative studies would be required to negate these 251 positive study outcomes. For the skeptics and debunkers among us who may want to disprove this overwhelming evidence, they could become like Sisyphus, trying to push a giant boulder (277 to 1,886 missing negative studies) to the top of a mountain, only to have to start over from the bottom the next day.

An Exemplary Study

While all of these listed studies are worthy of further description, the one by Brown and Harris is especially telling. Like the

ACE study described in chapter 1, it is worth looking at here in some detail. It evolved from a combined clinical and community sample of 114 depressed women who were compared to 282 matched controls.[108] The authors looked at demographics, life circumstances and stressful events—both recent and past—in the lives of these women. Of the 114 depressed women, 41 were out-patients and 73 were inpatients. While Brown and Harris had considered genetic transmission as a possible important factor, they found that its role was small. Rather, as summarized in the Appendix in Table A.10 (index cases), they found that from 49 to 83 percent of the depressed women had suffered one or more *severe, long-term losses* or *threats* of major trauma in their recent and/or distant past, which was highly statistically different from these kinds of events that the control women had experienced. When they broke down their other characteristics, they found six general areas that were an important influence on whether or not they became depressed, as shown in the hexagon diagram in Figure 5.1. These areas included: 1) *Low resources* (e.g., low socioeconomic status, isolation from safe others), 2) *Vulnerability factors* (no safe person with whom to express their pain, loss of their mother before age 11, having three children under age 14, and unemployment, especially if living in a blue-collar family), and 3) *Low self-esteem* (even though this finding is almost universal among those with depression, and also for those who are in active grief,[705] as well as being common among trauma survivors).

Against this backdrop, Brown and Harris found that a serious provoking or triggering stressor—such as a severe loss, or threat of loss, or a severe long-term difficulty—occurring within the previous year was also commonly present among those who were depressed. Those women who became depressed tended to have *several* of the background vulnerability factors. On top of that, they tended to have a recent serious stressor, such as a divorce or job loss by their husband. *My sense is that their "depression" could also be called "grief," and by that simple reframe it may improve their chances for healing.* This is because Brown and Harris found that those who did *not* become depressed tended to have the protective findings of: 1) *no vulnerability factors,* 2) a *safe person with whom to talk,* 3) a *healthy self-esteem,* and 4) were actively *working through their grief* as it came up. This study shows that people with depression commonly have not only a history of past trauma, but also often have a severe or serious recent trauma that can be addressed and expressed in order to help them heal.[108] Their findings validate the use of a trauma-focused psychotherapy approach to assist people with depression in their healing.

Depression and grief are two sides of the same coin. Depending on which side the experiencers and their clinicians may look can determine their subsequent clinical outcome and possibly even their long-term fate. Labeled as "depression," they may sense a loss of control and a need to be "fixed" from an outside source, including chemicals or even the trauma of electroshock. Pick the other side of the coin and the experiencer is empowered to move through the pain with the assistance of a clinician and other resources, as summarized in Table 12.1 on page 148 and explained in the text. Two special interest groups—the drug companies and the insurance/managed care companies— promote the former: a limited kind of fixing from the outside. But armed with increasing knowledge of their diagnostic and recovery choices as presented in this book and elsewhere (e.g.,

Figure 5.1. Major Findings in a Study
of 114 Depressed Versus 282 Control Women

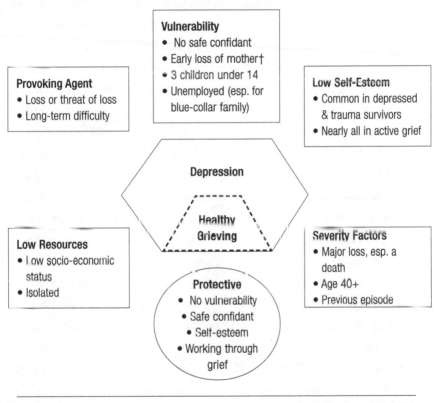

Vulnerability
- No safe confidant
- Early loss of mother†
- 3 children under 14
- Unemployed (esp. for blue-collar family)

Provoking Agent
- Loss or threat of loss
- Long-term difficulty

Low Self-Esteem
- Common in depressed & trauma survivors
- Nearly all in active grief

Depression

Healthy Grieving

Low Resources
- Low socio-economic status
- Isolated

Protective
- No vulnerability
- Safe confidant
- Self-esteem
- Working through grief

Severity Factors
- Major loss, esp. a death
- Age 40+
- Previous episode

Compiled from Brown & Harris 1978

† Did not look for/report other childhood trauma

refs. 150, 174, 186, 296, 360, 798, 807), trauma survivors and their clinicians are choosing an empowering trauma-focused approach.

Nearly 25 years after the Brown and Harris report, research psychiatrist Kenneth Kendler and his colleagues found similar results.[426] In a nine-year follow-up study of 1,942 adult women twins, they reported 18 significant associations with being depressed. These included: 1) a history of *childhood trauma,* 2) early *teen problems* (neurotic, low self-esteem, anxiety and behavior problems), 3) later teen problems (school, social support lack, substance misuse and more traumas), 4) *adult problems* (divorce, past depression) and 5) *recent* marital and other life *stress.* They showed a telling visual representation of the complex interrelationships among these many factors, as compiled in Figure 5.2. Note that at least 10 of these associated factors are directly related to having a history of trauma. Their assumed proof for "genetic risk" was having a twin or parent with a history of "depression," which to me is weak evidence.

Kendler is one of the most prominent researchers in the field of psychiatry, genetics and mental health. He and his colleagues said, "Two of the most widely replicated findings for major depression are its greater prevalence in women after adolescence and its causal association with stressful life events". Supported by these data from Kendler and colleagues,[424-6] and others,[433-4] my current estimation is that at least two-thirds of depression is most likely caused by childhood and other trauma, and that at best one-third may have other factors at play, including environmental toxins and possibly genetics. Of course, in a given person, the cause may not be "all or none." It may be *both/and*—nature *and* nurture.

It is important to understand how the toxic process of trauma comes about.

From this vast clinical literature and the observations and experience of countless therapists, it is clear that trauma plays a major role in the genesis of depression in a sizable percentage of people who have it. In the following chapters I will describe further how trauma may cause depression and other disorders.

Figure 5.2. Predictors for Depression Among 1,942 Adult Twins

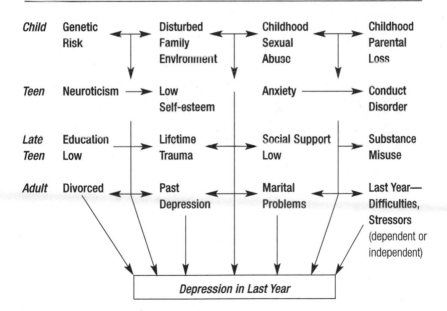

Compiled from Kendler et al. 2002—*see original article for detailed connections found*

6   THE PROCESS OF TRAUMA AND LOW SELF-ESTEEM

Trauma is any event, usually a nonordinary one that significantly harms the body, self or spirit. It covers a broad range of hurtful experiences including traumas that involve the physical, sexual, mental or emotional realms of our being. Throughout this book I have referred to the main kinds of childhood trauma as including *sexual* abuse (CSA), *physical* abuse (CPA), and *psychological* or *emotional* abuse. Child emotional and physical *neglect* are also traumatic, as is *witnessing verbal or physical violence,* especially within the family, and having a mentally ill household member.[254] Loss of a parent or parent figure through separation, divorce or death is also traumatic.[108] These traumas may occur under different guises that may go unrecognized by the victim, perpetrator and observer as being traumatic, as summarized in Figure 6.1.

Childhood and other trauma experiences are complex. Clinical and research psychologist William Friedrich said, "To simply place a broad label on a child as sexually abused may allow for a simple categorization, but it obscures the heterogeneity, severity, and co-occurrence of maltreatment experiences."[276] Each kind of abuse usually occurs in combination with one or more of the others, with *psychological/emotional* abuse being the *most common* and *nearly always present* in the background of the other three main trauma types, as shown in Figure 6.2.

Attempts to isolate each of these traumas and study them is difficult, if not usually impossible. Some researchers have tried to sort out just which subsequent effects or disorders may link to each specific kind of trauma. Some of them have reported negative results, especially for child sexual abuse, when they compared that specific abuse with other traumas. This kind of faulty reasoning and research can reflect a kind of isolation bias and often results in erroneous conclusions. As Friedrich points out, this kind of mindset can become counter productive, since the *sexual abuse nearly always* occurs in the presence of other traumas, and usually in a seriously dysfunctional family.[276]

There are several avenues through which we can explore the genesis of trauma and its effects. I believe that one of the most basic of these ways comes from the areas of self-psychology and object relations theory, which I describe below. Expanding upon and eventually transcending the works of earlier clinicians and writers, since the 1930s these observers have described a more sophisticated and accurate, though often subtle, process of how the child gets wounded in the context of child abuse and neglect.[143, 370, 515, 797-8, 816] The following is a summary of how this often happens.

Figure 6.1. Childhood Trauma Versus Healthy Parenting

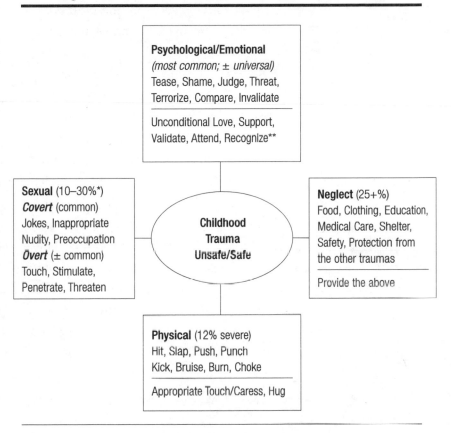

*These figures are estimates of the incidence & prevalence of these types of childhood trauma, based on data from the literature. Paradoxically, statistics based on reports to *child protective services* may show the opposite of the actual occurrence of trauma. These figures are (occurrence/reports): *neglect* (25+%/50+%), *physical* (12%/18%), *sexual* (10-30%/9%), *emotional* (90%/4%). Most *published* clinical & *research data* are on (in order of most common study data): sexual, physical, these two combined, psychological & very little on neglect.
**Healthy parenting descriptors are shown below the line in 3 boxes as appropriate.

Figure 6.2. Venn Diagram of the Spectrum of Childhood Trauma

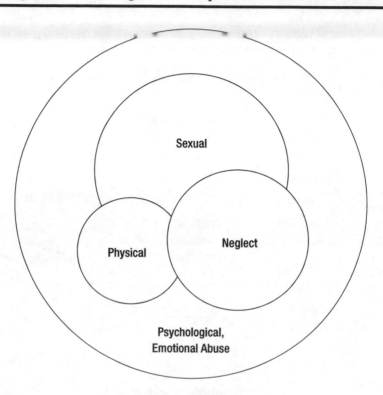

Each may be overt, covert (subtle), or both.

(estimated & expanded from Muenzenmaier et al. 1993, Anda et al. 2002)

THE PROCESS OF WOUNDING

1. Previously traumatized and wounded themselves, the child's parents feel inadequate, bad and unfulfilled, i.e., they feel shame and emptiness.
2. They unconsciously project those charged feelings onto others, especially onto their spouse and their vulnerable children. They may also exhibit and project grandiosity (e.g., "I always know what's best for you!"—when they don't). They look outside of themselves to feel whole.
3. In a need to stabilize the parents and to survive, the child denies that the parents are inadequate and mistreating. With the unhealthy boundaries that the child has learned from its parents and others, the child internalizes (takes in, introjects, accepts) the parents' projected inadequacy and shame. A common fantasy is that, "If I'm really good and perfect, they will love me and they won't reject or abandon me." The child idealizes the parents.

> **Case History 6.1:** This dynamic of the child idealizing the parents is illustrated in the following case history, as told by Chuck, who was a forty-eight-year-old health professional.
>
> "I've felt empty and sad for as long as I can remember, but I never really knew that I had been abused. I tried individual psychotherapy for a few months and a self-help group for nine months at age thirty-two, which resulted in my beginning to awaken to some of my feelings and potential. It was not until age forty-two, after attending several Adult Children of Alcoholics meetings, that although I didn't want to attend, and even resisted, I began to remember having been mentally and emotionally abused as a child. The memories didn't come back

suddenly or all at once, but trickled into my awareness, little by little over several years.

"During that time I found a birthday card that I had made at age eight for my father. I had written 'You are Superman, You're so super,' and I drew a color picture in crayons of Superman, which I gradually realized was a clue to my having idealized him, even though he was almost never there for me as a father. And when he was there, he often emotionally abused me. The abuse was often subtle to me, and included especially teasing, shaming, threatening and making vague demands. My father was a rageaholic and compulsive gambler, and my mother was a meddler and controller. Looking back, I can see that both of them were wounded, too.

"After years of trying all kinds of self-improvement techniques, it was only after I began to remember having been abused that I could focus on what and how I could heal that old poisonous stuff inside that I'd been carrying around all of these years."

4. The child's vulnerable true self* is wounded so often, that to protect that self it defensively submerges ("splits off") deep within the unconscious part of its psyche. *The child goes into hiding* (Figure 6.3). The "child in hiding" represents what may appear at first to be a way that helps us to survive. Its downside is that going into hiding and staying there keeps us alienated

---

*Other terms for the real self include *true self,* our *true identity, existential self, heart, soul* and *child within.*[143, 370, 575, 797-8, 816] This is opposed to the *false self,* also called the ego or codependent self, which is an assistant or kind of "sidekick" to the true self that can help us negotiate our family and our world. (I use the term *ego* here in a more simple and expanded way from its conventional understandings, wherein it was previously viewed, perhaps with some confusion, as *both* true self *and* false self.)

from the power of knowing and being our true self.

By its true self going into hiding, the child becomes alienated from its present experience in a number of ways—*and* from past experiences by forgetting much of what actually happened. The child becomes alienated from its internal experience—which includes emotional responses to abuse of fear, shame, grief and anger. The child also becomes alienated from its perception of what is occurring externally with others: "Daddy's not drunk. He was so tired he fell asleep on the lawn."

Figure 6.3 The Child Goes into Hiding

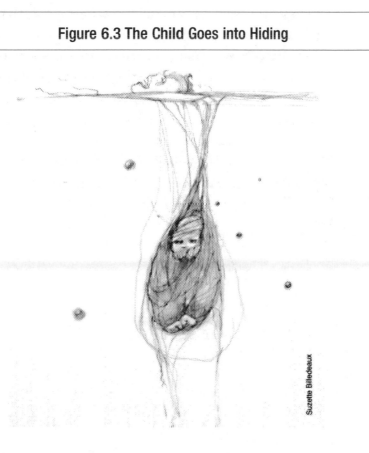

Suzette Billedeaux

When the true self is in hiding—which it does to try to survive an otherwise unbearable life experience—it is unable to encode its impactful memories in a conscious and currently useful way. Yet, paradoxically it somehow stores these memories in its unconscious mind as "old tapes," unfinished business, stored painful energy or ungrieved grief, much of which the object relations psychologists call "object representations"*.[816]

5. When children are not allowed to express their grief in a healthy way, their true self will try to find its own way out and express its painful experiences, like an enclosed abscess that is waiting to drain. But unexpressed pain may be stored as toxic energy and may then manifest in their life as a physical, mental, emotional or spiritual disorder, or more usually as a combination of these. Another term for this repeated attempt to express its trauma and grief is *repetition compulsion*.[476, 794-5]

6. The true self takes in whatever else it is told—both verbally and nonverbally—about itself and about others, and stores it in its unconscious (mostly) and its conscious mind (sometimes and to some degree).

---

*The establishment of the false self may include some aspects of traumatic forgetting (dissociative amnesia) that are accompanied by the behaviors and responses that allow us to try to stabilize the family and avoid further abuse. *Unconscious blocking* appears to be the major factor here, and *misappraisal* (e.g., misnaming what happened as normal or deserved) is also important in the genesis of the amnesia. Denial or *cognitive avoidance* is also often part of traumatic forgetting and is primarily a cognitive and emotional screen that reinterprets reality and substitutes a false reality according to the demands of the abuser(s) and emotional and physical survival. As kinds of traumatic memory distortions, these characteristically involve a dissociation and/or censoring of some aspects of the traumas, such as the emotional pain of the abuse, and may involve the amnesia for some, most or even all of the traumatic experiences, and the substitution of an idealized past for the truth.[103, 104, 798]

7. What it takes in are messages from major and impactful relationships, primarily parents, but these may also include siblings, grandparents, clergy, and other authority and parent figures. The *experiential representations* of these relationships in the unconscious memory that continue to affect these children as adults are called "objects" or "object representations" by the object relations theorists. These messages and representations are laden with feelings, and tend to occur in "part-objects" (e.g., good parent, bad parent, aggressive child, shy child and so on). The more self-destructive messages tend to be deposited in the false self or "internal saboteur," also described as the internalized rejecting or otherwise mistreating parent.[816]

8. Hurting, confused and feeling unable to run their own life, the person eventually turns that function over to the false self.

9. A tension builds. The true self is always striving to come alive and to evolve. At the same time, the "negative ego" (the destructive part of the false self) attacks the true self, thus forcing it to stay submerged, keeping self-esteem low. Also, the child's grieving of its losses and traumas is not supported. Because of all of the above, the child's development is disordered and boundaries become unhealthy.* This resulting "psychopathology" or "lesion" has been called a "schizoid compromise",[320] and a "splitting off of the true self".[816] The outcome can be a developmental delay, arrest or failure.

---

*Children and adolescents need to be given and taught healthy boundaries, which help them feel safe and function better. Parents who are loose or inconsistent with boundaries are subtly traumatizing their child.[797]

10. Some results include traumatic forgetting, chronic emptiness, fear, sadness and confusion, and often periodic
explosions of self-destructive and other destructive behavior—both impulsive and compulsive—that allow some
release of the tension and a glimpse of the true self.

11. The consequences of the continued emptiness and/or
repeated destructive behavior keep the true self stifled or
submerged. Not living from and as their real self—with a
full awareness of their experiences—and with no safe
people to talk to about them, often dissociated and numb,
in order to survive they may forget, dissociate or otherwise
shut out most of their painful experiences.[103, 104, 794, 795] The
person maintains a low sense of self-esteem, remains
unhappy, yet wishes and seeks fulfillment. Compulsions
and addictions (and other repetition compulsions) can provide temporary fulfillment, but lead to more suffering and
ultimately block fulfillment and serenity.

RECOVERY

12. Recovery and growth are discovering and gently
unearthing the true self (child within) so that it can exist
and express itself in a healthy way, day to day. It also
means restructuring the false self or ego to become a more
flexible assistant ("positive ego") to the true self. Some
other results: growth, creativity and aliveness.

13. Such self-discovery and recovery is usually best accomplished gradually and in the presence of safe, compassion-
ate, skilled and supportive people. Recovery is a cyclical
process, and while it has its moments of peace, joy and

liberating self-discovery, it is also common to experience periods in which confusion, symptoms and suffering intensify. Participation in supportive recovery groups teaches the person how to deal with these cycles as they experience how others deal with their emotions, symptoms and with their growth and accomplishments in the recovery process. With commitment to and active participation in recovery, this healing process may take from three to five years or more.[798]

14. By listening, sharing and reflecting in a safe environment, the trauma survivor begins to remember what happened. They begin to reconstruct the physical, mental and emotional fragments of their memory that were previously buried deep within their unconscious mind. This crucial and healing kind of uncovering and remembering involves a process that evolves slowly over time.

15. During recovery the survivor learns to experience, express and tolerate emotional pain, and by doing so experience its movement and transient nature. This is the opposite of being overwhelmed by and mired in the stagnant pain and numbness of depression, which is commonly accompanied by disabling anxiety (i.e., fear).

In the next chapter I will further describe the process of trauma by reviewing what we know about how it effects our self-esteem and our ability to have a healthy relationship or "attachment" with our parents and others. I will also continue to address the process of recovery and healing.

BB1

We care about your opinions. Please take a moment to fill out this Reader Survey card and mail it back to us.
As a special **"thank you"** we'll send you exciting news about interesting books and a valuable **Gift Certificate.**

Please PRINT using ALL CAPS

First Name

Last Name

MI

Address

City

ST

Zip

Phone # (____) ____ – ____

Fax # (____) ____ – ____

Email

(1) Gender:
____ Female ____ Male

(2) Age:
____ 12 or under
____ 13-19
____ 20-39
____ 40-59
____ 60+

(3) Marital Status
____ Married
____ Single
____ Divorced/Widowed

(4) Did you receive this book as a gift?
____ Yes ____ No

(5) How many Health Communications books have you bought or read?
____ 1 ____ 2-4 ____ 5+

(6) How did you find out about this book?
Please fill in ONE.
1) ____ Recommendation
2) ____ Store Display
3) ____ Bestseller List
4) ____ Online
5) ____ Advertisement
6) ____ Catalog/Mailing
7) ____ Interview/Review (TV, Radio, Print)

(7) Where do you usually buy books?
Please fill in your top TWO choices.
1) ____ Bookstore
2) ____ Religious Bookstore
3) ____ Online
4) ____ Book Club/Mail Order
5) ____ Price Club (Costco, Sam's Club, etc.)
6) ____ Retail Store (Target, Wal-Mart, etc.)

(9) What subjects do you enjoy reading about most? Rank only **FIVE**. *Use 1 for your favorite, 2 for second favorite, etc.*

	1	2	3	4	5
1) Parenting/Family	○	○	○	○	○
2) Relationships	○	○	○	○	○
3) Recovery/Addictions	○	○	○	○	○
4) Health/Nutrition	○	○	○	○	○
5) Christianity	○	○	○	○	○
6) Spirituality/Inspiration	○	○	○	○	○
7) Business Self-Help	○	○	○	○	○
8) Teen Issues	○	○	○	○	○
9) Sports	○	○	○	○	○

(14) What attracts you most to a book?
(Please rank 1-4 in order of preference.)

	1	2	3	4
1) Title	○	○	○	○
2) Cover Design	○	○	○	○
3) Author	○	○	○	○
4) Content	○	○	○	○

TAPE IN MIDDLE; DO NOT STAPLE

BUSINESS REPLY MAIL

FIRST-CLASS MAIL PERMIT NO 45 DEERFIELD BEACH, FL

POSTAGE WILL BE PAID BY ADDRESSEE

HEALTH COMMUNICATIONS, INC.
3201 SW 15TH STREET
DEERFIELD BEACH FL 33442-9875

FOLD HERE

Comments:

7 THE PROCESS OF TRAUMA—CONTINUED

THE EFFECTS OF SHAME

In the previous chapter I described one view of the process of the genesis and effects of trauma. Each traumatized person has their own experience and effects. Two of the more unifying and core experiences of trauma are PTSD,[421,646] and a pervasive, underlying belief and feeling of *shame*. Shame has several guises. If shame is the umbrella, its spokes are low self-esteem or self-worth, self-hate, embarrassment, shyness and often even grandiosity. It reflects a decreased awareness of the true self, which may have been lost as the most hurtful effect of childhood trauma. Burdened with shame, we may not be able to care for ourself in a healthy way.

While few researchers have looked for it, nearly all of those who did found shame to be significantly present in the trauma survivors that they evaluated. In their 31 diverse reports, they called it *low self-esteem*. As listed on page 13, low self-esteem is a *DSM-IV* diagnostic criterion for depression. But more important, it is a frequent, if not universal, effect of repeated childhood trauma.

Clinical Studies

I found 17 independent clinical studies that evaluated 2,946 childhood trauma survivors and their controls, as shown in Table 7.1. All seventeen found a significant decrease in self-esteem among the trauma survivors when compared with the controls, as well as the occurrence of a significant increase in multiple and varied co-morbidities.

Community Studies

I found ten studies of 2,520 people from diverse international communities, all of which showed a significant decrease in self-esteem and increased co-morbidities (Table 7.2). All ten indirectly suggested or found that the low self-esteem was *the most substantial predictor of mental disorders.*

Prospective Studies

Supporting these above twenty-seven reports were four that used perhaps the most reliable research method, the prospective study, wherein people are evaluated and monitored long-term. Here, a total of 863 children and adults who were survivors of childhood trauma, and their controls, were followed for up to twelve years, and all of the traumatized samples showed a significant decrease in self-esteem and a significant increase in multiple co-morbidities (Table 7.3). One twelve-year follow-up study showed that with trauma-focused treatment there was substantial improvement in these disorders and symptoms over time,[132] and another emphasized the need for earlier and stronger treatment to help lessen the detrimental effects of the trauma.[733]

Using multiple and varied research methods, these thirty-one studies by independent authors on diverse populations found that among 6,329 people, low self-esteem was a common and important finding among the trauma survivors. It is thus useful to include an evaluation of a person's self-esteem and if appropriate, address it in their recovery plan.

Shame (low self-esteem) is a common and debilitating long-term effect of repeated childhood trauma. It blocks our motivation to heal. I summarize some effective ways to address it under "Recovery Aids" at the end of this chapter.

ATTACHMENT THEORY

The effects of childhood trauma hurt, and they are many and varied. Since the 1930s, clinicians and researchers have made countless observations that have substantiated the above patterns and dynamics on the process of wounding. Over the past twenty years a new generation of researchers has focused on the behavior of eleven- to sixteen-month-old infants when they are exposed to a specific stressor. Called the "strange situation," they looked at the way children react when their mother leaves them briefly with a stranger and then returns. Based on their results in thirteen reports published from 1981 through 1993, they have found four common infant reactions. The first is *ideal*. It arises from having a mother who is sensitive and appropriately attentive and responsive in her long-term care of her child. When stressed in this experimental way, the infant rapidly seeks the attachment figure (the mother), and when she returns, tends to be easily soothed, comforted and reassured by

Table 7.1. Low Self-Esteem and Childhood Trauma:

Year/Author	Study Characteristics	Self-Esteem
1977 James	7 CSA vs. 14 controls, all adolescents	↓
1979 Courtois	31 women incest survivors, by advertise- ments & mental health agencies	↓ (87%)
1983 van Buskirk & Cole	8 women CSA incest (6 bisexual/gay)	↓
1984 Bagley et al. (Prospective study)	149 CSA women vs. 471 controls	↓
1992 Toth et al.	153 children lower SES 46 abused, 35 neglected, 72 controls	↓
1992 Grayston et al.	CSA girls vs. Controls	↓
1993 Moeller, Bachman & Moeller	354 abused ♀ (CSA, PA, EA) vs. 314 controls in a gynecological practice	↓ 2.3x self-esteem (self-confidence)
1994 Roesler & McKenzie	188 CSA adults mean age 40 (20 men)	↓
1995 Mennen & Meadow	135 girls 6-18 with CSA evaluated	↓
1995 Stern et al.	84 CSA children, 85 controls	↓
1995 Lanz	77 CSA vs. 164 controls, all pregnant single adolescents	↓
1997 Meyer et al.	65 CSA teens, 136 controls	↓
1998 Classen et al.	27 CSA women	↓
1999 Armsworth, Stronck & Carlson	36 women CSA vs. 35 controls	↓
2001 Cecil & Matson	57 teens, 192 controls	↓
2001 Reynolds et al.	45 CT children, 5-11 yo	↓
2001 Hunt et al.	119 CT children	↓
SUMMARY **17 Studies**	**2,946 CTs & controls**	↓

↓ = decreased, SES = socio-economic status, CT = childhood trauma, SA = sexual abuse

Results from 17 Clinical Studies

Other Effects of Trauma	Comments
↑ delinquency; seductive, sensitive	Controls (½ from community, ½ institutionalized)
Difficulty trusting; 79% dif. relating to men; 40% never married; 80% sexual problems	No controls, though an important early study
Weak boundaries. Pick men like father (cold, dominant), can't trust, don't enjoy sex	Mothers dependent on fathers. (2 mothers knew of incest = co-abuse)
70–80% of those with ↓ social support are depressed & often suicidal	↑ childhood stress, CSA & self-esteem & ↓ social support put person at high risk for dep. & suicide
↑ aggressive behavior (co-morbid with depression)	
↑ depression, anxiety, SA/CD, obesity, fatigue & PMS, gynecological problems, tension, crime victim, pessimistic	Found 16 dysfunctional char's. of parents of abused [0% of perps were women]
↑ depression, dissociation, PTSD, sexual dysfunction	Showed CSA a significant factor in these findings
↑ depression, anxiety	Force & penetration = more symptoms
↑ depression, behavior problems	
↑ anxiety, SA, delinquency, ↓ support, family relations	Controls not being normal adolescents may bias against the degree of differences
↑ depression	
↑ depression, anxiety	
3-9x dep. + 2x suicide, 1.9-5x anxiety 13 x psych, hospitalization 2-11x eat dis.	↑ adult victimization
↑ depression	
↑ depression, PTSD, behavior problems	
↑ depression, anxiety	

Co-morbidity common

Table 7.2. Low Self-Esteem and Childhood

Year/Author	Study Characteristics	Self-esteem
1985 Ramsay & Bagley	CSA 83 of 377 women (random sample)	↓ 4x
1986 Bagley & Ramsay	45 ex-prostitutes (73% CSA) vs. controls (29% CSA)	↓ 10x (71 vs. 7%)
1986 Brunngraber	21 CSA women (incest)	↓
1987 Alexander & Lupfer	149 CSA c college students vs. 437 controls	↓
1989 Rew	34 CSA/55 nursing students	↓
1989 Morrow & Sorell	101 lower SES adolescent girls	↓
1993 Nash et al.	56 CSA vs. 49 controls (43% clinical)	↓
1999 Liem & Boudewyn	145 CSA vs. 542 controls, college students	↓
1996 Romans et al.	225 CSA, 252 controls	↓
2000 Muller & Lemieux	66 CSA/PA	↓
SUMMARY		
10 studies 1985-2000	**2,520 CTs & controls**	↓

Trauma: 10 Community Studies

Other Effects of Trauma	Comments
2x depression; 3.7x suicidal; 5x self-harm	8x had received psychiatric treatment
5x depression/suicide (80 v 16%)	All ex-prostitutes were severely abused as children
↑ SA/CD, hyperactive, somatization	
↑ vulnerability to further sexual assault	↓ family concept, empathy & support, even if perp was not in family
↑ depression	
↑ depression	Graded response to trauma severity
↑ dissociation (family dysfunction may be important)	↓ self-esteem = feel damaged & inadequate
↑ depression	
Other factors operative	
Predicted psychopathology	No control group

Co-morbidity common

Table 7.3. Low Self-Esteem and Childhood

Year/Author	Study Characteristics	Self-Esteem
1984 Bagley & McDonald	57 CT girls (20 CSA) vs. 30 controls Followed 8 years	2x ↓
1985 Bagley et al.	149 CSA women vs. 471 controls, prospective	↓
1997 Tebbutt et al.	84 children: (¼ boys) CSA followed at 0, 18 mos & 5 yrs	↓ 43%
2000 Cameron	72 women, 51 for the full 5 surveys over 12 years follow-up	↓ 88%
SUMMARY		
4 studies 1984–2000	**863 CTs & controls**	↓

her, and is thereby soon ready to explore the environment again.[546] Called a *secure* attachment, this kind differs from the other three types of infant attachment reactions when they have been previously traumatized or neglected outside of the experimental situation. These reactions may be a part of the early experience of many survivors of childhood trauma. All three have a fearful or anxious attachment with their mother, and I summarize their basic features in Table 7.4.

Trauma: Four *Prospective* Studies

Other Effects of Trauma	Comments
↑ depression, sexual problems, neurosis-related to separation from mother, physical abuse & neglect	Vulnerable & hopeless, without recovery work became involved in repeated abusive relationships
↑ depression, 70–80% of those with low social support are depressed & often suicidal	↑ childhood stress, CSA & ↓ self-esteem & social support put at high risk for depression & suicide
↑ depression, behavior problems (46%)	↑ other traumas during follow-up Need for earlier & stronger treatment
↑ 7x depression; 77% anxiety; 82% ED; 78% sexual problems; 83% PTSD; 75% GYN; 67% headaches/jaw paim	With trauma-focused treatment there was substantial improvement in these disorders & symptoms over time
Co-morbidity common	Trauma-focused treatment helps (one study)

ED = eating disorder, PTSD = post-traumatic stress disorder

These "attachment" reactions represent a snapshot of the early parent-child relationship and have provided us with more understanding of how early trauma may affect a child. Child protection service workers and clinicians can use these kinds of observations in their work. While some have criticized the limitations of attachment theory,[323] I believe that these observations support some of the above-described dynamics, in part, of how the child gets wounded.

Risky Families

Numerous studies report the prior trauma and psychopathology of the parents, parent figures, siblings and the child's other relatives. While summarizing these is not the focus of this book, one study may serve as an example. Goodwin and colleagues looked at one hundred mothers of sexually and/or physically abused children, and found these mothers were *eight times* more likely to have been *sexually abused* themselves *as children,* when compared to five hundred controls.[305] Based on their own prior wounding, these mothers may not have been able to protect their children from abuse, and thereby became *co-abusers* or *enablers* of the abuse (which I describe further in my book *Memory and Abuse*).

What other risk factors may predispose a family to abuse its children? Brown and colleagues looked carefully at this question and found seventeen significant characteristics of *mothers* that put the child at a high risk for being abused. They also found three characteristics of *fathers,* six of *children* and five of the *family* as a whole that predisposed the presence of child abuse and neglect. As shown in Table 7.4, these characteristics are associated with risk factors of from 5 to 11.8 times those found among the control or "normal" samples.[109] These are very high numbers. *Impaired, troubled* or disordered parents put their *children* at *especially high risk* for being *abused* or *neglected.* To help break the transgenerational cycle of abuse, we need to take these data seriously and develop effective ways to use this information to prevent future childhood trauma.

Table 7.4. Attachment Theory—How a One-Year-Old Infant Responds in Relationships: An Introduction

(compiled & expanded from refs. 238 & 546)

Attachment Characteristic	Secure/ Healthy	Avoidant/ Unresponsive	Ambivalent	Disorganized /Disoriented
Care of child	Sensitive* (Type B)	Rejecting (A) &/or Intrusive	Uninvolved (C)	Erratic, (D) Abuse
Child's response to stress**	Child soothed, returns to play	Avoidance, aggression	Clingy, fussy Don't relax	Freezes, Confused
Child feels or behaves	Secure, connected, confident	Avoids mother ± accepts strangers	Fear/withdraw Preoccupied ↓ exploring	Disoriented, Disorganized
Heart rate & cortisol	Normal	↑	↑	↑ ↑
Shuts down by	Remains open	9–12 months	?	?
Secure in future relations	+	Aggressive, delinquent	Less secure, Needy q Dependence	?
Learns Empathy	+	–	±	±
Attracts secure relationships	+	–	Needy/ Rejection cycle	–
Comments	Healthy relationships	?	Vulnerable, Easily victimized	?
Early experience of	Healthy Adults	Trauma survivors	Trauma survivors	Trauma survivors

* To young (infancy-toddler) child's behavior and needs. ** Stress = Mother leaves, stranger enters, alone with child a while, then mother returns. ↑ = increased, + = yes, – = no, ? = unknown

RECOVERY AIDS

In my work assisting trauma survivors in recovery I have observed an *almost universal* finding of *low self-esteem* among them. The belief and painful feeling of shame declares that "I am bad, not enough, flawed, inadequate, imperfect and even rotten at my core." Shame appears to be taught and learned, repeatedly implanted by offenders, which their victims incorporate into their beings. This subtle yet toxic process often begins at birth and can continue as child abuse, and continued traumas may be repeated throughout an adult's life. Active shame blocks healing.

A recovery program can slowly address and heal the effects of trauma, including the shame. Primary in healing shame is first to name it accurately, in whatever guise it may manifest itself. *Naming* things accurately gives us *personal power.* It is important to differentiate shame from guilt. Sometimes confused with shame, guilt is a painful feeling that comes from making a mistake, doing something wrong—or not doing it right. We can heal guilt by apologizing or making amends to the person we may have wronged, and, if appropriate, perhaps even asking for forgiveness. Guilt is about *doing* or not doing.

Shame is about *being* or not being. In guilt, we have done something wrong which we can more easily correct. In shame, we *are* something wrong, and we can see no way to correct it. Often fostered by some organized religions as "original sin," we feel as though we are born defective and bad. From this collective shaming trauma, our false self then maintains the shame. As one patient said, "I have a tape recorder in my head that reminds me of how bad I am." Another said, "There is this constant broadcast in the pit of my being telling me I'm not good

Table 7.5. Risk (Odds Ratios) for Child Abuse and Neglect According to Risk Factors (from refs. 109 & 149)

Risk Factor	Physical Abuse	Sexual Abuse	Neglect	Any/2 or more +	
Mother					
Younger	3.5x	2.3x	2.2x	2.4x	+
Sociopathic	4.9x	6.3x	4.4x	4.9x	+
Low Education	2.6x		5x	3x	+
Low Soc-economic			2.7–5x		
Low Relig. Attend.	2.2x			1.6x	
Low Self-Esteem			2.7x	2.3x	
On Welfare	3.7x		11x	5x	+
Seriously Ill	2x		2.2x	2x	+
Early separation from	4x		3.6x	2.8x	+
Low involvement by	2.7x			2.3x	
Alienation			2.7x	2x	
Hostility/Anger			2.3/2.8x	1.9x	
Dissatisfaction with child	2.4x		5x	3.2x	+
Non-white			4.4x	2.6x	
External locus of control	2.2x		1.8x	1.6x	+
Preg. complication	2.5x				
Single parent	2.3x		2.6x	2x	+
Child					
Handicapped		11.8x			
Girl/Unwanted		2.4x/3x	2.7x		
Low verbal IQ			2x		
Anxious withdrawn					
Harshly punished		3.2x	2x		
Bad temperament				2x	+
Father					
Involvement by/warmth	3.2x		3.5/2.1x	3/2.6x	+
Mental Illness			2.3x		
Stepfather		3.3x			
Family					
Low Harmony	2–2.4x		2.4–2.6x	1.7x	+
Large Size			3.2x	1.8x	
Low income			3x	3x	+
Parent dies		2.6x			
Neg. life events		4.4x			

24% had 4 or more risk factors; 3% had no risk factors. + = had 2 or more factors

enough." Shame can be so pervasive that it can stop people from going into recovery because they believe they don't deserve to or that they will never feel better.

> **Case History 7.1:** Sharon was a forty-four-year-old woman who came to me complaining of a strong and painful sense of insecurity. She had been physically abused and neglected throughout her childhood. Over time, in group therapy, as she worked, she realized that it was really shame or low self-esteem that was robbing her of what she called "a sense of being unable to root myself so I could feel secure." She often described her "battle" as trying to box her way out of a canvas bag. No matter how hard she struggled, she couldn't see and free herself. Over time, she shared her burdensome feeling and experience of shame to the therapy group and revealed it from many different angles. Eventually she was able to grieve for her lost childhood. With compassion and acceptance from the group, Sharon eventually was able to feel compassion for herself, realizing how severely she had been treated. She told the group that the voices inside her head telling her how bad she was weren't quite so loud anymore, and she could now often hear her real self soothing her.

A major way to heal shame is to share our experience of it with safe people.[797, 798] An effective way to do that is to tell our story or narrative, bit by bit, of what happened to us in our trauma experience.[583] This process may be accomplished in individual therapy or counseling, during heart-to-heart talks with a trusted friend, and in group therapy or a self-help group. Each time that we share our shame, we express it, and thereby expel it outside of our self. By doing so, we paradoxically own that we experienced it, and then we can get rid of it. Shame usually takes a long time to heal.

While there are some data-based studies that show an overall improvement using group treatment (see next volume) and contact with therapists,[277] most of the experience on healing low self-esteem (i.e., shame) is anecdotal, although it is based on decades of careful observation on countless trauma survivors as they heal.[272, 413, 414, 450, 600, 601, 793, 798] These reports also validate ways to help heal shame from a rich and consistent perspective. If someone believes that they are mentally ill, this may aggravate and compound that shame. Shame will likely rear its subtle but ugly head numerous times during recovery. However, participating in a recovery program will eventually affirm our inherent goodness.

8   THE NEUROBIOLOGY
OF TRAUMA

We have long pursued the cause of mental illness. But in our search for its biological truths, could we have missed a fundamental connection? In my introduction to this book I raised the *nature* versus *nurture* question, and proposed that the cause of most mental illness was not either/or. Rather, it appears that its cause is *both/and:* nature *and* nurture.

When we've looked at the biology of people with mental illness we have found several abnormalities in brain structure, function and chemistry among some people.* From that association between disorder and abnormal biology, we assumed that biology most probably caused the disorder.

But we may have missed a larger connection. We may have missed the big picture. This is because for only the last twenty-five years, and especially for the past ten, some biological researchers have added childhood trauma to the possible variables that they

---

* In spite of our continued assumption that these abnormalities are genetically transmitted, so far we have found no abnormal genes for people with common mental disorders (e.g., refs. 82, 178, 572, 573, 759). Bremner said, "Thirty years after the start of the biological revolution in psychiatry, we still haven't found the gene for schizophrenia or mania."[82]

looked at among people with mental illness. When they did, they found that repeated trauma in childhood also caused similar—if not the same—abnormalities of brain structure, function and chemistry.

AN EVOLVING NEW THEORY

Our prior assumption was that the discovered abnormal biology caused the mental illness. But we can look at it another way. If we include trauma as another legitimate variable to examine, we can arrive at another conclusion. The trauma may have caused *both* the abnormal biology and the mental illness.

As I show throughout this and the next book, a *history* of childhood trauma is *strongly* associated with several common mental disorders, including depression, anxiety disorders, addictions, post-traumatic stress disorder and dissociative disorders. It is also *moderately* to *strongly* associated with personality disorders and psychoses, violence and some behavior problems. A few bold researchers have proposed that this relationship may be causal of some of these mental disorders.[56, 67, 82, 426-6]

Since 1991, researchers have found an association between having a history of childhood trauma and abnormal brain biology, which I describe below. With childhood trauma as a valid third variable, we can now look at the relationship among the three variables (trauma, biology and mental disorder) in another way, as shown in Figure 8.1. Our old theory was that abnormal brain biology caused mental illness. Now, perhaps a more plausible theory is that childhood trauma causes *both* of the two variables of abnormal brain biology and some mental illnesses.

If childhood trauma causes *brain damage* and the related *mental illness,* then we can say that these two conditions are its *consequences.* By understanding that childhood trauma is the base cause of some mental illnesses, their prevention becomes a reasonable possibility. We can prevent some mental disorders by not abusing and neglecting our children.

But what is the evidence for this theory? What data do we have that supports it? As this book goes to press, I have found forty-one studies that show a significant association between the history of childhood trauma and abnormal brain structure, function and chemistry, which I summarize below. What these tell us is that repeated childhood trauma damages the brain and some of its functioning. Among these brain areas are the prefrontal cortex (the thinking and interpreting brain) and the limbic system (the emotional brain), including the hippocampus, amygdala, and the

Figure 8.1. Relationship of Childhood Trauma
to Effects and Assumptions

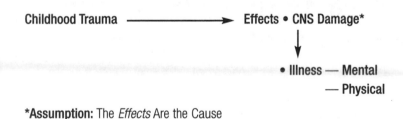

Childhood Trauma ⟶ Effects • CNS Damage*

↓

• Illness — Mental
— Physical

*Assumption: The *Effects* Are the Cause

Correction: Childhood **Trauma** Is the *Cause*
CNS Damage & **Illness** Are the *Consequences***

**We continue to learn more about how background factors, such as genetic influences and environmental toxins, may cause mental illness &/or interact with trauma. For example, could a genetically transmitted mental disorder so affect a parent that they abuse or neglect their child?

A Cause for Hope

This new information should not discourage trauma survivors. Instead of looking at the glass as being half empty—
believing we are damaged, I believe that our glass is actually
half full. This is because knowing this information supports
everything we have learned about the process of healing by
using a trauma-based recovery program. I describe this
recovery program throughout these two volumes. Rather than
being discouraging or suggesting hopelessness, this new
information is actually empowering. Knowing the truth about
the cause of our pain usually hurts at first. But by working on
our recovery in the company of safe people, and with
patience and persistence, this possible truth eventually can
set us free.

As a corollary, a patient once complained to me that she
was afraid to admit how bad or hurtful her abuse was. She
said that if she admitted the severity of it, then she would
have to accept how damaged she is. I worked with her to
understand that she never had healthy parenting, and if she
could admit that, then she could be open to learn how to be
a good parent to herself. She could learn how to take good
care of herself—begin to eat healthily, exercise and take
time for creative endeavors. She then realized that her mind
may be hurt and need healing, but her true self
(child within) was never damaged—it was in hiding and
might come out if she learned the skills of a protective good
parent to take care of herself.

vermis of the cerebellum, as shown in Table 8.1. This table
shows eight key areas of the brain according to their location,
function, and it clarifies some of the detrimental effects that
trauma has on each of them.

Healthy Families

Cared for by healthy parents, normal infants and children learn to calm and soothe themselves by internalizing the nurturing behaviors of their caregivers.[715] As they grow and develop, their brain and peripheral nervous system develop in tandem, so that these key brain areas work in harmony with one another to help handle ordinary stress. When the child encounters a stressful situation, its sympathetic nervous system is automatically activated in a "fight or flight" response. Once the stress is handled appropriately, these healthily developed key brain areas act to modulate or calm the stress reaction, toning it down once again to a normal resting state. The child can now relax and tend to its tasks of being a normal healthy child. (A snapshot example of this response has been repeatedly shown in the healthy, or "type B" reaction in attachment theory research, described in the previous chapter on page 85.)

Unhealthy Families

If a child is repeatedly abused or neglected, its brain and nervous system are highly likely to be damaged to varying degrees. Accumulating research data has shown the following: Repeated trauma to developing infants or older children damages their *prefrontal cortex* (which performs "executive" functions such as thinking, focusing, reasoning, controlling behavior and self-soothing), *corpus callosum* (the fiber bundle connecting the two cerebral hemispheres), the *hippocampus* (learning, memory, emotional balance), *amygdala* (emotion processing and balance), *cerebellar vermis* (helps calm an overexcited limbic system), *HPA axis* (hypothalamic-pituitary-adrenal axis, which is a major part of

Table 8.1. Characteristics of Brain Structures

(compiled from refs. 12, 80, 82, 198, 203

Brain Structure	Location	Function
Reticular Activating System (RAS)	Multisystem network throughout limbic system & brain, consisting of 1–5 below & more	Alerts cortex of threats & modulates fear/anxiety/stress response
1 **Locus Coeruleus** (LC) & 2 **Ventral Tegmental Nucleus** (VTN)	Bilateral nuclei above pons; VTN extends into medulla	Norepinephrine regulation in brain; LC interacts with ANS, immunity & HPA
3 **Hippocampus**	Between amygdala & midbrain	Processes memory, learning, fear/stress & ANS activities
4 **Amygdala**	Between hippocampus & cortex	Processes feelings & emotional memory
5 **Hypothalamic-Pituitary-Adrenal axis** (HPA)	Extends widely in body	Regulates hormones
Cerebellar vermis	Behind midbrain	Modulates an overexcited limbic system
Cerebral hemispheres (medial prefrontal cortex)/**Corpus callosum**	Dominant structures/ connect hemispheres	Uses & balances messages from lower structures constructively or destructively

*All are more complex than this introductory table summarizes. ANS = autonomic nervous system

& Their Relation to Trauma*

continued from p. 96, refs. 416, 584-8, 665)

Kind of Stress

Acute	Chronic	Comment
Processes fear & acute stress	Chronic distress programmed into experience	Programming (repetition) produces many of the ongoing effects of trauma
Activity reflects degree of emotional arousal, e.g., calm/alert	As others; may be involved in PTSD	Determines charge or valence of incoming information
↑ cortisol damages synapse & dendrite structure	Atrophy, ↓ memory & learning, ↑ PTSD symptoms	Has ↑ # of cortisol receptors; *continues neuronal growth throughout life*
Reactions vary	Atrophy; reactions become programmed, e.g., "highjack"	Connected to thalamus, cortex & RAS
Influenced by above, which ↑ cortisol may damage	Damage whole body, including the above structures	Can damage or nourish some of the above structures
Cortisol may damage	Marked ↓ blood flow overexcited limbic system	Coordinates balance, emotions, hemispheric switching
	↓ integration, aggravating, constructive, functioning	Planning, execution, response inhibition, fear response extinction

"Highjack" = extreme emotional over-reaction through amygdala

the body's hormone system),* the *serotonin/dopamine/GABA* system, and the *sympathetic nervous* system (Figure 8.2 and Table 8.2).

To better understand these brain structures and functions, it may be helpful to summarize a bird's-eye view of their relevant anatomy and physiology. The nervous system consists of the brain and peripheral nervous system. The brain (cerebrum) has two large softball-sized halves (hemispheres) squeezed together inside the top of our skull, both of which connect to the adjoining deep lying (mid-brain) structures, which include the limbic system, which helps us handle our learning, memory and emotion. The mid-brain continues as the brain stem, which then becomes the spinal cord, from which the peripheral nerves branch out to work our muscles and organs. Throughout this large structure of the brain and peripheral nervous system is a crucial subsystem of chemical messengers called *neurotransmitters*, as shown in Figure 8.2.

These complex systems are each interconnected, directly or indirectly, with the other brain structures/systems. Like a skilled symphony orchestra under the direction of an expert conductor, in normal health these interact to help us recognize, then process, and finally calm the stresses of everyday life. But if the brain structures and systems are damaged and disrupted from repeated childhood trauma, they may be unskilled, out of tune with one another, and the conductor will often be missing. Instead of a harmonious and pleasing symphony, they will often produce a cacophony of painful noise—inside and out—that doesn't know

---

*Activation of the HPA axis is one of the main manifestations of our response to stress. The adrenal cortex, stimulated by adrenocortropic hormone (ACTH) from the pituitary gland, releases glucocorticoids (including especially cortisol). The hippocampus contains a high density of glucocorticoid receptors and plays a vital role in the feedback system that regulates the activation of the HPA axis.

Figure 8.2. Simplified Scheme of Brain System Relationships*

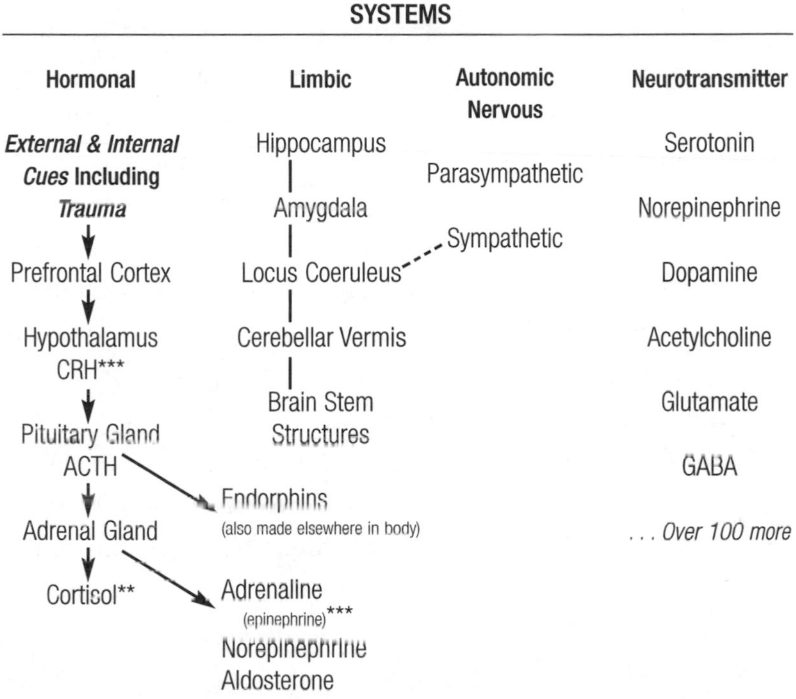

SYSTEMS

Hormonal	Limbic	Autonomic Nervous	Neurotransmitter
External & Internal Cues Including *Trauma*	Hippocampus | Amygdala | Locus Coeruleus	Parasympathetic --- Sympathetic	Serotonin Norepinephrine
↓			Dopamine
Prefrontal Cortex			
↓	Cerebellar Vermis		Acetylcholine
Hypothalamus CRH***	|		
↓	Brain Stem		Glutamate
Pituitary Gland ACTH	Structures		GABA
↓	Endorphins (also made elsewhere in body)		... *Over 100 more*
Adrenal Gland			
↓	Adrenaline (epinephrine)***		
Cortisol**	Norepinephrine Aldosterone		

* All have a complex function and interrelationship with one another. Other systems, such as the neuro-*receptor* systems, also exist and play an important role.

** *Cortisol* helps in normal healthy functioning by increasing energy release and metabolism, but like a double-edged sword, in repeated trauma—through high concentrations and disordered metabolism—it can damage the brain and other organs (e.g., suppress inflammatory and immune response) and block memory. [560a]

*** Epinephrine and norepinephrine in healthy people increase cardiovascular and respiratory response, perspiration, blood to muscles, mental activity and cellular metabolism. But repeated trauma can cause vascular and other vital organ damage. CRH = corticotropin releasing hormone (also has neurotransmitter properties); ACTH = adrenocorticotropic hormone; GABA = gamma aminobutyric acid.

how to quiet itself. Imagine a symphony orchestra constantly trying to tune up but being unable to play. With this kind and degree of brain damage, it is not surprising that trauma survivors of all ages are often hurting and, at times, attempting to get rid of it—

projecting their pain onto others and often acting it out in other ways, including being depressed.

In early childhood the brain is extremely sensitive and mal-leable to experiences that are both positive (healthy nurturing) and negative (abuse and neglect).[82, 613a, 782] Repeated trauma can thus have long-term detrimental impacts on children's ability to think, feel, relate and function, now and later in their lives. We have a vast confluence of data from studies on central nervous system (CNS) "plasticity"—the study of CNS organization as a function of experience. *Disruptions* of *experience-dependent* brain and nerve chemical signals during early growth and devel-opment may lead to major abnormalities in neurodevelopment, often resulting in mental illness. Neuroscientists Michael Weiss and Sheldon Wagner said, "Much like working on clay, which becomes more difficult as the clay hardens, age and time harden the plasticity of the CNS. In some systems (such as seeing and hearing) the clay is hard by the end of the first year. For others (thinking and speaking), the opportunity to adjust the develop-mental path persists into later childhood."[782]

Weiss and Wagner conclude, "Infants are born with approxi-mately one hundred billion neurons. This is about all we need to be Einsteins or Beethovens. But what differentiates [them] from a newborn is not the number of neurons, but the connections that these neurons make (the synaptic connections). By adulthood, these neurons branch out to each other to form about one hun-dred trillion connections. This thousand-fold increase is due almost solely to the effects of experience. Experience not only creates connections, it also prunes connections. . . . There are thousands of studies documenting the unequivocal effect of early experience on development. The conclusions from these studies are obvious: deprivation or abuse as early experience leads to less optimal development, and enriched experience can lead to enhanced development."

DEPRESSION AND BRAIN ATROPHY

Researchers have found abnormal brain structure, chemistry and function in several mental disorders, including depression, alcoholism and schizophrenia. For example, using recent techniques such as magnetic resonance imaging (MRI), positron emission tomography (PET) and spectroscopy, independent investigators looking at diverse groups of depressed people have found significant atrophy of certain brain structures. These include substantial brain areas: 1) the frontal lobes (3 positive reports/1 negative report), 2) orbital frontal lobes (2 reports), 3) subgenual frontal lobes (1/1 reports), 4) caudate nucleus (2/3 reports), 5) hippocampus (9/3 reports), 6) putamen (1/1 reports). As a whole, this atrophy is shown further by 5 separate reports of significant enlargement of the brain ventricles (the two tissue-empty but fluid-filled areas, one inside each cerebral hemisphere). Four studies also showed enlargement of the amygdala. In all, these total 44 separate studies.[82a] These brain areas are all interconnected and involved in the stress response, in which cortisol is elevated (which appears to damage the hippocampus, verbal memory and thinking).

What does this information mean? One possibility is that the atrophy is somehow significantly related to or perhaps it may even cause the depression. Some of these studies looked for a history of childhood trauma among its subjects, and found a significant link between the trauma and both the brain atrophy and depression. Few found no association. A more rational explanation, based on all of the reports that I have summarized in this book, is that, in a majority of people with these three findings, the repeated childhood trauma is the most likely cause of both the brain atrophy and the depression. I will present this evidence in the next chapter.

NEUROBIOLOGY OF ANTIDEPRESSANT DRUGS AND PLACEBO

We are discovering neurobiological changes related to the use of both antidepressant drugs and placebo. For example, in a study of seventeen depressed men given either fluoxetine (Prozac) or placebo for six weeks in a double-blinded fashion, those responding to *placebo* had increased glucose metabolism in several key brain areas (prefrontal, anterior cingulate, premotor, parietal, posterior insula and posterior cingulate). They also showed a decreased metabolism in other brain areas (subgenual cingulate, parahippocampus and thalamus). These changes overlapped with those seen in the people who responded to fluoxetine. But fluoxetine response was also associated with other changes in the brain (brain stem, striatum, anterior insula and hippocampus).[487] I discuss ADP drugs and placebo further in chapters 10 and 11.

In the next chapter I will continue describing the neurobiology of trauma by summarizing the evidence for trauma's effects on the structure and function of the brain, the neuroendocrine system, and neurological functioning.

9   THE NEUROBIOLOGY OF TRAUMA: THE EVIDENCE

Structural/Anatomical Brain Damage

In my research on the neurobiology of trauma, I found forty-four data based, peer-reviewed, published studies that give us evidence that repeated childhood trauma damages the brain's anatomy, physiology and overall functioning.

Concomitant with the advances in the technology of magnetic resonance imaging (MRI) since 1995, I found three of these forty-four studies that reported atrophy (shrinkage) of most or parts of the *cerebral cortex* among people with repeated childhood trauma, when compared with control subjects. One of these found indirect evidence of decreased prefrontal cortex size.[201]* While damage to any part of the brain is usually detrimental to a person's psychological and behavioral health, injury to the cerebral cortex, especially its prefrontal area, can be especially

---

* Another study not listed in Table 9.1 reported a large degree (32 percent) of atrophy of the orbitofrontal cortex among fifteen recently depressed people when they were compared to twenty normal controls. Since the literature (and my clinical experience) strongly suggests that at least two-thirds of depressed people have a significant history of repeated childhood trauma, it may be reasonable to assume that at least ten of these fifteen depressed people were also trauma survivors.[34]

debilitating, since it is so instrumental in such tasks as thinking, focusing, reasoning, controlling behavior and self-soothing.

I also found nine studies on the *hippocampus* among trauma survivors (Table 9.1). All of these showed a significant atrophy (shrinkage in size or volume of either the left or the right hippocampus, or both of them) among trauma survivors. As summarized in Table 8.1, the hippocampus is a crucial organ for processing our emotions, learning and memory. To complete its job, it interacts with the rest of the limbic system, brain and body. If any one or more of these crucial parts of our brain are damaged by repeated childhood trauma, short circuits may occur, leaving its owner at a disadvantage.

In these studies, the amount of shrinkage of the hippocampus varied from 5 to 26 percent among trauma survivors as compared to control subjects. The *amygdala* was found to be atrophied by from 8 to 9.8 percent in two studies. With no change found in one study, most of the remaining five studies did not look at the amygdala's size. While the hippocampus is a large enough organ to discern on the MRI, the amygdala is relatively smaller and may be harder to see. Four of these studies showed a significant association between atrophy of the hippocampus or amygdala and symptoms of traumatic stress such as depression, irritability and memory deficits, as shown in Table 9.1. Two also reported atrophy of the *corpus callosum,* which is important in relaying messages between the two cerebral hemispheres.*

---

*An additional study (not listed in Table 9.1) showed a bilateral atrophy of the hippocampus among twelve adolescent alcoholics when compared with twenty-four controls, but showed no difference in cerebral size.[202] Since the literature (and, again, my clinical experience) showed that most adolescents with alcoholism or other chemical dependence have a history of repeated childhood trauma, in addition to alcoholic drinking, past trauma may be another factor in causing atrophy of this important brain structure.

In summary, these thirteen studies were published from 1995 to 2002. Three of them looked at the *cerebral cortex,* eight addressed the *hippocampus*—two of which also looked at the *amygdala*—and another two examined the *corpus callosum* (the large nerve bundles that interconnect the two hemispheres). All twelve showed a *significant atrophy* of these important parts of the brain. Remarkably, *nearly every study* that has looked at these two important variables of brain structure and childhood trauma has *found a significant link.*

Damaged Hormone and Neurotransmitter Systems

In addition to structural damage, repeated childhood trauma may disrupt the brain's hormonal and neurotransmitter systems. For these, I found seventeen studies on over 1,375 children that showed significant defects in the functioning of their hypothalamic-pituitary-adrenal (HPA) axis, the hormones that it produces and their neurotransmitters that act in concert with these to help them function mentally, emotionally and physically (summarized in Table 9.2). From the hypothalamus and its adjoining pituitary gland, the brain releases corticotrophin-releasing hormone (CRH) and adrenocorticotropic hormone (ACTH), which then stimulates the adrenal gland to secrete the stress hormone cortisol. High cortisol levels can impair normal memory in healthy people[560a] and may be a factor in dissociative amnesia among trauma survivors.

The secretion rate of all three of these hormones is normally high in the early morning, and low in the late afternoon and evening. Acute stress disrupts this cycle temporarily. But repeated childhood traumas disrupt it and other metabolic

Table 9.1. Brain Atrophy

Date/Author	Sample Evaluated
Cerebrum (Two Main Brain Hemispheres)	
1999 DeBellis et al.	44 CT child/teens with PTSD, 61 controls
2000 De Bellis et al.	11 CT children, 11 controls
2001 Carrion et. al.	24 CT children with PTSD, 24 controls
Hippocampus (HC)/Amygdala	
1995 Bremner et al. 1996	22 combat veterans, 22 controls
1996 Gurvitz et al.	7 combat veterans with PTSD, 7 combat veterans, no PTSD
1997 Stein et al.	21 CSA women, most with PTSD &/or DID, 21 controls
1997 Bremner et al.	17 severe CS/PA adults with PTSD, 17 controls
2000 Driessen et al.	21 CT & BPD women, + controls
2001 Teicher et al.	18 CSA, 29 controls
2002 DeBellis et al.	12 teen alcoholics, most CT (?), 24 controls
Vythilingham et al.	46 women, CT vs. controls
Corpus Callosum (CC)	
1997 DeBellis et al.	CT children
Teicher et al.	CT children
1995–2002 **13 studies**	**3 on Cerebral Cortex, 9 on Hippocampus,** **2 on Amygdala, 2 on Corpus Callosum**

CSA = childhood sexual abuse, EEG = electroencephalogram, CT = childhood trauma,

and Trauma

Findings

Cerebrum (Two Main Brain Hemispheres)

↓ 7% brain size; ↓ CC size; ≈ age onset trauma; NSD HC size (may delay until older)

Evidence of ↓ size of anterior cingulate area of medial prefrontal cerebral cortex

↓ brain and hippocampus size

Hippocampus (HC)/Amygdala

8% ↓ right HC size, associated with short-term memory deficits

26% ↓ bilateral HC size (≈ trauma severity), normal amygdala/whole brain size

5% ↓ HC size, ≈ dissociative symptoms

↓ 12% size left HC & related memory deficits

↓ 16% size left HC, 8% amygdala

↓ 9.8% size amygdala, ≈ depression, irritability, hostility

↓ HC bilateral; other brain functions normal

↓ 15-18% size left hippocampus

Corpus Callosum (CC)

↓ size corpus callosum

Pending

All had significant atrophy associated with a history of repeated trauma

BPD =borderline personality disorder, ≈ = proportional to, NSD = no significant difference, DID = dissociative identity disorder

Table 9.2. Hormonal/Neurotransmitter

Date/Author	Sample Evaluated
1991 Queiroz et al.	CT children vs. controls
Kaufman et al.	30 CT children vs. controls
Putnam	13 CSA girls, prospective
1996 Hart et al.	197 CT children in daycare vs. controls
1994 De Bellis et al. a & b	13 CSA girls vs. 13 controls; + 21 CT controls
1995 Hart et al.	49 CT children vs. controls
1996 Goenjian et al.	CT teens with PTSD (earthquake)
1997 Carlson & Earls	CT young Romanian children
De Bellis et al.	CSA girls
Kaufman et al.	13 CT children with ongoing stress, 13 depressed, 13 controls
Stein et al.	19 severe CSA women, 21 controls, given low dose (0.5 mg) DST
1999 De Bellis et al.	18 CT children with PTSD, 10 overanxious, 24 controls
2000 a & b Cicchetti & Rogosch	384 & 371 CT children vs. controls
Heim et al.	40 CT women ± depressed, 11 depressed, 20 controls
2002 Carrion et al.	51 CT children with PTSD, 31 controls
	1,375 + CT & controls
1991–2002 17 studies	

CSA = childhood sexual abuse, EEG = electroencephalogram, CT = childhood trauma, NSD = no significant difference, DA = dopamine, NE = norepinephrine, EPI = epinephrine, * = prospective CRH = corticotropin-releasing hormone

Defects & Childhood Trauma

Findings

↑ urine NE in CT boys; related to abandonment? (cited in De Bellis 2001)

HPA axis dysregulation

↑ diurnal cortisol secretion, possibly due to ↑ central CRH secretion

HPA axis dysregulation

↓ basal, CRH stimulated & total ACTH, nl cortisol/same measures; suggest HPA axis dys-regulation. ↑ depression & suicidality, ↑ urinary catecholamines & metabolites

Cortisol response failure under stress

HPA axis dysregulation

Disturbed circadian rhythm of HPA axis

↑ urinary catocholamines

↑ ACTH response to CRH, normal cortisol under high stress (as with chronic traumatized animals); possibly from ↑ central CRH secretion

Enhanced DST, similar to combat-related PTSD (severely depressed do not have suppressed DST). 3x depression, 5x dissociation

↑ urine DA, NE, EPI, ↑ depression, suicidality, ↑ global functioning

Abnormal cortisol levels

Abnormal ACTH & plasma cortisol after CRH

↑ cortisol, adrenal activity

Defects in HPA axis, hormones & neurotransmitters—*Replicated*

HPA = hypothalamic-pituitary-adrenal axis, DST = dexamethasone suppression test, EEG = electrooncephalogram; catecholamines = neurotransmitters such as DA, NE, EPI & their metabolites.

functioning long-term. This leaves the child and adolescent, and later the adult, with an abnormally functioning master gland (hypothalamus/pituitary), which often results in sleep disruption and a disrupted response to stress, and often damages and disrupts other brain organs and systems. All of this apparently trauma-induced disordered metabolism can be associated with or result in depression, suicidality and PTSD (most did not look for other mental disorders), as several of these studies show (Table 9.2). As with the trauma-associated brain structural damage described above, the analogy of the detrimental neurobiological effects of combat trauma may also apply here, since these disordered hormone effects are similar to those found in several studies on combat veterans with PTSD.

Other Trauma-Related Brain Function Damage

The remaining damages found so far include some other functions of the brain and nervous system. Here, I found fourteen studies that were published from 1974 to 2002, which I show as but examples, since I suspect that there are several more. These trauma-related effects include: decreased *neurological function* years later, decreased *verbal* and *performance skills* and *IQ,* decreased *mental development* (personal, social and motor), abnormal *EEGs, seizures, depression* and *substance abuse* (Table 9.3). Three of these studies found an abnormal relationship between the two brain hemispheres, which also may be correlated with various mental disorders.

Summary

I summarize these study results in Table 9.4. While the number (forty-four) of these studies is not as large as those that link trauma with mental disorders (nearly three hundred), most of their findings have been replicated by diverse and independent investigators. Replication is one of the strong markers of validity in scientific research (described on page 37). These replicated and consistent results are especially meaningful in our work with children and adults with mental disorders.

Animal Studies

Finally, I include two articles that review the literature on the effects of trauma on animals, mostly conducted on rats and non-human primates. These reviews show the same structural, hormonal, neurotransmitter, and some of the functional defects and damage as do the above studies on traumatized children (Table 9.6). As do others (e.g., in refs. 82, 197, 198 & 643), the authors of the second review say that the early trauma may represent the *underlying biological substrate* of an *increased vulnerability* to subsequent stress and *mental illness*. They recommend taking a trauma history on all mentally ill patients and underscore the importance for the development of novel treatments.[347]

Related Treatment

Others and I believe that these novel treatments are already available in the form of a trauma-focused program of recovery. These include especially individual and group psychotherapy

Table 9.3. Decreased Brain/Neurological Function &

Date/Author	Sample Evaluated
1974 Martin et al.	58 physically abused children (no evidence of head trauma)
Sandgrund et al.	60 abused, 30 neglected, 30 controls
1977 Applebaum	30 abused, 30 controls (2 months to 2.5 years old)
1983 Friedrich et al.	11 physically abused preschoolers 4-5.6 years old
1978 Davies et al.	CSA (incest)
1993, 98 Ito et al.	30 children, CT vs. controls
1994 Teicher et al.	115 child/teen psych unit CTs vs. controls
1995 Schiffer et al.	CT adults vs. controls re: hemispheric activity
1997 Putnam et al.	13 CSA girls
Teicher et al.	15 severe CT, 15 controls
Teicher et al.	104 children, CT vs. controls
1999 Irwin et al.	CTs evaluated
2001 Read et al.	Childhood trauma vs. controls
2002 Anderson et al.	8 CSA 18–22 years old vs. 16 controls, cerebellar vermis relax. time (blood flow to)
14 Example Studies 1974–2002	**More than 565 CTs + Controls**

CSA = childhood sexual abuse, EEG = electroencephalogram, CT = childhood trauma, ≈ = proportional to, NSD = no significant difference

Childhood Trauma: Example Results from 14 Studies

Findings

Neurological dysfunction 4.5 years later

Decreased verbal, performance skills & IQ

Decreased mental (personal, social & language) & motor development

Decreased verbal, memory & cognitive skills

77% abnormal EEG, 27% seizures

Left brain, reversed cerebral structural symmetry

2–3x clinically significant FFG abnormalities

↓ right brain integration

2 years earlier puberty, 2x auto-antibodies

CTs had brain dominance reversed on coherence EEG

↓ cortical development, 7x neuropsychological test deficits

Defects in smooth pursuit eye movement tasks significantly related to childhood trauma

2–3x non-specific EEG abnormalities

Lower blood flow in CTs, correlates with temporal lobe seizure symptoms ≈ ↑ drug use & depression

Decreased brain & other neurological function

EEG = electroencephalogram

that assists the whole person in healing from their trauma-related effects and issues.[33, 34, 96, 151, 174, 186, 753, 797, 798] The recovery aids of eye movement desensitization and reprocessing (EMDR),[675] and at times judiciously selected and used psychoactive drugs such as buspirone for excessive fear or an antidepressant drug for a time may help take the edge off of the person's extreme pain. The aim of healing is not to eliminate emotional pain. Rather, a major goal is to get to know it and ultimately befriend our pain. We identify and accurately name the trauma, truthfully describe where it came from, connect the trauma to current conflicts and issues, and while doing so, we grieve. We express and grieve the pain that we never got to express and grieve (since our unconscious goal when we were mistreated was to survive). And once we know our pain, we can gradually let it go (something we may not have been able to do when we identified exclusively with being depressed).

Key in the area of healing is the role of the prefrontal cortex in the process of reacting to both external triggers and cues and the process of healing. Looking back at Figure 8.2, we can see that essentially every brain structure, system, hormone and neurotransmitter tend to automatically react to messages transmitted to them by and through the prefrontal cortex. We also usually have little or no control over the external cues that we encounter in our environment from moment to moment. But we do have control over how we process these triggers and cues in our *prefrontal cortex*. Thus, through its "executive" functions, such as thinking, focusing, reasoning, controlling our personal behavior and self-soothing, we can, over time, during our recovery work learn to use this crucial part of our brain to our advantage. We can learn to begin to see things differently and react in more constructive and healthy ways. While this idea may at first sound simple, it is not. Rather it involves a long process of experiencing our pain and learning from it, including its meanings for us on multiple levels.

Effective "treatment" is not something that someone else does to us. It is not found outside of our self. Successful treatment is self-treatment in the form of an ongoing motivation and dedication to heal, and then applying patience and persistence to complete it. That completion may take a long time. Finally, treatment, or better, *recovery* from the effects of repeated childhood trauma is usually best accomplished in stages that include stabilization of the surface disorder (Stage One), doing the original pain work (Stage Two, which usually takes the longest) and then eventually making constructive meaning out of it all (Stage Three), which I describe further on page 163 and chapter 14.

*   *   *

Some have postulated that children may have a delayed effect of showing such brain damage (just as the "sleeper" effect for mental and behavioral disorders suggested by Frank Putnum[605] and Dan Brown[105]), since their *brains may not show damage early in life* in spite of continuing abuse and neglect. It is remarkable that even with this possible reservation, some children who were studied showed the same brain damage as did combat veterans. It is as though they have been living through their own physical, mental, emotional and sexual combat zones in the presence of their abusers, who are most often their parents, and sometimes their siblings and other relatives.

Table 9.4. Summary of Neurobiological

Finding	Long-Term Effect
Brain size	↓ 7%
Hippocampus size	↓ 5–26%
Amygdala size	↓ 8–9.8%
Corpus Callosum	↓ size
HPA axis rhythm	Disturbed
Cortisol secretion	↑ diurnal secretion
Urine NE, Epi, DA**	↑
EEG	Abnormal
Brain function***	↓
SUMMARY	
Brain Structure, Hormones & Function	Significant Abnormalities

* ≈ = significantly associated with
**NE, Epi, DA = norepinephrine, epinephrine (adrenalin), dopamine [all stimulants of the nervous system];
DST = dexamethasone suppression test; EEG = electroencephalogram (brain wave test)
***Mental (personal, verbal, language, thinking, emotional, social), motor development, hemisphere balance.

Findings in Trauma

References

De Bellis et al. 1999 *(≈* age onset trauma)*, Bremner 2002 *(medial prefrontal cortex)*; Carrion 2001

Bremner et al. 1995, 6 & 7 *(≈ short-term memory deficits)*; Gurvitz et al.1996 *(≈ trauma severity)*; Stein et al. 1997 *(≈ dissociative symptoms)*; Dreissen et al. 2001; De Bellis et al. 2002; Vythilingham et al. 2002

Dreissen et al. 2001, Teicher et al. 2001 *(≈ depression, irritability, hostility)*

De Bellis et al. 1997, Teicher et al. 1997

De Bellis et al. 1994, Goenjian et al. 1996, Carlson & Earls 1997, Kaufman et al. 1997, Heim et al. 2001

Kaufman et al. 1991, Putnam 1991, Hart et al. 1996 *(all possibly due to ↑ oontral CRH secretion)*, Hart et al. 1995 *(response failure under stress)*, Stein et al. 1997 *(↑ DST ~ 3x depression, 5x dissociation);* Carrion et al. 2002

Queiroz 1991; De Bellis et al. 1994, 1997, 1999 *(~ ↑ dopression, suicidality, ↓ global functioning)*

Davies et al. 1978; Teicher et al. 1994, 1997; Read et al. 2001

Martin et al. 1974, Sandgrund et al. 1974, Applebaum 1977, Friedrich 1983, Ito et al. 1993, Schiffer 1995, Teicher et al. 1997 *(7x neuropsychological test deficits)*, Irwin et al. 1999, Anderson et al. 2002 *(≈ drug use & depression)*

41 Studies show significant decrease in brain structure size (atrophy), function & neuro-hormonal/neurotransmitter function (1974–2002)

Table 9.5. Brain Damage in Traumatized Animals: Example Literature Reviews

Date/Author	Study	Findings
2000 Kaufman et al.	Review of traumatized animal research 1978–2000	↓ size HC, amygdala, frontal cortex, GABA receptor binding, other abnormalities
2001 Heim & Nemeroff	Review of traumatized animal and human research 1988–2001	Early trauma damages the HPA axis by CRH dysregulation and other neurotransmitter abnormalities. Recommends addressing trauma history in mentally ill patients.

HC = hippocampus; CRH = corticotropin releasing hormone (also has neurotransmitter properties); GABA = gamma aminobutyric acid; HPA = hypothalamic-pituitary-adrenal axis.

Chronic childhood trauma also fragments overall brain functioning, causing significant difficulty focusing, learning and relating to others. Repeated trauma impairs the normal stress response in several ways, including through a mechanism called "kindling." This occurs when the brain or one of its parts becomes hypersensitive to lower stimuli than would ordinarily set it off.[705] Chronic stress also damages the body's immune system, including the thymus gland, and may make the traumatized person more vulnerable to infections and autoimmune diseases.[82, 301a]

All of these injurious effects on the brain and the body leave the person at a distinct disadvantage in surviving and coping with life. No single illness or syndrome describes or simplifies the results of these effects. Instead, trauma survivors may have *any one* or a *combination* of acute and chronic mental disorders. These are often accompanied by one or more physical illnesses, as the ACE study and others have shown.[254] Trauma survivors often have difficulty focusing and are easily distracted. They commonly have learning and behavior problems (ADHD/ADD, conduct disorder, oppositional defiant disorder), emotional blunting and lability (depression, anxiety disorder, etc.), extreme emotional pain and covering it (addictions), age regressions and flashbacks (dissociative disorders), difficulty testing reality (psychotic symptoms and signs), learned malfunctioning in relationships with self and others (personality disorders), somatization (physical functional and organic disease). They frequently have a combination of the above. Underlying, and a major part of, most of these is posttraumatic stress disorder. Underlying PTSD is a wounded and violent society that is mostly unaware of all of the above. I say more about these "co-morbid" conditions in chapter 12.

While we need further research to learn more about these upsetting effects, their mere existence is distressing and has profound implications in the areas of medicine, psychiatry, psychology and the law. For example, with this knowledge we cannot continue to allow parents and others to abuse and neglect their children. We need to educate the public, especially people having children. We cannot continue to support our health insurance companies (under the name of "managed care"), as they repeatedly disallow payment coverage for appropriate and effective recovery methods such as trauma-focused individual and group psychotherapy. We need to rethink our assumptions and conclusions about the causes of mental illness.

Child abuse is not about small numbers. It is a dramatically common phenomenon. Data show that in the United States one in three girls and one in four to five boys are sexually abused.[103, 104, 798] At least one in ten children are seriously physically abused (enough to cause physical injuries). At least one in four children are neglected. Well over half of children are psychologically and emotionally abused. We cannot afford to live in denial anymore. We need to address this problem head-on. Hopefully, we will also see the world's violence decrease as we stop our violence to our children.

10 DO ANTIDEPRESSANT DRUGS WORK?

Yes, they do appear to work, but at best by only a few percentage points (e.g., 2 to 10 percent) better than placebo. More likely, for most people they work only about as well as placebo. But, with their high expense and fairly high incidence of toxic side effects, are they worth it? Here are some considerations.

Saying that antidepressant drugs (ADPs) may not work flies in the face of seemingly firm medical opinion and could put more demands on clinicians and threaten to damage the large incomes and profits of the drug industry.[523] Antidepressant drugs may have selected uses, and in some cases could even be life-saving. But could we have bought into using these sometime helpful drugs too enthusiastically and often prematurely? For example, the long-term usefulness of benzodiazepine sedative drugs (e.g., the Valium, Ativan, Xanax family) proved to be largely untrue but only after we learned painful lessons over a four-decade span of clinical and personal experience about their limited efficacy, bothersome and sometimes dangerous side effects, and high addiction rates.

We have also had the same four decades of experience with modern antidepressants. These drugs include four kinds, starting with 1) the monoamine oxidase inhibitor ADPs (MAOIs), and then 2) the tricyclic ADPs, and over the past twenty years 3) the highly marketed selective serotonin reuptake inhibitors (SSRIs) and finally 4) the atypical ADPs. In spite of these categorical differences and the drug companies' heavy promotion of their individual drugs, numerous therapeutic trials have shown that none of these different categories or kinds of antidepressants is any better than another, nor is any individual brand name any better.[335-345, 523]

DRUG PROMOTIONS

Drug companies that make psychiatric drugs are big business. While over time they have produced some effective drugs, such as antibiotics and diuretics, drug companies are not generally run by clinicians, they do not take a Hippocratic oath, and they do not appear to always act in the best interest of sick people. They function in most ways like any other big business. Their only regulation, often with minimal success, is by limited agencies of the federal government. Most of the psychiatric drug types they have produced were discovered by accident, as shown in Table 10.1. Most of these drugs are nonspecific in their action. That is, they tend to have broad-spectrum effects, both positive and negative, beneficial and toxic. Most of the drug company clinical trials are limited to only a few weeks' duration, yet they and their representatives regularly recommend that patients take their drugs long-term, often without full knowledge of toxic and detrimental consequences that come only later (remember thalidomide).

Behind the Scenes

Behind the scenes, many psychiatrists on the faculty of medical schools and testing companies, and others who give lectures and workshops about psychiatric drugs, are paid by drug companies to do much of their research and help promote their drugs.[47a, 68b] A recent survey of one hundred authors of published *clinical practice guidelines,* which offer "state-of-the-art" diagnostic and treatment advice to physicians, nurses and allied clinicians, revealed that 87 percent of the authors had been paid by drug companies and/or were their prior employees or consultants.[149] Might this represent what lawyers would call a conflict of interest? Thirty years ago, medical ethics probably would not have allowed this kind of behavior. While this information is minimally disclosed to most of the speakers' continuing education audiences, it is not published in the medical journal articles in which they write about these drugs and is not usually known to the general public. As this book goes to press, apparently instigated by critics, some medical journals have just begun to require such disclosure of the authors of its published articles.[149, 182, 187, 288, 469, 470, 498, 543, 618, 686, 740] Another study found that *over half* of the U.S. Food and Drug Administration's (FDA) *advisory committee* members are paid by drug companies that have an interest in FDA decisions.[187, 226] These kinds of deceptions can have important implications and cautions for all of medicine and psychiatry.[47a, 68b, 165a]

Regarding the clinical trials of each drug, there is no requirement by the government or any other authority that the drug company report any negative results to clinicians or the public. Instead, they tend to report only positive results. Similar to the tobacco companies, many drug companies have tended to deny

Table 10.1. Many Psychiatric Drugs Were Accidentally Discovered (compiled from ref. 749)

Drug Category & Prototype	First Used	Accidental (original use)	Effects (found later)	Toxic Effects (examples)
Antipsychotics: Chlorpromazine (Thorazine)	1954	Dyes; antihistamine	Antipsychotic	Tardive dyskinesia
MAOIs: Iproniazid	1956	Tuberculosis	Antidepressant (ADP)	HT crisis, headaches (tyramine)
Tricyclics: Imipramine* (Tofranil)	1958	"Hypnotic"—actually often stimulating	Sedation, ADP, stimulation	Several toxic effects
Benzodiazepines: Chlordiazepoxide (Librium)	1960	Sedated psychotics	Sedated others	Addiction, dissociation, dysfunction
Lithium	1970	Epilepsy, arthritis, kidney stones	Antimania	Requires blood-level monitoring
SSRIs: Fluoxetine (Prozac)	1984	Sedation, antianxiety	Sedation, ADP/ stimulation	Akathisia, anorgasmia, weight gain, etc.

*Initially found in experimental animals to ↓ dopamine, norepinephrine and serotonin. HT = hypertensive, ADP = antidepressant, MAOI = Monoamine oxidase inhibitor

or minimize the toxic effects of their drugs, as shown in a few examples in Tables 10.1, 10.2, and A.13 (in the Appendix). They downplay these toxic effects in various ways, including calling them "side effects," when they actually often indicate drug *toxicity*. One of the more bothersome effects of most of the ADPs, some antipsychotics, and all of the benzodiazepine drugs is a *painful* and often *confusing, prolonged* and *disabling withdrawal syndrome*. Drug companies have tended to deny the existence of such withdrawal, claiming instead that the symptoms are simply a "reemergence" of the original complaints. After being pressured for years to disclose this information as a warning to clinicians and pharmacists, they finally began to list cursory warnings, some of which I show in Appendix A.13 on page 232.

Drug companies tend to assign drugs their names not by their chemical properties, but for marketing purposes only. They make up both the generic and trade or brand names, which usually have nothing to do with the drug's chemical structure. More deception: They may also disguise the names of some drugs to make more money from them, including when their patent for a drug has expired. For example, Serafem for the treatment of severe premenstrual problems (premenstrual dysphoric disorder) is actually only Prozac (fluoxetine), and Zyban for helping people stop smoking is simply Welbutrin (bupropion).

Even though many antidepressant drugs have been shown to differ only very little in effectiveness from placebo (sugar pills),[339, 435a, 446-8, 523-8, 721] drug companies have frequently exaggerated this small and often insignificant difference in their advertisements to physicians and other clinicians in medical journals. And seventeen years later, when the patent runs out for a particular drug, they may change their original promotional claims. For example,

Table 10.2. Adverse Effects of Selected Psychiatric Drugs:

Drug	Adverse Effect	Drug Co. Report
Fluoxetine (Prozac) (may *also apply to other SSRIs*)	Stimulation, agitation, mania (divided into these 3 effects to make % appear lower?)	9% (vs. 3% for placebo, i.e., a 3-fold difference)
SSRIs (selective serotonin reuptake inhibitors; see Table 10.1)	Akathisia (severe, painful stimulation & agitation)	Rare
	Suicidality & homicidality* (commonly associated with akathisia)	Nonexistent to rare
	Sexual dysfunction, anorgasmia, loss of desire/erection	5%
	Weight gain	Rare
	Withdrawal syndrome, painful & often disabling	Rare
Benzodiazepines, Other ADPs,** Antipsychotics	Withdrawal syndrome, painful & often disabling	Rare, if ever (initial reports)
Tobacco/Nicotine (for comparison)	Cancer, lung & heart disease, addiction, early death	Denied the existence of any health risks
SUMMARY		
Several Common Psychiatric Drugs	**Numerous adverse effects**	**Denied or minimized**

* May also occur with some antipsychotic drugs.
** ADP = antidepressant drug
*** See February 2003 issue of *Consumer Reports* magazine for updated information about problematic drug advertising.[165a]

Differences Between Drug Company & Independent Reports

Independent Reports	Comments
25 to 30% (3 times drug company reports)	A high percentage, despite *large numbers* of subjects also *given antianxiety drugs* during trials
9% (a very large difference)	This overstimulation usually occurs in first few weeks of SSRI use.
Risk (.25 to 4+ times), with high risk for fluoxetine. Jick's prospective study showed . . .	. . . A common association, even when controlled for factors such as prior ADP use &/or suicidality[396]
70 to 80% *(a 16- to 18-fold difference)*	How might this marked difference occur?
Common	High % of users complain of weight gain
Common	Some drug companies are finally admitting it is real. (Table A.13)
Common	Minimized a long time, despite Hollister's early warning report in 1978
Clear proof of these toxic consequences	Some drug company behavior is similar.
Show there are significant problems	**Drug companies do not tend to give us accurate warnings.*****

in 1984 Eli Lilly launched Prozac (fluoxetine) as one of the first "effective" SSRI antidepressant drugs. Over the next seventeen years, associated with heavy marketing and promotion, it made billions of dollars from its sales to health consumers who took their clinicians' word that it was effective for lessening their symptoms of depression. In late 2001, when its patent ran out on exclusive rights to making and selling fluoxetine as Prozac, they appear to have changed their tune. At this point, Lilly representatives published evidence that Prozac was *no better than a placebo* (sugar pill) to treat depression.[249, 299a, 725] Why? Because not only had their patent run out on Prozac, but now they had a new antidepressant (generic name duloxetine) to market and sell to clinicians and the public that was "more effective." How might the public interpret this kind of behavior? Could the company have known it all along? How did this knowledge pass the academics who conducted the clinical trials for Lilly? And how and why did it pass the government agency that originally approved the licensing of Prozac?

MY CLINICAL EXPERIENCE

My own clinical experience includes: 1) hearing more than four hundred (a conservative estimate) of my patients recount their experiences of having "depression" for which they had been prescribed by others one or many ADPs—and often a string of them—mostly unsuccessfully, and 2) prescribing these drugs myself for more than over two hundred of my own patients (also a conservative estimate). (My approach has always been to look first for the cause of the symptoms of depression that the patient could address, with or without my or others' assistance, to help lessen their pain.)

Unpredictable

From that experience, I observed that about a third of my patients reported experiencing an acceptable relief of their symptoms of depression *for a time;* another third had some, though not ideal relief for a time; and the final third reported no relief. I say "for a time" because they usually reported that most of their relief lasted for only a few weeks or months, and then their symptoms returned—although a small number said they were helped for a year or more. Many reported only a *partial* relief of their symptoms, and their overall quality of life had not significantly improved. Many of them went on to try a different ADP, which had about the same one-third/one-third/one-third effect described above. Their histories often included having tried a string of several to as many as eight or ten different ADPs, mostly tricyclics and SSRIs, and since 1990 mostly the latter. Of course, many of them stopped taking one or more ADPs because of their bothersome or even intolerable side effects.

ADPs are unpredictable in their actions, results and toxic effects. Different people may react in totally opposite ways to the same drug. For example, I have seen one person become quite sedated on paroxetine (Paxil), and another feel overstimulated on the same drug and dose. I have seen similar results from other ADP drugs. And more often than not, when they do work, people tend to benefit from these drugs only somewhat, if at all. The following is a summary of a patient I assisted in her recovery.

> **Case History 10.1:** Margaret was a forty-six-year-old divorced woman who grew up in a troubled family wherein she experienced repeated physical, mental and emotional abuse. She presented with a long history of recurring episodes of major depression, with a strong component of anxiety. Over the years she had seen several different clinicians and had been diagnosed with depression. She was treated over time with eight different antidepressant drugs, most of which had little or no lasting effect on her depressive symptoms. On further evaluation I found her to fulfill the *DSM-IV* diagnostic criteria for PTSD. When she voluntarily withdrew from taking her current antidepressant drug, she became more aware of her childhood trauma history and the effects that it caused, including her anxiety and depression. She slowly began to express these painful experiences to safe people, and over the next few months her mood began to lift. She is currently still working a recovery program in group and individual therapy.

Margaret's story represents a common experience that I have observed among childhood trauma survivors. After the trauma, they develop one or more painful conditions or disorders, such as depression, an anxiety disorder, PTSD, an addiction or the like, and often seek aid from physical medicine or mental health clinicians in the community. These clinicians focus on the presenting complaints and make a limited diagnosis based on *DSM* or other diagnostic criteria.[611-613] Influenced by health insurance companies, they then prescribe or recommend a limited form of treatment, such as drugs or, less often, brief psychotherapy. They tend not to connect the person's current problems with their past traumas, and thereby may miss a major opportunity to make an effective therapeutic intervention, which I describe in the next two chapters.

Having realized some of the above dynamics, psychiatrist J. Douglas Bremner describes his experience.[82] He said:

> *I asked some of my more experienced psychiatric colleagues at Yale whether or not they felt that childhood abuse was an important topic for research study for a psychiatrist. They gave me their opinions that childhood abuse was not very common, and in any case was not an important topic. . . . I then asked the other psychiatrists and social workers in the psychiatric clinic at the VA [Veterans Administration Hospital] if they would be willing to screen their patients for a history of childhood abuse, in order to participate in my studies using brain imaging to examine the effects of abuse on the brain. They felt that they couldn't ask their patients about anything in their childhoods, because if their patients had been abused, that subject would make them much more upset, and then the psychiatrists and social workers would have trouble dealing with them. I offered to screen everyone coming into the clinic for abuse myself, and to take on as my personal patients anyone who became extremely upset as a result of this screening. Fascinatingly, the results of the screening procedure were the opposite of my colleagues' fears. The patients who did have abuse histories were extremely appreciative that at last their psychiatrists were finally figuring out how to properly assess them as patients.*

At times a trial of antidepressant drugs may be indicated and helpful for some childhood trauma survivors, but that should not be the primary treatment aid. Here, the primary focus should be on the gradual cognitive and experiential connecting of the person's current pain and issues with their past trauma, which is often best accomplished by using the recovery aids described in the next chapter. In this context, when they are effective, ADP drugs may take the edge off of otherwise distracting and disabling pain, so that the person can work more constructively on healing from the long-term trauma effects.

For the minority of people with depression who grew up in a healthy family, ADP drugs or individual psychotherapy—or a combination of both—may be effective in lessening their symptoms. I have assisted some such people as well. However, knowing how common childhood trauma is and that full trauma memories may be slow to emerge, even for them I keep an open ear for that possibility. Our mistake may have been to assume that there is no connection between past trauma and subsequent mental illness.

When I read the independent London researcher Charles Medawar's comprehensive review of the state of our understanding of ADPs, I noticed that his summary, and others', supported what I had observed in my clinical experience: that ADP drugs are not as effective as we would like them to be and/or as the drug companies would like us to believe.[523] For example, regarding ADPs, he wrote, ". . . patients generally respond (some very well, others less so) in about 50–70% of cases".[523] Research psychiatrist John Greden said, ". . . up to 70 percent of patients being treated for depression are not finding satisfactory relief of their depressive symptoms".[313] In this chapter and the next I will summarize some of Medawar's and others' most salient findings. I recommend that anyone interested in this topic read their original articles, some of which are available on the Internet.

RECENT HISTORY OF ANTIDEPRESSANT DRUGS

During the past forty years, the politics of marketing and prescribing these and other drugs developed and escalated hand-in-hand with ". . . the biological approach to psychiatry—treating mental illness as a genetically influenced disorder of brain chemistry—[which] has been [either] a smashing success"[697] or a subtle failure.[409]

In the 1950s, monoamine oxidase inhibitors (MAOIs) were discovered and developed from the finding that some patients with tuberculosis who took the antibiotic drug *iproniazid* experienced a lifted mood[759] (Table 10.1). This finding led to drug companies and some academics looking for more profits by theorizing a possible biochemical basis for depression and developing drugs to try to treat it, in that they speculated that depression might be due to a lack of brain noradrenaline (also called norepinephrine), and later thought caused by a lack of another neurotransmitter, serotonin (5-hydroxytryptamine). Unknown to many clinicians and others, both of these theories were eventually disproved.[339, 523, 759]

Until the 1980s, up to 80 percent of cases of depression were thought to be self-limiting. This observation may have been related to the fact that in the 1960s some drug companies began a slow marketing campaign to find "depressed" patients—who should naturally be prescribed their patented ADP drugs.

Psychiatrist and author Frank Ayd said, "To a certain extent, it was necessary for Merck [a drug company in the 1960s and beyond] to educate the physicians in order to market the illness [depression] so they would know what to prescribe for that illness, which was Merck's drug [amytriptyline/Elavil]" (Ayd in

Healy[345]). This process continues even today. Drug companies develop psychoactive drugs and then teach physicians how to use them. With pressure from the "managed care" arms of insurance companies, other professions commonly buy into this process. As an example, currently psychologists are lobbying government agencies to allow them to prescribe psychiatric drugs. As psychiatrist Ashley Wazana of McGill University said, "The tail seems to be wagging the dog."[345] Today drug companies are further violating ethical guidelines by marketing their drugs to the public through often misleading TV commercials.[165a]

Like all good business people, to keep them financially well afloat, the drug companies looked for more and better drugs. When they found more kinds of tricyclic antidepressant drugs in the 1960s and 1970s and the SSRIs in the 1980s, they escalated their marketing campaign to try to convince clinicians and the public that depression was common and, of course, that those afflicted needed their drugs.

Over time, drug companies have presented a storyline of the medical necessity to treat the world's now large "depressed" population, which they had themselves assumed and promoted, with any one or a combination of their own ADPs or benzodiazepine sedative drugs long-term. With minimal evidence, they appear to have planned, believed and marketed that depression was a genetically transmitted biochemical brain disorder. After more than forty years of clinical and research experience, we now know that much of that storyline has been embellished to some extent by the drug companies in concert with some academics, and others in government agencies and the helping professions. Most of what they have promoted appears to be untrue.

I will describe more problems with antidepressant drugs in the next chapter.

11 DO ANTIDEPRESSANT DRUGS WORK?

MORE CONCERNS

DRUG VERSUS PLACEBO: BIASES AND PROBLEMS

From numerous clinical trials, the therapeutic differences between the efficacy of ADP drugs when compared to placebo have been neither great nor impressive. Even so, with the growing belief in and promotion of the "biologic basis" of depression and the discounting of placebo factors at work in these trials, intense marketing and subtle politics seem to have overtaken the data, such that prescribing ADPs has, since at least the early 1980s, become routine. Clinical and research psychiatrist David Healy said, "Almost anyone who was unhappy for any reason could now be diagnosed as depressed. It was at this point, I believe, that psychiatrists unwittingly handed the agenda over to the pharmaceutical industry"[345].

But problems, often carefully hidden or overlooked, developed. Unfortunately, many companies' original drug *trials,* for example, have tended to have several important *biases.*

1. Many of their test patients also *took other psychoactive drugs* at the *same time* that they were being "tested" on an ADP. In several studies, 25 percent of these "trial" patients were also taking benzodiazepine drugs at the same time. Medawar notes that the *one* study that did not permit the use of other drugs was the *only one* of four trial studies to find *no* statistically *significant difference* between treatment results for fluoxetine (Prozac) and placebo.[523] This means that in each of the other three (i.e., 75 percent of these fluoxetine [Prozac] trials), *other drugs were allowed to contaminate the results*—and that these were therefore not appropriately conducted or "clean" trials.

2. A second flaw was that among all four of the pivotal trials on fluoxetine (Prozac), the investigators used what is called a *placebo washout* period to *exclude the early responders to placebo*. In this manipulative procedure, *all of the test subjects* received placebo for the first week, and every one of them whose Hamilton Depression Scale rating dropped below 80 percent of their original value was [inappropriately] excluded.[523] The investigators may argue that "half" of the eliminated subjects would have been given the fluoxetine anyway. But we don't know that for a

---

*Originally, early in the forty-year sequence of properly conducted ADP drug trials, Smith and colleagues found that the median placebo improvement response rate was 46 percent (versus 61 percent) for active drugs. But later, these often hidden placebo washouts reduced the actual placebo response rate by about 13 percent (a potentially significant figure) from 46 percent down to 33 percent.[709a] Some thirty years later, in 1998, Kirsch and Sapirstein calculated the mean effect sizes (i.e., effectiveness) for changes in depression among 2,318 patients who had been randomly assigned to either antidepressant medication or placebo in nineteen double-blind clinical trials. They found that the effect size for active medications that are *not regarded to be antidepressants* was as large as that for those classified as antidepressants, and in both cases, these "inactive placebos" produced improvement that was at least 75 percent of the effect of the active drug. A more careful

fact, since many drug companies often vary their drug/ placebo ratios (I have seen ratios of 4/1), so why tamper with proven experimental procedure and introduce such a potentially major bias into the credibility of any important drug trial?*

3. A third potential flaw is that trials on SSRIs before 1990 typically *lasted* for only about *six weeks,* and more recently for only *eight weeks.* This is hardly enough time for drug companies to provide clinicians with crucial data to make informed decisions about whether to prescribe an ADP for a several-month period or longer—which drug companies and their spokespeople recommend (some suggest that depressed people take their drugs for a year to life).

4. A fourth flaw is that the *double-blind procedure* (where neither researcher nor subject knows whether drug or placebo was taken) is *often blocked or invalidated* when the person experiences one or more *side effects* from the drug, thus potentially *telling* both researcher and subject that they have in fact *taken the active drug.*

5. A fifth potential problem involves the inherent *motivation bias* of the drug company that develops the drug. A drug company has to spend several million dollars to develop a

---

examination of pre- and post-effect sizes, i.e., the differences among depressed individuals assigned to no-treatment or wait-list control groups, suggested that about one-quarter of the drug response is caused by the administration of an active medication, *one half is a placebo effect,* and the remaining *quarter* is caused by other nonspecific factors. Research psychologist Irving Kirsch (1998) said, "What is the proportion of the response to antidepressant medication that is duplicated by placebo administration? Sapirstein and I calculated this figure to be about 75 percent (Kirsch & Sapirstein, 1998). Joffe and colleagues' (1996) data indicate the figure to be 65 percent. Pharmaceutical company statistics yield an estimate of 71 percent (Kirsch 1998). These data, all of which are from published sources, indicate that, at best, the pharmacological effect of antidepressant medication is somewhere between 25 and 35 percent of the total drug response." [446-448]

new drug, as it jumps through the numerous hoops that are required for licensure. The enormous cost of every new drug project that does not result in a licensed and successful drug can be a financial drain on their coffers, and so there is naturally great pressure to produce "positive" results from their trials. Could it be that the researchers that they pay, within and outside the company, sometimes find positive results because their salaries and grants depend on it? Another variation on this influence may involve Heisenberg's classic *Uncertainty Principle,* which says that the experimenter inherently influences the results of the experiment, and that by the simple act of *observing,* this influence unknowingly occurs.

6. A sixth potential bias is that investigators and reporters can *misreport* or *misinterpret* a subject's HAM-D Scale (Hamilton Depression Scale, used almost universally in ADP drug trials). As clinical and research psychiatrist Bruce Greyson said, "The 'gold standard' scale for measuring depression in drug studies is the Hamilton Depression Scale [HAM-D], and most drug studies use as a criterion for improvement a 50 percent decrease in a patient's score. On the HAM-D, generally 7 points is considered depressed, and 15 is severely depressed; so if a patient enters a drug study with a HAM-D score of 32, and after 4 weeks of Prozac has a score of 16, that's counted as a successful treatment because the patient's score fell by 50 percent, even though they still score in the 'severely depressed' range!"[317]

   This potential bias may be associated with how the drug companies, researchers and now probably most psychiatrists and other helping professionals define "improvement."

Greyson added, "With the advent of the *DSM-III* and then *DSM-IV*, psychiatrists got away from identifying depression in terms of how the patient feels, and started defining it with their 'Chinese-menu' symptom lists. So now to be depressed you need to have at least five symptoms, only one of which is feeling sad; the others are diminished interest in activities, weight change, sleep change, psychomotor change, feelings of worthlessness, diminished concentration, and recurrent thoughts of death (as shown in table 2.3 on page 17). What that means is that if antidepressants correct your insomnia and restore your appetite and give you more energy, they can by definition make you no longer depressed, even though you still feel like death warmed over. And there are lots of data to show that antidepressants do just that: They help correct what are called the 'vegetative signs of depression'—the decreased sleep, appetite, energy, libido, etc. but don't necessarily help you feel any better." [317]

David Healy said that when drug companies test their antidepressants, they generally measure not only depression (by scales like the HAM-D) but also the reported quality of life. But although they are quick to publish the improved depression scores, they almost never make public the quality-of-life data, because antidepressants don't, in fact, improve quality of life, and in some cases, they worsen it. [339, 344]

When combined with these six serious potential and often real drug trial biases, the information summarized in this book shows that ADPs are, as a whole, at best only a few percentage points better than placebo. More realistically they are *about equal* to placebo in their effectiveness in helping ameliorate depression. Plus, their downside is that they are *expensive,* as shown in Table 12.3 in the next chapter, they have *bothersome side effects* (Table 10.2 on page 126)*,* and rarely, especially if involved in drug interactions and overdoses, they can be fatal.[39, 339, 396]

ANALYSIS OF DRUG VERSUS PLACEBO TRIALS

Perhaps even stronger evidence comes from recent independent analyses of the numerous clinical drug trials that were previously conducted or sponsored by the drug companies themselves. For example, research psychiatrist Arif Khan and colleagues evaluated the treatment trials for nine FDA-approved *antidepressant* drugs between 1985 and 2000 on 10,030 depressed patients who participated in fifty-two trials evaluating ninety-three treatment arms of a new or prior drug.[435a] They also looked at thirteen FDA-approved *antianxiety* drug trials on 8,340 anxious patients between 1985 and 2000 who participated in forty trials evaluating seventy-five treatment arms of a new or prior drug. Their remarkable finding was that *fewer than half* (48 percent, 45/93) of the *antidepressant drug* treatment trial arms showed superiority to placebo. Among *antianxiety* drugs, the same percentage of 48 percent (36/75) showed superiority over placebo. These data show that conventional drug treatments for depression and anxiety are superior to placebo *less than half the time.* Thus, in over half of the trials (52 percent), the response to antidepressants and anxiolytics was *indistinguishable* from that of *placebo.* These results replicate previous reports by independent researchers on the small difference between antidepressant drugs and placebo.[435a, 446, 448, 721] They also call into serious question the proposal that placebo controls can be done away with in clinical trials. Based on these data, if new antidepressants and anxiolytics were tested against "standard" treatment rather than placebo, about half of the trials would yield invalid results.[435a]

Prozac (fluoxetine) took seven trials to find two that showed superiority over placebo, and Paxil (paroxtine) and Zoloft (sertraline) required even more.[456a] These few analyzed drug trial studies are thus the most positive results that the drug companies could complete in order to submit their most new-drug favorable findings to the FDA for approval. Thus, Khan et al's study was not able to look at the five negative studies that showed that Prozac was no better than placebo because its drug company had apparently not submitted them to the FDA.[456a]

The same applies to other drug makers. In fact, drug companies have among the most minimal of requirements that the Food and Drug Administration has ruled as being adequate to show the "effectiveness" of any new ADP drug. Their only requirement is to produce two placebo-controlled, randomized, double-blind studies that show a 50 percent improvement on the Hamilton Depression Scale over five to eight weeks of taking the drug that significantly exceeds the antidepressant effectiveness of placebo, which often is by only a few percentage points. For example, two study results in the neighborhood of 55 percent success for drug receivers compared to 45 percent of placebo receivers would possibly warrant FDA approval, even if the same studies had failed to show any drug advantage six times previously.

For most people who take them, antidepressant drugs don't work well. An ideal ADP drug would specifically lessen the symptoms of depression without causing bothersome or toxic side effects. But there is no such ideal drug today. In spite of drug company claims to the contrary, these drugs tend to have broad and nonspecific effects, many of which prompt people to stop taking them, such as oversedation, overstimulation, weight gain and anorgasmia—to name some of the more common ones. In the field of medicine we call these "shotgun" effects, as opposed to a single-bullet kind of effect. Clinical and research psychiatrist Thomas Moore said, "Antidepressant drugs are a kind of bull in a China shop" (Moore in Healy 2002).[345] Harvard psychiatrist and author Joseph Glenmullen said, "Normal functioning of the brain is impaired by antidepressant drugs" (in Healy[345]). When they do work, for some people they may be just as effective at lower than recommended doses (especially in elderly people), which we have learned over time with many of the ADP drugs. In this book, I am not saying that we should not use them at all. I believe that for some people they may help to some degree, even though for a majority who use them they do not work as well as we would like.

Risks and Benefits

Another way to look at this problem is to compare the relative risk for taking a drug to its potential benefit. For at least thirty years, physicians and other health professionals have been aware of the importance of weighing these two key realities. While they have spoken of risk-benefit ratios and more recently risk-benefit analysis, I have not found a clear description and discussion of them for commonly used psychiatric drugs.

Based on my thirty-year experience in the fields of addiction medicine and trauma psychology, I have estimated the risk-benefit ratios of commonly and some uncommonly used psychiatric drugs (see Table 11.1). I also base this information on my knowledge of the literature (e.g., refs. 39, 74, 339, 523, 676, to name a few). Given this overview, readers may make their own inquiries and decisions regarding their and others' personal situations wherein any of these drugs may be involved.

In my clinical work, I have seen many patients who wasted money and time trying antidepressant drugs, who went through painful withdrawal periods, and of course, many others who have suffered toxic effects of antidepressants, many of whom received little or no relief from their depressive symptoms as well. I have also seen countless patients who became addicted to stimulants and benzodiazepines, frequently prescribed for depressed and anxious people, who went through painful withdrawals and drug-seeking behaviors. By contrast, I have never seen a patient addicted to barbiturates, the antianxiety drug buspirone or to major tranquilizers, although I know that especially the latter are often toxic.

Based on his vast clinical and research career on depression and ADP drugs, David Healy said, "With the increasing use of these drugs, there has been a huge upsurge in the numbers of people who are depressed. This is not what is supposed to happen when treatments work. . . . Their capacity to sell to us far outstrips their capacity to help us. This is the point at which the antidepressants become part of the problem of depression rather than part of the solution"[345] Psychiatrist Joseph Glenmullen said, "I don't think there is an epidemic of depression, but there is an epidemic of prescribing antidepressant drugs".[345]

Perhaps their biggest detriment has to do with the way that antidepressant drugs have been used for their more than forty years of existence. This use has too often allowed the helping professions that recommend and prescribe them often to *overlook* what appears to be the most common cause of or association with depression: a history of trauma, most commonly *repeated childhood trauma.* These traumatic experiences appear to be woven into a web of other subtle and overt factors that may predate depression or aggravate it. These factors may include: 1) the presence of other "co-morbid" disorders; 2) a poor to marginal diet or nutrition; 3) a lack of regular exercise; 4) an overexposure to a television, movie and print media that commonly portrays a negative distortion of our human potential and reality; 5) an out-of-date and often ineffective educational system; 6) a religious system that is often not nourishing to our spirits; and 7) ongoing traumas and significant stressors in the person's adult life.

Even though ADP drugs have become a mainstay of treatment of depressive symptoms today, there are at least twelve other treatment aids, which is in part why I subtitled this book, "Choices for Healing." I discuss these potential choices in the next chapter.

Table 11.1 Risk-Benefit Ratio Analysis of Common Psychiatric Drugs
The Ideal Ratio Is as Close to Zero as Possible

(ratios estimated by author 2002)

Drug	Estimated R/B Ratio	Risk	Benefit
SSRI Antidepressant*	Medium (See also Table 10.2)	• 25-80% bothersome adverse effects, including akathesia & suicide/ homicide; • 33-86% have a withdrawal syndrome	On average, most are only 2-10% better than placebo in reducing symptoms of depression by 50%
Benzodiazepine Sedative**	Medium to high	• High addiction rate • Block healthy feelings & grieving • High withdrawal rate & potential long disability	Excellent for acute severe fear (anxiety) The longer taken, the less effective (drug tolerance) in reducing fear
Busplrone (Anti-fear/ anxiety)***	Low	Low risk	About 80% helped
Major Tranquilizers****	Medium to High	• Tardive dyskinesia • Withdrawal syndrome	Helps some psychotics function Helps family & staff
Placebo †	Zero	Lowest risk	33-70% helped in depression [446-8, 523-6]

Comments

* Of 2/3 of people who are helped some, 1/3 are helped partially & 1/3 are helped more. Often help lasts for only a few months. The last 1/3 of people are not helped at all.

** If used, do so for only a few days to avoid risk effects. For serious ongoing fear (anxiety): buspirone plus psycho-social-spiritual aids (see Table 12.1) may help.

*** Takes edge off fear (anxiety); helps many with PTSD & panic. Expensive (as for most drugs)

**** See *The Truth about Mental Illness* for further comments

† Show how poorly many drugs work

12 CHOICES FOR HEALING DEPRESSION

Depression is complex. Depending on the cause(s), one person with it may respond better to one or more of the following recovery aids, while another with the same condition may benefit from others. However, most people will find help in using a combination of several of them. Seeking out the right combination for oneself is often empowering, too, and in itself may be another kind of treatment aid.

ADDRESSING THE CAUSE

Addressing and treating the most likely cause of any problem should be a "given" for all presenting problems in medicine, psychiatry, psychology and the other health professions (see Table 12.1). But somehow for depression and some other mental and physical disorders, many otherwise well-trained and well-meaning clinicians tend often to use a "one size fits all" approach. Promoted and supported by the drug industry and commonly enforced by the managed care business, as described throughout

Table 12.1. Treatment Aids for Depression: Some Clinically Significant Differences author's & others' estimates

(compiled and expanded from references cited in text)

Aid	Estimated Effectiveness	Acceptability	Toxicity	Cost
Addressing the cause	++−++++*	Fair to good	Depends on other aids used	Depends on methods
Positive company	+−++++	Good	Low	Generally low
Individual psychotherapy	+−++++	Varies	Usually none to low	Moderate to high
Group therapy	+−++++	Low to good	Low	Low to moderate
Bibliotherapy	0−+++	Common	Rare	Low
Stop smoking	+−++	Varies	None	Low
Regular exercise	+−+++	Fair to good	Low	Low
Nutrition, diet	+−++	Fair to good	Low	Low
Recovery from co-morbidity	+−++++	Fair to excellent	Low	Varies
Sleep restriction	+−++	Fair to excellent	Low	Low
Morning light exposure	+−++	Fair to excellent	Low	Low
Spirituality	+−++++	Good to excellent	Low	Low

* Potential for being effective: 0 = None; + = 25%; ++ = 50%; +++ = 75%; ++++ = 100%.
Result usually depends on motivation, persistence and hard work of the individual, combined with the knowledge and skills of the clinician(s) and the rapport between them. This process cannot be rushed.

this book, this stereotyped approach is to prescribe one or more ADP drugs, with—though more often without—a few brief psychotherapy sessions (if the patient is lucky).

If clinicians used this kind of nonspecific approach for every problem and disorder among all the patients and clients that they saw, they would not only be practicing substandard health care, but they would likely be harming some of their patients and thereby risk being sued for malpractice. But most health care consumers are unaware of the importance of making a *differential diagnosis,* which includes carefully considering all of their causal and therapeutic options, especially in the area of mental health.

Any one or a combination of the following situations or problems may be a factor in aggravating and at times causing the symptoms of depression, as I show throughout this book. These may include: 1) a history of significant trauma during childhood or later in life, 2) a recent major stressor (e.g., major work, personal or relationship discord), 3) a recent major change (e.g., job change or loss, separation, divorce, geographical move, childbirth, disability, loss of a loved one), 4) excessive use of alcohol or other psychoactive drugs, whether legal or illegal, 5) some prescribed drugs (e.g., some antihypertensives, such as propranolol, H$_2$ blockers for stomach ulcers, oral contraceptives and corticosteroids), and 6) debilitating physical illness. Because they are so common and amenable to treatment and recovery work, in this book I have focused on the stressors and especially on the traumas. If the above factors are ruled out over time, a familial or genetic factor can be considered (although we can't change our genes—even if a real genetic defect were ever proven).

To arrive at a more precise diagnosis and treatment plan may take a few to many extra minutes, or an extra evaluation session or two, or even more. But doing so can ultimately save both cli-nician and patient time and trouble in the long run, and usually leads to prescribing or recommending a more appropriate and effective treatment.

POSITIVE COMPANY

At the turn of the twentieth century, Kraepelin prescribed for depression removal from a negative human environment and submersion in the company of happy people (secure, upbeat, optimistic, safe).[381] Meyer added a related "common sense" ver-sion of psychotherapy, characterized by "...kindly, humane over-tones and a searching practical use of the patient's life history and current situation . . . [giving] careful attention to the . . . [per-son's] milieu and how the patient might. . . best be served by it." Meyer also attended to sleep and nutrition, occupational therapy, hydrotherapy and recreation, following a regime of work, rest and play, socialization, and discussion with clinicians.[381]

But why would these modern pioneers recommend such an approach to what some today believe is a genetic-biological problem? Could it have been that they either observed or sur-mised trauma as a causal factor and/or saw that such a prescrip-tion actually helped people to recover more effectively? Almost a century later, psychotherapist and author Susan Forward and Craig Buck in their book *Toxic Parents* described toxic people, including parents. By this they mean those who—usually unin-tentionally—physically, sexually, mentally and/or emotionally mistreat their children.[271a] But it may not be simply problem par-ents. It may be the total family and household environment that people need to get away from to recover. For example, in the adverse childhood experiences (ACE) study, Felitti and colleagues noted that 59 percent of a general clinical population reported having experienced childhood trauma. About 19 percent of respondents reported having had a mentally ill person in the family.[254] Can a mentally ill—for example, depressed—parent impact their child from a young age such that the child takes on some or many of the attitudes, moods and behaviors that the child saw modeled by the parent? The ACE study and others suggested so.[434] It is not just our troubled families that can harm children. Our television and motion picture media constantly bombard us with mostly mindless and frequently violent programs.[568] News shows and newspapers tend to cover only the negative. This constant exposure to the negative is likely an important factor in the origin of some of our stress.

In my work assisting trauma survivors for more than twenty-five years, I have noticed how hard it can be for them to accept a safe relationship—for example, one that is usually found in most individual and group psychotherapy settings. Yet this is the place for them to feel safe enough to risk being real and expressing their true self, as they heal from the painful effects of trauma.

INDIVIDUAL THERAPY OR COUNSELING

Individual therapy can be a good way to start healing from depression. Ideally, the clinician will evaluate the person as to the most likely cause of their symptoms and problems, their treatment options and the best course of treatment and recovery. Here it is important to have a comfortable clinician-patient rapport. If there is a history of childhood trauma and the depressed person wants to work on it, it is important that the therapist have a knowledge and skills base in this area from which to guide them. A major healing component of both individual and group therapy is through the process of telling our story of what happened and expressing our pain to safe others over time.[170, 360, 371, 582-3, 798] I describe some examples of studies that show the efficacy of individual and group therapy in the next volume.

Psychiatrist Paul Fink said that psychodynamically oriented therapists further address the cause by considering the possibility of an unconscious conflict that may drive the depression.[261a] Rather than seeing conscious or real events as the *only* cause, they explore whether these may also be the stimulus or trigger for deeper issues. For example, in depressed patients who have been traumatized there is often repressed anger at the abuser and at the parent who did not protect or believe them when they asked for help. They commonly feel guilt and shame over their anger. Many have experienced serious losses, and their depression may also be driven by fear of abandonment by important others.

Therapists may view addressing causes differently. Some are satisfied to discover past important events. Others go deeper, seeking the meaning of the link between the depression and the childhood and other trauma. Finding these connections may be essential to ending the recurring depressions that may be stimulated by trauma and related "events." Examples include: the anniversary of a death, a specific holiday, a passing fantasy of wanting to kill someone, or other single events which may be otherwise considered "irrelevant." In one case, a successful woman became depressed on major holidays. Her uncle had repeatedly raped her from when she was age six to sixteen when he visited on these holidays. Her hate for him became manifested by her then and subsequent anxious depression at holiday times. Her depression had protected her from acting on her rage. This kind of analysis can assist people to make the appropriate connections, get a deep cognitive and emotional understanding of their pain, and eventually get free of it.[261a]

Psychotherapy can address and assure that the person understands how their actively participating helps in their recovery at all levels, plus the importance of appropriate follow up treatment. No matter what kind—psychodynamic, cognitive, behavioral or interpersonal—*regular* therapy sessions are often especially helpful. At least ten weekly sessions are ideal to start the recovery process, to insure that the person follows the recovery plan, and determine whether they are benefiting from it. Some patients take a "flight into health" (suddenly and inappropriately feeling better) to avoid therapy. Fink said, "In one case I had early in my career, such a person was prematurely discharged and killed herself. Experienced therapists know how to recognize and prevent it. Other recommended life style changes, as well as a trial of ADP drugs, are usually secondary to psychotherapy and may also be hard to accomplish. For example, stopping smoking, exercising, and addressing co-morbidity may help, but alone may not be enough to relieve the depression."[261a]

GROUP THERAPY

Group therapy has been shown to be an effective aid in helping people heal from depression. Some clinicians recommend group therapy as a treatment of choice for adult survivors of trauma, many of whom have depression or other disorders as a presenting problem. In treating countless trauma survivors, in both individual and group therapy, I have noticed that with or without ADP drugs many experience an improvement of their depression over the first few months of their recovery work (some may also worsen for a time, only to gradually improve later). Feeling better temporarily, there is a temptation to stop the therapy. But to heal the effects of trauma generally takes several years of continued recovery work. The focus of the group is crucial here. For "depressed" trauma survivors, the most effective focus of the group is to help the members connect their current pain, disorders and issues with their recent and especially their past trauma. An education group is not group psychotherapy, although it may be helpful if it teaches about the effects of trauma and how to heal from them. The effectiveness of a general therapy group is somewhere in between an education group and a trauma-focused (Stage Two recovery) group. The term "trauma-focused" means addressing all of the person's trauma effects, including their needs for healthy boundaries and other life skills.[296]

BIBLIOTHERAPY

Reading about what depression and other disorders are, how they develop and how to deal with them can help.[803] Countless books are available. I have listed a limited selection in the references,[170, 171, 179] and there are many other helpful books that are not included here. *Caution:* Some books on depression and other mental disorders may have a narrow focus, describing only a genetic and biological theory of causation, leaving out trauma as

Table 12.2. Co-Morbidity Estimates: The Co-Occurrence of Disorders

(See also chapters 2 and 3 of reference 655a, and 643)

Disorder	Depression	Anxiety Disorders	Chemical Dependence	PTSD	Personality Disorders	Schizophrenia	Medical Problems
Depression	-------	Over half	Common 9–93% (secondary depression)	To 80%	Common	Common	Common
Anxiety	Over half	-------	Common (primary & secondary anxiety)	Usual in PTSD	Common	Usual	Common
Chemical Dependence	9–98% (secondary depression)	Common (primary & secondary anxiety)	-------	Common	To 65% esp ASPD & BPD	10–15%	Common
PTSD	To 80%		Common	-------	Common		Common
Personality Disorders	Common	Common	To 65% esp ASFD & BPD	Common	-------		
Schizophrenia	Common	Usual	10–15%	Common		-------	
Medical problems	Common		Common	Common			-------

a common factor and recommending drugs as the treatment of choice. These kinds of books and articles, including some found on the Internet, can be counterproductive in that they may imply that the afflicted person somehow has something inherently wrong with them, which can worsen their already low self-esteem and distract them from discovering and addressing the more likely causes of their pain.

STOP SMOKING

Since smoking cigarettes and other tobacco products has been shown to aggravate depression, and may at times cause it, stopping smoking can be an aid to decrease the symptoms and severity of depression.[216, 254, 811] Like stopping drinking and drugging for an alcoholic or drug-dependent person, the beneficial effects of stopping smoking may take a few weeks or more after the smoker has completed an often emotionally painful withdrawal period from the nicotine and smoking behavior.

REGULAR EXERCISE

For many people, regular exercise is a natural antidepressant and may work by stimulating the body's release of endorphins— one of the body's natural painkillers. Making ourself exercise regularly may take great self-discipline and internal motivation. To be most effective, we should exercise probably at least three times weekly. If the exertion during exercise is mild, it should be almost daily. All such exercise should be carried to the person's

Figure 12.1. Venn Diagram of Estimated Common Co-Morbidity Among Childhood Trauma Survivors

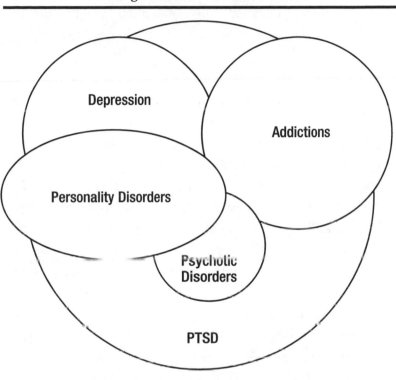

Anxicty/anxicty disorder is common among all of these five disorders.
Dissociative disorders also share co-morbidity with them.
Childhood trauma is the *common base* of all of them.

individual physical tolerance. Eventually, the most benefit tends
to come from aerobic exercise. While regular exercise works best
for short-term improvement,[339] although promising, its long-term
effectiveness has not been adequately determined.[477]

RECOVERY FROM CO-MORBIDITY

Initially, in the 1960s, co-morbidity was defined as two or
more disorders present in the same person at the same time.
Later, it has come to mean their occurrence at any time during a
person's life span. Depression often happens in the presence of
other mental or physical disorders, the more common of which
I show in Table 12.2. Sometimes depression may come as a
result of them. For example, almost *any* debilitating or life-
threatening illness, mental or physical, can so disrupt our
abilities that we feel somehow swept into substantial dis-
couragement or despair. Losing our physical or mental functioning can be disruptive, distressing and draining, and therefore
"depressing." Rather than see such emotional pain as a natural
part of the grieving process when we have a major loss, we—
and those around us—may erroneously call it "depression,"
when it in fact may not be. What the person may need to do
instead is to talk with safe people about feelings and concerns
regarding their actual or potential losses. But to do that may
seem too painful, time-consuming or unreliable. Primed with
the mindset that most painful feelings are "depression," we may
settle for that label, without considering other possibilities and
alternatives. While some studies have shown that it is harder to
heal with more co-morbidity, I have found that it may depend

more on the *kind* of co-morbid disorder present and whether the childhood trauma is seriously addressed in a *stage-wise* sequence, which I cover in chapter 14.

It is natural to develop the symptoms of depression when we have lost an important part of our ability to function mentally, emotionally, physically, socially or financially. This kind of loss may *result from* our having a mental or physical disorder, such as PTSD, schizophrenia, alcoholism or a stroke. "Depression" is a common presenting or concomitant finding among people with all sorts of debilitating conditions. For example, symptoms of depression have been reported to occur in up to 80 percent of people with PTSD, 65 percent with schizophrenia, 50 percent or more with some personality disorders and in more than half (with a wide range of from 9 to 98 percent) of people with alcoholism and other chemical dependence.[420, 655a]

Depression can be a consequence of repeated or ongoing alcohol or other drug intoxication and withdrawal. Alternatively, people can drink alcohol or take drugs to self-medicate depression.[643] (Depression may also be due to living with an addict in the past or currently.) To illustrate co-morbidity further, I show an example of the interrelationships among various disorders in Figure 12.1.

Co-morbidity is a hallmark of repeated childhood trauma. The more *severe* the trauma, the *younger* the age when the person is traumatized, and the *longer* the repetition, the more common the resulting co-morbidity. Subsequently, the more the existence of the trauma is *not validated* and *not prevented* by others around the child, the more severe the co-morbidity is likely to become.[66-7, 263-4] Finally, the more the effects of the trauma are treated with "Band-Aids," such as giving a depressed trauma survivor antidepressant or other psychoactive drugs alone, the more likely the co-morbidity will become entrenched. The person is then commonly left confused, ashamed and hopeless. The way to break this vicious cycle is to take a complete trauma history, and if present, to connect the depression or whichever other co-morbid disorder is present, to the trauma and begin to address their pain from this perspective.

Throughout this book and the next I have presented close to some three hundred published databased articles describing the associations and effects of trauma. In most of these, co-morbidity as the concurrent presence of two or more disorders that are associated with having a history of childhood trauma was a *replicated* finding. This result was true even among the several *prospective* studies, which emphasized the close relationship between trauma and co-morbidity. The co-morbidity was more common and with a higher number of disorders according to the *degree* of trauma *severity,* perpetrated at a *younger age,* that is *repeated,* and finally *unaddressed* (i.e., ignoring the existence of the trauma, the child's feelings and the need for protection from it). These were commonly associated with the subsequent occurrence of a high degree of multiple co-morbidity. In his recent book *The Trauma Model: A Solution to the Problem of Comorbidity in Psychiatry,* clinical and research psychiatrist Colin Ross describes the close connection between common and less common mental disorders and childhood trauma in more detail.[643]

Alcoholism/Chemical Dependence and Depression

Alcoholism and other chemical dependence have a special relationship to depression in that for many afflicted people their harmful chemical abuse tends to cause or aggravate the depression. This relationship has been demonstrated by the common result of a lessening or even disappearance of the depressive symptoms when the person stops using alcohol or other drugs for from one to several weeks. (A related issue is that *family* members of alcoholics often become depressed themselves. This raises the question of whether depression is genetic in transmission or whether, instead, people develop symptoms of depression associated with experiencing the traumas of an active alcoholic or CD family. My colleagues Rob Anda, Vincent Felitti, others and I have recently shown that it is not the parental alcoholism itself that causes the depression, but the adverse childhood experiences that are associated.[10]

Other chemically dependent people may drink or use other drugs excessively, in part, *because they are depressed.* Clinical and research psychiatrist Martin Keeler said that ". . . a precise diagnosis of depression can only be made when the patient is neither intoxicated nor experiencing alcohol [or other drug] withdrawal. . . ."[420] A related and more general observation is that active chemical dependence can and often does *mimic many mental disorders,* so that many clinicians who work in the addictions field follow Keeler's approach when their early withdrawing patients manifest symptoms or signs of mental illness. Clinical experience shows that when these other co-morbid problems or disorders are attended to and treated appropriately, the depression and other mental disorders to one degree or another may improve. If a clinician had prescribed a psychoactive drug when such a patient had just stopped drinking or drugging, an observer may assume that the drug had caused the improvement, when a more likely cause would be their abstaining from the alcohol or other addictive drug. If the mental disorder does not

improve with up to two months of abstinence, we can assume
that it may be a separate disorder and look for other causes, and
then treat it accordingly.

Based on the above, we can construct the following diagram:

Mental &/or   Other mental &/or
physical disorders ⟷ physical disorders

Because these co-morbid disorders may interact with one
another as described above and in other ways, it can be difficult
to heal from co-morbidity. Complicating the picture even more,
while at the same time paradoxically simplifying it, is the relationship of trauma with mental and physical illness. The following diagram, although overly simplified, may help us further
understand the relationship of co-morbidity:

Mental &/or   Other mental &/or
physical disorders ⟷ physical disorders

Either or both may be caused by
or associated with
childhood or other trauma

SLEEP RESTRICTION AND MORNING LIGHT THERAPY

Sleep restriction or deprivation has been used to treat depression in Europe for years. Some have called it the single most effective treatment, although its downside is that its antidepressant effect is transient, usually lasting no more than a few days.[249] Morning light treatment consists of exposing the person to daylight in the morning for from thirty to sixty minutes, which also has an effective, although similarly transient, antidepressant effect. Initially used for "seasonal affective dysphoric disorder" ("winter blues" or "SAD"), it has recently been used to treat and possibly prevent depression as well.[211a] When combined, these two inexpensive and effective methods can help speed a person's recovery from the discomfort of their depressive symptoms. Like most of the above recovery aids, these are readily available for the depressed person (or people around them to suggest), since they may be used without a prescription. Interestingly, a few inpatient treatment programs in the United States have begun to add these methods to their treatment approach, believing that they may have an additive or even a "booster" effect to concomitantly used antidepressant drugs.[249] Patients who use these methods feel improved, encouraged and often motivated to return to their daily productive lives.

SPIRITUALITY

Spirituality is about our relationship with our self, others and the Universe (Higher Power, God/Goddess/All-That-Is), and it is much more. While many aspects of religion are a part of it,

Table 12.3. Drug & Electro-Convulsive Treatment Aids for Depression: Some Clinically Significant Differences

according to author's & others' estimates from references 74, 75, 339, 381

Aid	Estimated Effectiveness	Acceptability	Toxicity	Cost
ADP drugs	+−+++ (toxicity may limit effectiveness)	Moderate; often depends on effectiveness, side effects & cost	Low to high	Moderate to high
Electroshock treatment (EST or ECT, C=convulsive)	+−++ (high toxicity may limit effectiveness)	Patients are often encouraged or "pushed" to receive it, so it is at best only semi-voluntary	Some to much impairment of memory, cognition & motivation (depends on number of shock "treatments")	Causes brain damage[75]

* Potential for being effective: 0 = None; + = 25%; ++ = 50%; +++ = 75%; ++++ = 100%.

spirituality contains and transcends organized religions. Thus spirituality is like the umbrella, and each religious path or faith is a spoke in that umbrella. If we have a loving and nourishing relationship with the God of our understanding, it is likely that we can use that relationship to help us heal. Prayer, meditation, working the Twelve Steps, other spiritual practices and more are choices that we can consider using.[17, 219, 786]

One concern is that some aspects of organized religion can be traumatic in their own right and can thus aggravate many mental and physical disorders. Here I refer to the overemphasis on sin, guilt and fear that some religions can foster. I have seen numerous patients over the years who have made these kinds of observations in their own recovery. When they eventually worked through and let go of much of their guilt, shame and fear, they often became able to use spirituality and/or religion as a nourishing recovery aid.

Since most of these above recovery aid choices are trauma-specific, they may also be used to an advantage to help heal from other kinds of "mental illness" that are trauma-related. Other methods may also help for those with concomitant PTSD, including eye movement desensitization and reprocessing (EMDR).[675] Neurotherapy (EEG biofeedback) may also help recovery from depression, which I describe in the next volume.

ELECTROSHOCK

In the last 2,400 years of recorded history, it has been only since the early 1960s that we have used *drugs* more seriously to try to treat depression. Initially barbaric and recently claimed "safe and effective" by those who administer it, *electroshock treatment* (EST, or ECT for electro*convulsive* treatment) has been used to try to help severely "depressed" people since 1940. But what do we know about it? In 1998, research psychiatrist Peter Breggin reviewed 184 articles and books on ECT and reported that ". . . most controlled studies of efficacy in depression indicate that the treatment is no better than placebo with no positive effect on the rate of suicide. . . . ECT is *closed-head electrical injury,* typically producing a delirium with global mental dysfunction (an acute organic brain syndrome). Significant irreversible effects from ECT are demonstrated by many studies, including: 1) Inventories of autobiographic and current events memories before and after ECT; 2) Retrospective subjective observations on memory; 3) Autopsy studies of animals and some of humans. ECT causes *severe* and *irreversible brain neuropathology,* including *cell death.* It can wipe out vast amounts of retrograde memory while producing *permanent cognitive dysfunction"* [my italics].[75]

This is disturbing information. Unfortunately, ECT has been increasingly used in North America, and there are ongoing attempts to promote its further use worldwide as "the most effective antidepressant." It is becoming a sizeable money-making business. Who is protecting the unaware patients? My guess is that most people who are subjected to ECT are survivors of moderate to severe childhood trauma, and a trauma-focused approach may be helpful—and certainly safer than ECT. Breggin concludes that "Contemporary ECT is more dangerous since the current doses are larger than those employed in earlier clinical and research studies. Elderly women, an especially vulnerable group, are becoming the most common target of ECT. Because of the lopsided risk/benefit ratio, because it is fundamentally traumatic in nature, because so many of the patients are vulnerable and unable to protect themselves, and because advocates of ECT fail to provide informed consent to patients—ECT should be banned."[75]

Long before drugs and ECT, we had an accumulating experience of much safer, supportive and healing nondrug recovery aids, many of which we have also recently learned more about in different ways. I show a summary of several characteristics of twelve of these in Table 12.1, and add electroshock treatment *only for comparison* and completeness in Table 12.3. I do not recommend it.

13   AN INITIAL APPROACH TO TREATING DEPRESSION

Depression and other mental disorders are difficult to heal. To do so usually takes persistence in using the recovery aids selected, and patience to complete the work.[792-3]

In selecting one or preferably more of these aids, the person should first determine what the likely origin is for their depressive symptoms. Looking at these from a statistical or "most likely" perspective, the most common causal factor or association with depression is having a history of childhood or other trauma. Significant loss or trauma in adult life may also be a causal or aggravating factor.

An affected person who has not determined the most likely cause of symptoms may consider consulting a helping professional. But in doing so they may encounter some difficulty in finding a clinician who can help most effectively, including one who has enough expertise and experience in evaluating and assisting a person who has a trauma history and manifests some of the effects of trauma. Identifying such a helping professional can involve a delicate balance of asking acquaintances who are trauma survivors in recovery and interviewing the clinicians they may recommend. Different kinds of helping professionals may view and treat depression differently. Thus, the person with symptoms of depression may ultimately benefit from asking around and interviewing any recommended helping professionals.

Others and I have recommended using psychotherapy as a treatment aid. But if chosen, even it may vary, since there are said to be more than four hundred different approaches. "Managed care" authorities will not usually approve of and pay for otherwise appropriate and effective long-term psychotherapy for depression and other "mental disorders," even though psychotherapy has been shown to be as effective as ADPs (see also sections in the next volume).

All of the above is part of why the recovery from or healing of "depression" is not a simple task—which the drug and managed "care" industries would have us believe. "Just buy and take our [marginally proven] drugs and you will be fine," or "Do what we authorize. . . ." Given our knowledge about the relationship between depression and trauma, I outline a rational approach to assessing a person with symptoms of depression in Figure 13.1 and Table 13.1.

Mild to Moderate Depression

Based on my clinical experience and knowledge of the literature, I outline suggestions for reducing the symptoms of depression, as shown in Table 13.1. For mild to moderate depression, it is usually most productive first to find the cause(s) of the symptoms and signs and address them. Since addictions, co-addictions and other disorders are common causes of depression and anxiety, their presence should be seriously considered.

Table 13.1. Reducing the Symptoms of Depression

(After first establishing that the diagnosis of depression is clear)

Mild to Moderate Depression

1. Find the cause(s) of the symptoms and signs, and address it (or them).
   Look for addictions, co-addictions and other disorders.

2. Use non-drug antidepressant recovery aids, including *regular exercise* to tolerance.
   Express any painful associated feelings and other important parts of your inner-life to safe
   people, including, ideally, a therapist.

3. If no help, reevaluate cause, and if appropriate, try another one or more non-drug
   recovery methods.

4. If still no help, see a trauma clinician for an evaluation to help rule out trauma as a causal
   factor

5. If still no help, strengthen the non-drug program above and at any time consider adding
   an appropriate ADP drug. (Watch for side effects and work closely with a physician
   regarding the most effective dose to take.)

Severe Depression *(i.e., suicidal, can't work or function and may need hospitalization)*

1. Find the cause(s) of the symptoms and signs and address it/them.
   Look for addictions, co-addictions and other disorders.

2. Begin a trial of an antidepressant drug, *plus* . . .

3. Use non-drug antidepressant recovery aids, including *regular exercise* to tolerance.
   Express any painful associated feelings and other important parts of your inner life to safe
   people, including a therapist.

4. If no help, institute numbers 3 and 4 from mild–moderate sequence above.

5. If still no help, consult a therapist who specializes in assisting depressed people.

Using nondrug antidepressant recovery aids, including *regular exercise* to tolerance, can be very helpful. Also, expressing any painful associated feelings and other important parts of our inner life to *safe* people over time—including, ideally, a therapist— will likely help us heal. I describe the characteristics of safe people elsewhere.[793]

If these do not help, reevaluating the cause, and if appropriate, trying another one or more non-drug recovery methods, can help. If still no improvement, consulting a trauma clinician for an evaluation or second opinion to help further rule out trauma as a causal factor may be productive. If still no help, strengthening the nondrug program and at any time considering adding an appropriate ADP drug can also assist in the healing process. (Watch for side effects of the drugs, and work closely with a physician regarding the most effective dose to take.)

Severe Depression

Severely depressed people may be suicidal, can't work or function, and they may need hospitalization. Here is where treatment with ADP drugs is indicated from the start, even though they may not work, or may work only partially and/or their side effects may prohibit their use. An obvious problem here is the three- to four-week delayed effect of ADPs, which speaks in favor of starting the *non-drug aids concomitantly* and seriously, since their beneficial effects often occur sooner. Until they improve satisfactorily, severely depressed people should also *see a health professional, ideally a psychotherapist, more often* as well. Otherwise, all of the principles for those with mild to moderate depression described above apply.

DIFFERENTIATING DEPRESSION FROM GRIEVING AND STUCK GRIEF

Most of our society is oriented to avoiding grief work. For example, mental health systems and other helping professionals may mislabel grieving people as being "depressed" or otherwise "mentally ill," when actually they are usually only trying to grieve. In Table 13.2, I outline some major points to consider in differentiating normal, healthy grief and grieving from depression.

Over the years I have noticed a progressive tendency of a large percentage of my patients, their friends and their clinicians to label them as being "depressed." When I evaluated them, it turned out that most were, in fact, not depressed. Rather, most had experienced several to numerous significant losses and traumas, yet had not been able to grieve them. No one had validated their pain by calling it *grief* and supporting their expressing it. Instead, they had nearly all called it "depression"—something that it usually was not. Their experience had been mislabeled. It was given the wrong name.

Grief and Grieving

Grief is something we can usually understand more easily than depression. I can grieve if I know what it is and if I have permission and support to do so. Here, I retain my personal power. But if I am told that I am "depressed," what can I do? I may not only have to mislabel my pain, but I may have to see a physician who will reinforce and maintain the misattribution and prescribe one or more of a series of expensive drugs with fairly high and uncomfortable side effects that may not work much better than a placebo. If all I do for my emotional pain is take the ADP drug, I may have given up my personal motivation and power to the chemical. Although taking the drug alone may be easier in the short run than engaging one or more of the nondrug recovery

Table 13.2. Differences Between Grieving and Depression

Characteristic	Grieving	Depression
Suicidal	0	+
Decreased: sleep, appetite, weight & functioning	±	+
Somatic symptoms, crying	±	±
Clear losses	+	± to 0
Numbness	Early	May be present as "stuck grief"
Awareness of feelings when supported	Yes, tend to feel more real	Tend less to none
Movement of feelings, not stuck, often with a **bittersweet** quality	Yes	No, stuck
Grief	Moves	May be stuck
Therapist's knowledge & acceptance of grieving as distinct from depression	Yes	Yes or no
Support system's knowledge & acceptance of grieving as distinct from depression	Yes	Usually no
Response to ADP drugs	± (Drug response is of no help in diagnosis)	± (Drug response is of no help in diagnosis)
Indication for ADP drugs	None when aware of grieving & it is supported	Usually
Need for acceptance & support	+	+
Potential for reduction of emotional pain	Good	Often incomplete resolution

aids in Table 12.1, I may be missing an opportunity that lasts to heal and grow.

Grieving has several characteristics that may help to distinguish it from depression, as shown in Table 13.2. These major differences include that:

1. The grieving person is not usually suicidal.
2. On taking a thorough history from them, they have clear losses and/or traumas.
3. They may be more aware of their painful feelings.
4. Ideally and *eventually* these feelings usually show some movement, at which time they also . . .
5. Often have a "bittersweet" character to them, and
6. They possess a good potential for reducing the experiencer's emotional pain.

Key in differentiating grief from depression is the knowledge, experience and acceptance of grieving as a distinct entity from depression by both the person's clinician and others in their support system.

With few exceptions, the symptoms and signs of grief and mild to moderate depression are almost identical, so that relying solely on the *DSM* diagnostic criteria to separate the two may be misleading. Depression is suggested by

1. The presence of suicidality
2. A more serious decrease in appetite, weight loss and functioning (although these are not always diagnostically reliable)
3. The absence of clear and significant losses or traumas

However, a favorable response to taking an ADP drug is not by itself diagnostic of depression,

At times it can be difficult to differentiate normal healthy grief and grieving from depression. For example, some people with depression are also trauma survivors, and they may have experienced recent significant losses. I have suspected for a long time that depression behaved like ungrieved grief that had somehow gotten "stuck" or stored up inside of us, like an abscess under the skin that is waiting to drain. The *pointing* of the abscess under the skin is perhaps manifested by many of the symptoms of depression. Thus, I have sometimes referred to depression as having a quality of "stuck grief." Reframing "depression" as stuck grief, i.e., a painful but ungrieved effect of trauma or major loss, can help facilitate a healthy expression and flow of grief and grieving. Also, many of my depressed patients who were unresponsive to ADP drugs have responded to one or a combination of the non-drug recovery aids in Table 12.1 on page 148. For these reasons and more, in some situations it may be difficult to differentiate these two common conditions. I describe the process of grieving in several of my books, including especially *Healing the Child Within* and *A Gift to Myself.*

*   *   *

With this information in hand, we can now expand this approach to treating trauma-based depression from a deeper perspective. In the next chapter, I describe the important stage-oriented sequence of healing from depression and other mental disorders.

Figure 13.1. Depression: Flow Chart for Decision Making

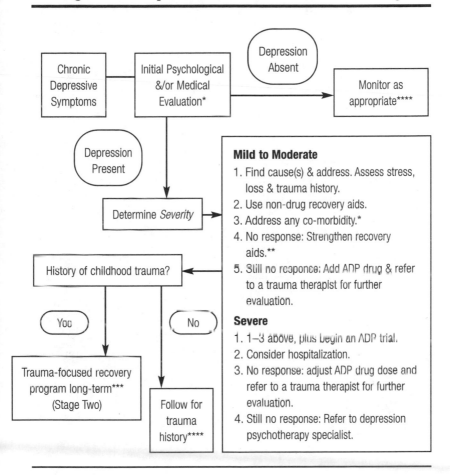

---

* Rule out more complex forms or co-morbidity with depression, e.g., PTSD, addiction, dissociative disorder, serious physical problems & effects of childhood trauma.

** Avoid using benzodiazepine sedative drugs to treat anxiety, insomnia or depression. Buspirone is a non-addicting and acceptable antianxiety drug.

*** Long-term group therapy, individual therapy, self-help group attendance, etc.

**** Because many trauma survivors authentically forget the trauma (dissociative amnesia),[7, 8, 103-4] or they may not be able to accurately name what happened to them as having been traumatic, keep an open mind that a substantial number may eventually remember a serious trauma history.[798]

14 THE STAGES AND PROCESS OF RECOVERY

Whether a person wants to heal from depression or another mental disorder (and some physical ones), taking a step back and looking at recovery from a broader and deeper perspective can help. A primary aid in doing so is knowing that recovery usually succeeds when approached in stages. In my work assisting people with various mental and emotional problems and disorders, I have found that using this sequential approach is helpful and at times can be crucial.[151, 174, 300, 473, 793, 797, 798]

For many mental and some physical disorders, we can benefit from paying attention to how the dimension of *time* relates to the process of healing. While all acute injuries need some time to heal, chronic ones tend to take more time. To help reach a successful repair and, eventually, growth, that time continuum can be divided into the following stages.

THE STAGES OF RECOVERY

Stage Zero

Stage Zero is active illness, and here recovery has not yet begun. It is manifested by the presence of any active disorder, such as a mental or physical one, including depression, an addiction or any other problem. In this stage, you see both symptoms and signs *and* other effects of whatever caused the illness. This active illness may be acute, recurring or chronic. Without recovery, it may continue indefinitely—unless the person becomes somehow motivated to begin a Stage One effort. At Stage Zero, recovery has not yet started, as shown in Table 14.1. (Note that this table reads from *bottom to top*.)

Stage One

Coming to treatment for any mental or physical disorder is the beginning of Stage One. It involves participating in a full recovery program to assist in healing the Stage Zero disorder. It is the standard kind of process that we most commonly consider as "treatment." If you are diabetic, you treat the diabetes by watching your diet, exercising, taking insulin and so forth. If you had "depression," you would often simply be prescribed an antidepressant drug, with little or no other investigation or intervention. Depending on the person and the problem, such a partial recovery program may be less likely to be as successful as a more complete regimen. Stage One is the conventional, superficial treatment of mental disorders often by using drugs alone. But this limited approach often does not work well. This is because

Table 14.1. Recovery and Duration According to Stages

Recovery Stage	Condition	Focus of Recovery	Approximate Duration
3	Human/spiritual	Spirituality	Ongoing
2	Past trauma effects	Trauma-specific recovery program	3–5+ years
1	Stage 0 disorder	Basic illness, full recovery program	Months to 3 years
0	Active illness	Usually none	Indefinite

Stage One people come in with a presenting disorder that is commonly the effect of the trauma.

Promoted by the drug and managed care industries for at least the last thirty years, drug treatment is usually strongly recommended and prescribed for depression and most other mental disorders. Unfortunately, this limited approach constitutes the bulk of their Stage One treatment today. Besides receiving drugs, a *minority* of people may get some brief counseling as well (if they are lucky enough to find a helping professional who recommends it—and if their managed care insurance company approves it). But that counseling is too often focused on only their current conflicts, and seldom on past traumas. Brief therapy can help, depending on how much healing work is accomplished. Eventually, people may discover or awaken to having had an experience of trauma in their childhood and/or adulthood, and begin to connect it to their having subsequent mental and emotional pain.

Stage Two

The typical motivation for beginning Stage One recovery is hurting too much—emotional pain, physical pain or debilitating disease. But eventually, somewhere during, or more often after, Stage One recovery, people may realize that they are still hurting. They realize that whatever they have done before hasn't worked as well as they had hoped—that the Stage One approach alone didn't help them enough. So they might then be more open to exploring other alternatives. That is where they can begin a more substantial healing—if they are lucky enough to find a helping professional who knows Stage Two work.

Stage Two recovery involves healing the effects of childhood and later trauma, including working through related core issues.[793] Once a person has a stable and solid Stage One recovery—one that has lasted for at least a few months to a year or longer—it may be time to consider looking into some of these Stage Two issues. Some mental disorders, especially those such as addictions (which often cause depression and anxiety), severe affective disorders (depressions and bipolar disorder*), some personality disorders, dissociative disorders and psychosis usually require a year or more to reach enough *stability* to be able to engage in Stage Two work. A trauma survivor may have grown up in an unhealthy, troubled or dysfunctional family. Many survivors may still be in a similar unhealthy environment, whether at home, in one or more relationships, or at work.

---

* As described in chapter 5, bipolar disorder (also called manic-depressive disorder) is an uncommon variation of depression. Some believe it is a separate disease, while others see it as being a part of the spectrum of depressive disorders. See notes and data on page 53 to 55.

How long does the Stage Two recovery process typically take? For a history of trauma that has become entrenched, which most are, it can take years to heal enough to find lasting peace. For some people it may take less time. There is no requirement or judgment on the amount of time it takes for a person to recover. It takes as long as it takes. My 25 years of experience in leading trauma-specific therapy groups has been that the members continually find relief when working or even when listening to others' work. In *A Gift to Myself,* I include numerous guidelines and experiential exercises to help facilitate Stage Two work, with a section at the end on how to assess when it may be time to stop therapy.[793]

It is helpful to make a personal *recovery plan,* a point I have emphasized throughout my prior books.* Making such a recovery plan gives us lots of advantages as we heal, one of which is to discover the usefulness of naming things accurately (see the chapter, "Naming Things Accurately," in my book *A Gift to Myself* for details).[793] For example, instead of "depression," if appropriate, consider calling it *grieving* from major losses and/or childhood trauma. And instead of saying "I deserved it," consider calling it *abuse* or *trauma.* These kinds of reframes can be effective as we heal. Doing so is important because what we deal with in therapy is often actually grieving, or stuck grief, and not a "mental disorder." "Depression" and "mental disorder" involves Stage Zero and Stage One thinking, and reframing depression as stuck grief— that is, needing to grieve but being somehow blocked from doing it—would be Stage Two thinking and understanding. As a

---

* I describe how to write a personal recovery plan in *A Gift to Myself* and "My Recovery Plan"[798a] (due out the fall of 2003). To obtain either, or a booklet version for each stage of recovery, please call Health Communications at 800-441-5569.

therapist, coming from that understanding is the need to help people identify and accurately name exactly what they are grieving from or about, thereby aiding them in their grieving in a healthy way.

What about a person who can't do more therapy because of managed care restrictions, budget constraints, low income and so on? We do the best with what we have. People who are motivated to heal can be creative. That's one reason I wrote my books—that is, for my patients, so they could save time and money by learning how to do the healing themselves, although with the help of safe others, including some therapists. Often, people go from one therapist to another, like people do with attempted intimate relationships. Some may fit. Others don't. They learn as much as they can with one teacher or guide and then go on to the next.

Stage Three

Stage Three recovery involves spirituality and its incorporation into daily life. Folding this strong recovery aid into our everyday flow is an ongoing and lifelong process. Stage Three is learning to realize spirituality. It is expanding the same question, "Who am I?" from Stage Two work, since that is a central question there, too. In Stage Three, the person is continuing to work on "Who am I?" in a deeper way. But now we also expand that question, "Who am I?" to the next interesting one: "What am I doing here?" and then "Where am I going?" Actually, Stage Three encompasses the whole process, from Stage Zero onward. Everything we do is spiritual, and by spiritual I am not talking about religion; I'm talking about *relationships* and *experiences* with self, others, and the Universe or God/Goddess/All-That-Is. Spirituality is about making meaning that may involve different levels of our life.[17] (See also pages 162 and 163).

Spirituality is a powerful tool. If the recovering person or their therapist does not understand spirituality, then one of the best places to learn about it is in most any Twelve Step fellowship group, no matter what the focus. Many people confuse spirituality with religion. While religions are kinds of "brand names," spirituality is the generic umbrella that embraces and transcends all religions. Psychological health is one of its goals. The healthier we are, the easier we can stay directly and authentically connected to ourselves and our Higher Power.

Having a spiritual connection to God, i.e., a sense of connection to a Higher Power, may be an association or aid for suicide prevention. For example, psychiatrist C. Bruce Greyson and researcher Barbara Harris Whitfield conducted research on twenty depressed patients who attempted suicide and were admitted to the psychiatric unit at the University of Connecticut Hospital. Those who had near-death experiences, in which they had a direct and powerful positive experience with a Higher Power, usually did not attempt suicide again.[317a, 786] They commonly said that they now had a sense of "cosmic unity." Other studies have replicated these results.[635a] Suicide attempters who didn't have a near-death experience, but who were given books to read about it, developed some of the same positive aftereffects and attitudes. Working a Twelve-Step program may lead us in the same direction, as numerous authors have described and countless individuals have experienced directly.

DIAGNOSIS AND THE RECOVERY STAGES

The *DSM* and similar diagnostic schemes and categories are useful mostly in Stages Zero and One. They can have some usefulness in Stage Two recovery, such as in the case of alerting clinicians when people may have a personality disorder or another one to which they may need to pay special attention. In all of these stages, *DSM* diagnoses are also useful for insurance reimbursement purposes, since the insurance industry requires a codified diagnosis before it will pay for health care. Beyond these considerations, I believe that the *DSM* diagnostic categories are not very useful. They are useless in Stage Three recovery work and, except for the above situations, in most of Stage Two. Even so, throughout this book and in the next, I refer to these diagnostic labels for purposes of accuracy in describing the strong associations that these forms of "mental illness" have with people with a history of childhood and subsequent trauma. I do this to point out how close mental illness was and is to repeated childhood and later trauma.

I'm not alone in these observations and opinions. As but four examples, Kutchins and Kirk,[464] Caplan,[133] Ross[638, 643] and Bremner[82] have described clear problems and deficiencies with the formulation and usefulness of the *DSM*. Regarding its relationship to childhood trauma, Bremner said:

> *This hypothesis of a common neurological deficit [among trauma survivors] could explain why there is such overlap among many disorders, and why clinicians are frustrated with the current diagnostic schema. The past half-century of psychiatry has been largely absorbed with an attempt to force clinicians*

to accept a "splitters" approach to psychiatric diagnosis which has led to finer and finer splitting of psychiatric diagnoses with successive versions of the DSM. An important foundation of this evolution of the psychiatric diagnosis is the absence of any theoretical foundation for diagnosis. This was largely a reaction to the previous era, in which psychoanalysis dominated psychiatric diagnosis and imbued a heavily dogmatic and theoretical foundation for it. However, cutting ourselves off from any theoretical foundations has had its price. It has led us into our currently absurd position of trying to justify why multiple psychiatric diagnoses—all spawned from the back of the DSM like the heads of the Hydra that sprouted after the single head called "anxiety neurosis" was lopped off by the so-called biological psychiatrists are actually distinct entities when all of the evidence points to the contrary. This situation has led us close to a grassroots revolution, in which the clinicians who actually see the patients are ready to assassinate the number crunchers who developed this idiotic scheme and are forcing the clinicians to comply with it in the name of "consistency of diagnosis" or "research protocol." In fact, these clinicians started ignoring the DSM years ago. However, if queried, they will spout the dogma like Protestants challenged by Catholic inquisitors in Spain during the fourteenth century. The fact is that it is time for us all to wake up and realize the truth—that these disorders are not truly distinct, that they have a common basis in neurology [i.e., trauma effects], and that we need to take a more enlightened approach to their evaluation and treatment.[82] (I discuss these ideas further in the Epilogue.)

This is a telling observation, one that many trauma-aware clinicians have made often. Bremner concludes,

> *Of course, the most relevant rationale to strengthen ourselves in terms of diagnosis is so that we can appropriately treat patients with trauma-related psychiatric disorders. If we can* properly diagnose trauma patients *[as trauma survivors], we can apply the* correct treatments *for these disorders. We are starting to learn more about treatments for trauma-related disorders, and the good news is that some treatments we have learned about in the past few years show considerable promise for disorders such as PTSD [my emphasis].*[82]

This leads us into the mental disorders other than depression that are commonly found to be variations among the effects of trauma. Indeed, some have suggested that if the *DSM* were to be rewritten with the truth about trauma effects more realistically in mind, it would become much smaller and most of it would consist of subcategories of a common diagnosis such as "post-trauma syndrome, manifested by *fill-in-the-blank*".[82, 96, 253, 360, 643, 715, 798] To bridge that conceptual gap, in the next book, the first chapter is appropriately on PTSD, which will provide us with an even firmer base from which to understand the multiple guises of the effects of repeated trauma. I continue with that and chapters on the other common mental disorders in the final volume, *The Truth About Mental Illness*.

Epilogue

Does childhood trauma cause depression? If we had only a few studies that looked at a small number of research subjects which showed a link between childhood trauma and a depression, the answer would be no. But that is not what we have.

In fact, we have exactly the opposite. We have 1) a large number of studies (251), 2) that used a *large number* of research *subjects* (159,793 people). These studies were conducted by 3) *multiple and independent researchers* who were 4) from *different countries,* and who 5) used several *different study designs* and methods (e.g., retrospective, prospective, index cases and meta-analysis) on 6) *diverse samples* of people (e.g., clinical, community and some forensic groups). Furthermore, the trauma-depression link was 7) *replicated* by nearly every one of these 251 peer-reviewed studies. The characteristics of this large number of scientifically conducted and published studies fulfill all of the criteria for quality research reports (as summarized in Table 4.2 on page 37), commonly including 8) highly meaningful *odds ratio* results and 9) a *graded response* pattern reported in all of the studies that looked for it.

Does childhood trauma cause depression? From the results of these reports the answer is "Yes, repeated childhood trauma causes depression and, as I show in the next volume, some other common and uncommon mental illnesses in a sizable number of people." Depending upon the amount of available evidence, for some disorders, such as depression and alcohol and other drug abuse and dependence, the evidence is overwhelming. For others, such as anxiety disorders, PTSD, eating disorders, psychoses and some personality disorders, the evidence is strong. For still others, such as behavior problems, including violence, and the occurrence of revictimization and somatization (which are not mental disorders, but happen commonly in association with them), it is firm. And for others, such as ADHD in children and ADD in adults, some evidence is present, but currently less convincing—perhaps because of the few studies published and the fact that most of the ones conducted on these disorders did not look for associated childhood trauma. (I discuss each of these disorders in some detail and describe their relationship to trauma in the next book.) I show a summary of the number of studies published to date that I found on depression and the number of people who were studied in Table 5.5 on page 55. A more graphic way to look at these data is shown in the bar graph in Figure E.1 and the pie chart in E.2.

From the above data and the other information detailed throughout this book, we can now reframe depression on and from a number of different levels and perspectives. These include the following.

FIGURE E.1 NUMBER OF STUDIES LINKING DEPRESSION
TO CHILDHOOD TRAUMA

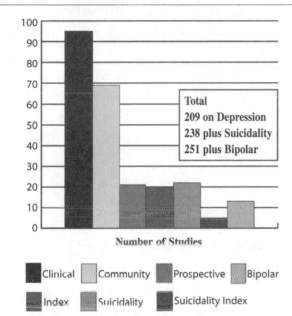

Total
209 on Depression
238 plus Suicidality
251 plus Bipolar

Number of Studies

Clinical Community Prospective Bipolar

Index Suicidality Suicidality Index

FIGURE E.2 NUMBER OF STUDIES LINKING DEPRESSION
TO CHILDHOOD TRAUMA: PIE CHART OF ABOVE DATA

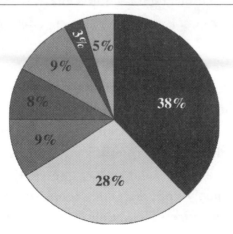

Depression: Levels of Development, Definition and Meaning
Bio-Psycho-Social-Political-Spiritual Dimensions

1) **Self loss**—Depression is a symptom of the subtle loss of the existence, acceptance, respect, honoring and love of our true self (real self, Child Within), first by others, then by self. The Child is repeatedly traumatized, and to survive, it goes into hiding.

2) **Pain defense**—a defense against the authentic feeling and expression of emotions (not allowed by many families), and against grieving of significant losses or traumas.[143, 476, 798, 816]

3) **Neurobiological effects**—a disruption and dysfunction, from the trauma, of one or more neurobiological systems and organs.[82, 194, 198, 203, 584-90, 734-8]

4) Resulting **significant ripple effects**—lack of energy, aliveness, expression, spontaneity and creativity of our true self. It is also a result of the cumulative frustration and eventual failure of our false self (ego) to work well.[143, 798]

5) **Insufficient explanation**—a non-specific group of symptoms that may be due to any one or more of a complex of associated, causal or triggering experiences or factors

6) **A symptom**—a non-specific group of symptoms that may be due to any one or more of a complex of associated, causal or triggering traumatic or other experiences.

7) **Disguised financial exploitation**—a marketing scheme by drug companies to sell their own minimally tested, patented and commonly toxic drugs that don't work well.[523]

8) **Existential effects**—emotional pain (sadness, hurt, fear,

anger, shame, guilt, numbness), physical symptoms and life inertia resulting from an accumulation of losses, hurts and traumas (loss or absence of: healthy parenting, true self, safe environment), and a lack of taught life skills (healthy: handling of feelings, boundaries, relationships and sense of humor); psychological visibility, self responsibility, independence, ability to give and receive love, and to do productive and meaningful work, and spirituality).

9) **Cumulative collective effects**—a nation, culture and world of wounded, hurting, numb, angry, distracted (by the depression and by addictions and compulsions), drugged, spiritually malnourished and creatively inhibited people.

Remedy—Find our true self and **heal it** with **safe people over time**. **Prevention—Stop abusing** and **neglecting our children** (and each other).

RECOMMENDATIONS

Having accumulated all of this information, what can we do with it? As a reader, you may already have some ideas. Perhaps we can explore them together. Feel free to modify these in any way that might best suit you. From my thirty-five-year experience as a physician (the last twenty-four years of which has been as a psychotherapist) and my research in the areas of mental illness and childhood trauma, I offer the following conclusions and recommendations.

1. Ideally, every person who has the symptoms of depression described in this book should be screened by a properly trained, experienced and licensed clinician who is knowledgeable about the effects of childhood trauma.

2. If there is a trauma history, the clinician can consider offering assistance to the person in a stage-oriented sequence, as described in chapter 14.

3. The concerned person and their clinician may consider using the flow chart or decision tree shown in this book on page 175 as possible guidelines.

4. A history of repeated childhood trauma, with or without retraumatization as an adult, may be appropriately considered to be an aggravating, if not possible causal factor in the genesis of depression. This consideration can have meaningful implications for the person's treatment and recovery.

5. Among several of these implications, the practice of connecting the two experiences of childhood and/or current trauma and depression now and in subsequent therapy and recovery-oriented situations can be healing.

6. This healing process may occur most successfully by using a wholistic trauma-focused and stage-oriented treatment and recovery program.

7. The program is usually best facilitated by using a supplemental, written personal recovery plan, ideally accomplished by the concerned person and reviewed by their clinician. To facilitate this process, I have included a copy of *My Recovery Plan for Stage Two Recovery* in Appendix B.

8. This whole process cannot be rushed, and usually takes a long time.

I wish you the best in your recovery, and if you are a clinician, in your helping others to heal.

Charles L. Whitfield, M.D.
January 2003
Atlanta, GA

CONTINUED EVIDENCE

After I had turned in my final manuscript of this book, within just two months, I found twenty-five more data-based published study reports linking depression to childhood and later trauma. I summarize these in Table E.1. I also found several more studies that linked suicidality with prior trauma.[664] These expand the total number of the already overwhelming number of 251 studies to more than 276 data-based peer-reviewed, published studies.

These additional findings show that:

1) There are likely more such studies that I have not yet found,

and 2) There will be an ongoing number of new such reports in the future.

I also found six additional studies that link low self-esteem to trauma (as discussed in chapter 6, with the same implications (e.g., references 21, 25, 275, 265, 271, 746)).

The Internet makes it easier to keep up with new studies by searching through programs such as PubMed (a free United States government service from the National Library of Medicine), Science Direct, and Ovid (both fairly expensive, by subscription only), as well as by regularly checking each journal's tables of contents for its new issue as it is published.

We are rich in information. The downside has been that its sources have been scattered over numerous journals and books that are hard to find without other resources, and often obscured within a vast literature of studies and articles that neither look for nor address trauma. This problem is in part what motivated me to write this book.

I hope that it has been useful to you.

Table E.1 Depression and Childhood Trauma: Continued Evidence

Year/Author	Study characteristics	Depression/ suicide/CT	Other effects of trauma	Comments
1980 Surtees & Ingham	19 depressives, 45 affective psychosis*	↑ recent stress, loss	*Plus 6 mixed PDs & schizoaffective	Index case study
1981 Finlay-Jones & Brown	164 women traumatized, 164 controls	↑	↑ anxiety	Recent traumas only
1983 Ageton 3-year follow-up	2,221 teen girls CSA	↑	↑ behavior problems, delinquency	3-4x revictimization Prospective
Herman	40 depressed women	↑	Co-morbidity	Index
1989 Fromuth & Burkhart	582 college men CT vs. controls	↑	↑ obsessive-compulsive . . .	hostility, ↑ psychoticism
Seng	105 teens, most CSA	↑	↑ SA/CD, behavior/ school problems	
Bryer et al.	36 women attempters	3x CT		Index
1990 Davidson & Smith	14 affective dis 14 anxiety, 9 PDs, 4 SA/CDs, 3 bulimics	84% CT	17/54 PTSD	Index
Metcalfe et al.	100 men psych in/outpatients	BPs had ↑ CSA	Psychotics had ↑ CSA	Index
1991 Bagley & Shewchuck	60 assaultive & CT youth 320 controls	↑	↑ anxiety, SA/CD, hyperactivity,	behavior problems, ↓ self-esteem
Bagley	750 women CT vs. controls	↑	↑ PTSD symptoms	↓ self-esteem
1992 Frazier & Cohen	82 women CT vs. controls	↑	↑ ED, SA/CD, anger, revictim.	↓ self-esteem
1993 Dubowitz et al.	93 CSA children 80 controls	↑	↑ behavior, hyperactive, schizoid	↑ ED (obese)
1994 Rodgers	5,362 people CT vs. controls	↑		41-year follow-up Prospective
Brown & Moran	404 women CT vs. controls	↑ , & longer course	Other current stressors	3-year prospective
Higgins & McCabe	199 college students, CT vs. controls	↑	↑ sexual problems	self-esteem

Table E.1 Depression and Childhood Trauma *(continued)*

Year/Author	Study characteristics	Depression/ suicide/CT	Other effects of trauma	Comments
Collings	284 college men	↑	↑ anxiety, phobia	↑ OCD, psychoticism, somatization
1995 Buist & Barnett	50 depressed women	54% CT	All postpartum depression	Index
Oakley-Browne et al.	777 women CT vs. controls	↑		
Oakley-Browne et al.	65 depressed 81 controls	4x CT		Index
Ullman & Siegel	155 women CT vs. controls	↑	↑ revictimization, physical problems, hospital/Dr visits	Community
1996 Portegijs	39 depressed 40 anxiety dis 51 somatizers	2.4 - 2.8 x CT 1.2 - 2.3 x 2 - 2.0 x		Index
1999 Saunders et al.	2,008 young women CSA/ rape vs. controls	2.5 x	SA/CD 2-5.1x, PTSD 3.1-3.4x	
2001 Kirkengen	34 CSA medical patients	↑	↑ anxiety, 29/34 severe EDs, 23 revictimized	26 psych hospitalization
2002 Harkness & Wildes	76 depressed women	↑ CT	↑ anxiety disorder	Index
25 Studies 1980-2002	**14,246 CT people & controls**	**↑ - 3 x CT or to 84% CT**		**9 index case 6 clin/7com 3 prospective**

FIGURE E.2 LOW SELF-ESTEEM AND CHILDHOOD TRAUMA: CONTINUED EVIDENCE

Year/Author	Study characteristics	Self-esteem	Other effects of trauma	Comments
1987 Tong et al.	49 CSA children vs. controls	↓ self-esteem	↑ aggression, behavior, & school problems	
1991 Hunter	52 CSA adults	↓ self-esteem	↑ relationship, body image . . .	↑ sexual identity problems

Appendix

Table A.1. Timeline of Selected Events

(Updated & expanded from

Date	Event
1896	Freud & Janet believe their patients' histories of trauma
1900–1985	Few publications on trauma as causal or associated with subsequent mental disorder. Freud's Oedipal theory. Idealization of the family
1940	Electroshock treatment begins
1940s	Continued accounts & reports of PTSD under different names[798]
1946–1962	Early descriptions of effects of child physical abuse
1952	*DSM-I* (First edition)
1960s	Emphasis on biological psychiatry begins. New and unproven: theories, sedatives, antidepressants & antipsychotics
1962	*DSM-II* (Second edition)
1973	Laws against child abuse enacted
1980	*DSM-III* (Third edition); PTSD included[7]
1985	Reports on effects of trauma begin to increase, and are published in clinical scientific literature.
1990	Biological psychiatry now entrenched. Anti-recovery movement begins
1978–94	Books on trauma as causal of mental/physical disorders
1994	*DSM-IV* (Fourth edition)[8]
1997–2003	↑ data on trauma as causal/assoc. with physical and mental disorders

in Mental Illness and Trauma

references 103 and 798)

Comment

Patients tell story, express their pain & improve (trauma/seduction theory & reality)

Freud's retraction of above in 1897–8 & following sets the stage for others' denial of the effects of trauma, propagating the myth of "the family" as always ideal & sacrosanct.[798]

A double-edged sword treatment (see text) Continuing denial of brain damage[75]

Descriptions of associated grieving

See, e.g., Caffey (1946), Silverman (1951–3) & Kempe (1962)[798]

106 diagnoses listed. No input from drug industry.

Drug industry, and academic psychiatry & medicine initiate & support this emphasis[335-345] Drug industry begins to "educate" physicians

182 diagnoses listed. General descriptions of disorders

Beginning of protecting abused and neglected children

265 diagnoses listed. More specific descriptions of disorders

Recovery movement grows; self-help books increase. Managed "care" increasingly promotes drug treatment.

Superficial critiques of trauma effects, including "false memory" hypothesis (still unproven)

See references . . . e.g., Brown & Harris 1978[108] and Herman 1992[360]

307 diagnoses listed, some apparently created by drug industry[133, 339, 345, 464]

e.g., ACE study,[254] McCauley et al.,[218] more than 276 others (see text)

Table A.2. Potential Results of Unresolved Trauma*

Problems	Characteristics
Life	Trauma changes a normal life (e.g., may alter: beliefs, thoughts, feelings, decisions, choices, expectations, behaviors; relationships; vulnerabilities; and life events). False self runs life.
Relationship	Choosing friends who have been or feel victimized (instead of healthier ones); loss of friends; irritability/aggression/bullying; re-victimization; withdrawal; isolation; boundary problems[797]
Thinking	Problems remembering and focusing; inhibited imagination, creativity, and choice-making ability; confusion; delayed information processing
Mental Health	Chronic or complex PTSD; alcohol/other drug problems; behavior, mood, anxiety, somatoform, eating, sleep, impulse control, personality, dissociative, and/or psychotic disorders, including depression
Lessening/ numbing emotional pain	A style of confusion, self-distraction, or distracting; alcohol or drug misuse or abuse; varying levels of dissociation; core recovery issues
Age Regressions	Ordinary age-regressions, sometimes with flashbacks & abreactions; dissociation, often leading to re-victimization
Repetitions (of the trauma)	Dangerous risk taking; reenactments of aspects of the event, such as promiscuity or prostitution after molestation, or feeling choked and exhausted anytime adrenaline increased; provoking attacks
Self-punishment	Provoking attacks on self or others; low self-care; repeated dysfunctional choices in relationships, with problematic results; self-mutilation; isolation, suicidality
Repeated somatic complaints or illness	Aches and pains (e.g., abdominal and other body aches, including back pain, headaches); decreased immune response; functional and organic illness; disability; ↑ Dr. office visits

* Expanded from Nader 2001; Felitti et al. 1998, Walker et al. 1999, McCaulley et al. 1997 and others.

Table A.3. Depression and Childhood Trauma:
96 Clinical Studies

Year/Author	Study Characteristics	Depression/ Suicide	Other Effects of Trauma
1937 Bender & Blau	16 CSA children	38% (6/16) depressed	↑ behavior problems
1942 Sloane & Karpinsky	5 CSA, incest	80 (4/5)	All promiscuous
1972 Lukianowicz	26 CSA girls, incest	↑	↑ anxiety, PDs, promiscuity, prostitution
1974 NIAAA Booz, Allen & Hamilton	50 CoAs intensely interviewed	↑	↑ SA/CD, promiscuity & teen pregnancy, etc. most grew up too fast
1975 Benward & Densen- Gerber	Interview of 118 CD ♀ inpatients, 52 CSA v. 66 controls	1.5x depressed (CSA v. non-CSA)	↑ antisocial behavior, CSA described as causative
1977 Browning & Boatman	14 CSA, incest	↑	↑ anxiety, hypersexual, runaways
1975 Molnar & Cameron	18 CSA teen girls	↑	↑ runaway
1979 Tsai et al.	90 women (30 each: clinical, non-clinical, controls)	↑	MMPI: ↑ Hs, Pd, Pa, Pt & Sc* ↓ social skills, family & sexual function
1981 Anderson et al.	155 CSA teen girls	↑	↑ anxiety, EDs, school problems
1981 Frank et al.	50 rape victims	↑ (psych drugs made worse)	↑ SA/CD drugs

Table A.3. continued on next page (See last page for key to abbreviations)

Table A.3. Depression and Childhood Trauma *(continued)*

Year/Author	Study Characteristics	Depression/ Suicide	Other Effects of Trauma
1983 Wolfe & Mosk	71 CTs, 35 controls, 6–16 years old	↑	↑ schizoid, somatic, aggressive, delinquent, hyperactive
1985 Lindberg & Distad	17 incest survivors	100% depressed 47% suicidal	100% PTSD, 2/17 SA/CD (12% = 2x gen pop)
1986 Friedrich et al.	85 CSA 3–12 year old children, clinical, forensic	↑	↑ anxiety, somatization, aggression, delinquency, hyperactivity, etc.
Bagley & Dann	65 CSA teen boys vs. 220 control in same Tx unit	↑	
Putnam et al.	96 CT patients	70–90%	↑ psychotic symptoms, SA/CD, EDs, PDs
Sloan & Leichner	5 CSA women on ED unit	↑ (3/5)	↑ sexual problems
Gorcey et al.	41 CSA 56 controls	↑	all psych outpatients
1987 Bryer et al.	66 women psych inpts	↑	50+% revictimized as adults, ↑ anxiety, paranoia, psychotic Sx
Beck & van der Kolk	12 chronically hospitalized psychotic women	3x CSA History	6x medical disorders, 3x drug abuse/CD
Livingston	13 CSA children mean age 10	77% (10/13)	Psychotic features common

Table A.3. Depression and Childhood Trauma *(continued)*

Year/Author	Study Characteristics	Depression/ Suicide	Other Effects of Trauma
Sansonnet- Hayden et al.	17 CSA of 54 teens in psych hospital	↑ 71% depression suicidality	
1988 Briere	133 women vs. 61 controls average age 27	↑	↑ dissociation (2x), SA/CD (4–9x), revictimization (8x), sleep, sex problems
Briere et al.	40 CSA, crisis ctr. 40 controls	↑	↑ dissociation, insomnia, anxiety, anger
McLeer et al.	31 children mean age 8	↑	48–75% PTSD
Schaefer et al.	36 CT 64 controls	↑	↑ anxiety, OCD, paranoid, psychoticism
1989 Stein et al.	51 women	↑	↑ SA/CD & anxiety/phobia
1989 Morrow & Sorell	101 lower SES adolescent girls	↑ , graded response	↓ self-esteem
Einbender & Friedrich	46 CSA girls, 6–14 YOs v. 46 controls	↑	↑ aggression, social problems, hyperactive, schizoid-obsessive, school, somatic & sex problems
1990 Jacobson & Herald	40 CSA, 100 psych inpatients	↑	↑ psychosis, SA/CD
Swett et al.	65 CT men 65 control psych outpts	↑	↑ anxiety, phobia, BPD

Table A.3. continued on next page

Table A.3. Depression and Childhood Trauma *(continued)*

Year/Author	Study Characteristics	Depression/ Suicide	Other Effects of Trauma
1990 Elliott & Tamowski	17 CSA children v. 17 controls	↑ symptoms (NS, compared to physically abused)	one of only 2 studies showing NSD (control bias?)
Goodwin et al.	20 severely CT women	90% (18/20)	↑ PTSD, SA/CD, dissociative
Hooper	60 CSA women 358 controls	2x	↑ neurosis
1991 Felitti	131 CSA v. 100 controls	2.6x	3.7x DOV, 1.6x GI probs & headaches 1.6–4.2x eating disorders
Brown & Andersen	166 patients	↑ + suicide	2x eating disorders, SA/CD
Kaufman	56 7–12 YO children, all CT	2–4x	
Wozencraft et al.	65 SA children	↑	
Bifulco et al.	21 F CSA v. 215 controls, random	5.1x	
Kaufman	56 CT children	12x [estimated]	
Kiser et al.	40 CT	↑	↑ anxiety, behavior problems
Brown & Garrison	132 CSA (incest) 250 controls	4–6x	20x anxiety, 2–6x ED, 30–38 SA/CD, 6x promiscuity, 2x migraines

Table A.3. Depression and Childhood Trauma *(continued)*

Year/Author	Study Characteristics	Depression/ Suicide	Other Effects of Trauma
1992 Pribor & Dinwiddie	2 women CT	4–9x	6x SA/CD, 6–15x anxiety/phobia
Walker et al.	14 ♀ severe CSA with chronic pelvic pain v. 86 controls	4.8–10.6x	4/x panic, 6x phobia, 23x somatization, 1.7–5.9x SA/CD, 2–2.5x sexual dysf., 7.6x chronic pelvic pain
Famularo et al.	61 CT children 35 controls	3.2–12x	↑ anxiety, SA/CD, behavior problems, PD, PTSD
1993 Handwerker	355 women 2/3 CT	2–4x	
Moeller, Bachman & Moeller	354 abused ♀ (CSA, PA, EA) v. 314 controls in a GYN practice [Found 16 defects of parents; 8% perps women]	2x/6.4x	SA (2.5x alc, 18x drug), 2x obesity, fatigue, PMS, 3x GYN problems, 3x high tension, 1.5x anxiety, 6.2x crime victim, 2.3x self-esteem, 3x pessimistic
Mueuzenmaier et al.	78 psych outpatients 65% CT	↑	↑ SA/CD, psychosis, revictimized, homeless
Swett & Halpert	71 of 88 women CS/PA v. 17 "no abuse." All on psych unit	↑ ("not signif," but "controls" were also psych inpatients = hi risk)	↑ anxiety, hostility & psychoticism, plus BPD APD, PD & Schizoid PD
Mullen et al.	298 CSA 294 controls ↑ family dysfunction	2.6 + 5.2x (2–74x suicide)	↑ ED. anxiety, SA/CD, ↑ family dysfunction, psych. inpt. & outpt.

Table A.3. continued on next page

Table A.3. Depression and Childhood Trauma *(continued)*

Year/Author	Study Characteristics	Depression/ Suicide	Other Effects of Trauma
1994 Goldberg et al.	201 patients	↑	↑ chronic pain (Depression is an expected natural consequence)
Rowan et al.	47 adult CSA survivors	↑	69% PTSD
Bartholow et al.	1001 men CT vs. controls	↑	↑ SA/CD, sexual identity problems
1995 Vize & Cooper*	180 psych. in- or outpatients	3x	3x bulimia 4.4x anorexia nervosa
Stern et al.	84 SA children 5–15 YO, 84 controls	2 + x	3 + x sexualized behavior, ↓ self-esteem
Windle et al.	802 alcoholics CT vs. controls	↑	↑ anxiety, APD
Mancini et al.	205 anxiety disordered 23–45% CT	↑	
Mennen & Meadow	135 girls 6–18 with CSA evaluated	↑	↑ anxiety ↓ self-esteem
Lanz	77 CSA vs. 164 controls, all pregnant single adol. [control bias?]	↑	↑ anxiety, SA, delinquency ↓ self-esteem, support, family rel'ns
Brodsky et al.	60 BPD ♀ psych inpt. 50% (30/60) CSA/PA	↑	↑ dissociation (50%) psych Tx, self-mutilation

Table A.3. Depression and Childhood Trauma *(continued)*

Year/Author	Study Characteristics	Depression/ Suicide	Other Effects of Trauma
1996 Toth & Cichetti	52 abused, 49 controls	↑	↑ school & social problems, emotional abuse important
Kumar et al.	111 adolescent psych inpatients CT vs. controls	No difference from controls (control bias?)	↑ inappropriate sexual behaviors
Ellason et al.	69 of 106 SA/CDs had CT Hx	↑	↑ PTSD, PD, dissociation
1997 Pillay & van der Veen	100 children CT	↑ (more if delayed disclosure)	↑ PTSD
Moisan et al.	60 boys SA (30 black, 30 Latino)	↑ ; [30% offenders were women]	↑ anger, hopelessness & somatization
Ferguson & Dacy	55 women CSA 55 controls	↑	↑ anxiety & dissociation
Caspar & Lyubomirsky	61 bulimics with ↑ CSA, 92 controls	↑	
1997 Pharris et al.	1,157 adolescents vs. controls	↑ Sx of depression	↑ suicidal thoughts & behavior
McCauley et al.	424 of 1,931 ♀ CS- &/or CPA	1.6x	↑ SA & medical disorders, revictimization
Ellason & Ross	144 CT survivors	↑	↑ dissociation, psychosis
Moyer et al.	65 CSA teens 136 controls	↑	↓ self-esteem

Table A.3. continued on next page

Table A.3. Depression and Childhood Trauma *(continued)*

Year/Author	Study Characteristics	Depression/ Suicide	Other Effects of Trauma
1998 Felliti et al.	9,508 patients ACE study, CT vs. controls	4.6–12.2x	2–10.3 self-destruction 4.7–10.3x SA/CD other co-morbidity
Kaplan et al.	99 adolescent pts. vs. 99 controls	2.9–9x	13–15 SA/CD 2–3x ADHD
Classen et al.	27 CSA women	↑	↑ anxiety ↓ self-esteem
Ackerman et al.	204 CT children	↑	↑ anxiety, phobia, PTSD, ADHD, behavior, PD
Kinard	150 CT children 148 controls	↑	Low rater agreement & denial?
1999 Grilo et al.	70 abuse Hx vs. 93 none	3.5x	2.5x suicidal, 1.9x BPD SX, 2.1x SA, 1.8x violent
Dickinson et al.	252 women CT vs. controls	↑	↑ PTSD, anxiety, phobia, ED, somatization
Fondacaro et al.	86 CSA, 125 controls prison inmates	↑	↑ SA/CD, anxiety, PTSD, panic, OCD, ASPD, schiz
Brown et al.	81 abused, 558 controls, children & adolescents	3–4x	8.4x repeated suicide attempts in CSA
Pelletier & Handy	40 CT, 20 controls	↑	↑ behavior problems

Table A.3. Depression and Childhood Trauma *(continued)*

Year/Author	Study Characteristics	Depression/ Suicide	Other Effects of Trauma
Gold et al.	187 adults CSA	↑ depression	↑ anxiety, aggressive & impulsive behavior, somatization, psychoticism
Harmer et al.	46 women, most CT, vs. gen population	↑	↑ parenting problems
2000 Kendal-Tackett et al.	65 CS/PA vs. 65 controls	3x	↑ surgeries, symptoms
Anderson et al.	45 bulimic inpatients, all CT	84%	58% PD, 22% SA/CD
Pelcovitz et al.	89 CT teens 96 controls	↑	↑ anxiety, PTSD, ODD
2001 Reynolds et al.	45 5–11 YOs, witnessed domestic violence, no controls	↑ depression	↑ PTSD, ADHD, conduct disorder ↓ self-esteem
Hurt et al.	119 CT children	↑	↑ anxiety ↓ self-esteem
Bulik et al.	30 identical twins, 1 bulimic	1.5x	↑ SA/CD (4x), anxiety 6x suggested environmental cause
2001 Johnson et al.	89 CSA adult	68% depressed	78% PTSD 22% dissociative disorder
2002 Frias-Armenta	150 women CT vs. controls	↑	↑ anxiety, SA/CD, APD, abuse own children

Table A.3. continued on next page

Table A.3. Depression and Childhood Trauma *(concluded)*

Year/Author	Study Characteristics	Depression/ Suicide	Other Effects of Trauma
Saigh et al.	151 children CT v. controls	↑	↑ anxiety, thought disorder, somatization
Cecil & Matson	57 CT teens 192 controls	↑	↑ self-esteem
King et al.	2,698 men CT v. controls	2.4x	↑ anxiety 1.7x, self-harm 2.6x
Johnson et al.	167 CT children	↑	↑ anxiety, anger
Runyon & Kenny	98 CT children	↑	
2003 Thompson et al.	51 CT, 21 adult rape victims, 25 controls	2.3x	3x anxiety, 2x SA/CD, 7x PTSD, ↑ eating disorders

SUMMARY

Clinical 96 Studies 1937–2003	**29,292 patients & controls (most sexual abuse, some physical, all likely psychological)**	**1.6 to 12.2x ↑ to 12x suicidal**	**Increased and often multiple Co-Morbidity. One kind of abuse commonly occurs with other kinds**

DOV = Doctor office visits, CSA = Child Sexual Abuse, CPA = Child Physical Abuse, CEA = Emotional Abuse, Sx = Symptom(s), CT = Childhood trauma, SA/CD = Substance abuse/chemical dependence, PD = Personality disorder, APD = Antisocial, BPD = Borderline personality disorder, NSD = No significant difference, Hx = History, x = times (risk factor or increase over control or general population), ODD = Oppositional defiant disorder, Tx = treatment, ED = eating disorder, ♀ = female, ADHD = attention deficit hyperactivity disorder, ↑ = increased

Table A.4. Depression and Childhood Trauma:
70 Community Studies

Year/Author	Study characteristics	Depression/ suicide	Other effects of trauma
1984 Bagley & McDonald	57 CT girls 30 controls	2x	↑ sexual problems ↓ self-esteem
Sedney & Brooks	51 CSA 51 controls	↑	
1986 Bagley & Ramsay	82 CSA women 285 controls	2x + 3.7 suicidal	4x low self-esteem, 5x self harm
Gold	191 people CT vs. controls	↑	
Bagley & Ramsay	45 ex-prostitutes (73% CSA) vs. controls (27%)	5x (80 vs. 16%) All ex-prostitutes were severely abused as children	10x low self-esteem (71 vs. 7%) (cited in Bagley & Young 1989/90)
Kilpatrick	285 CSA vs. 210 controls	↑ graded relationship ↑ revictimization	Staying with CD partner as adult ↓ self-esteem
Herman et al.	205 CSA women	↑	50% substantial effects
Fromuth	383 college women CSA vs. controls	↑ ± ↓ parental support a major factor	↑ anxiety, paranoia, psychoticism, somatization
1987 Conte & Scheurman	369 CSA children, 318 controls	↑	↑ anxiety, panic, behavior problems, somatization ↓ self-esteem
Briere & Runtz	152 adult women health crisis center (67 CSA [44%] vs. 85 controls)	Most common presenting problems (33/23%) (others: rel'n probs 27%, anxiety 14%)	↑ SA (2.6x alcsm, 9x drug), 2x anxiety, 2x anger, self harm, sexual problems, muscle tension

Table A.4. Depression and Childhood Trauma *(continued)*

Year/Author	Study characteristics	Depression/ suicide	Other effects of trauma
1987 Gorcey et al.	41 CSA survivors,* 56 controls	↑ *(Some clinical subjects)	↑ anxiety, sexual problems
1988 Briere & Runtz	41 CSA women undergradates vs. 237 controls	↑	↑ anxiety, dissociation, medical disorders
Stein et al (LA Epidem. Catch- ment Area study)	2,683, overt CSA only vs. controls	3+x	2-10x anx. disorder, 2x SA, 9x schiz, 5xOCD, 3.8x APD 2.2x any mental disorder
Burnam et al. LAECA study continued	432 CSA vs. 2693 controls	↑ Younger age abused = more mental disorders	↑ SA, anxiety disorders, OCD. No: ↑ mania, schiz, APD
Dimock	25 CSA men	↑ in all	
Mullen et al.	99 CSA/CPA vs. 215 controls adults ↑ depression	Those abused as adults also affected ↑ anxiety	phobia
Peters	71 CSA 48 controls	↑	↑ SA/CD, psych hospitalization
Murphy et al.	120 CSA, 81 adult SA victims, 184 controls	↑	
1989 Rew	34 CSA/55 nursing studs	↑	↓ self esteem
Mechanic & Hansell	288 CT teens 507 controls	↑	↑ anxiety, somatization
Shapiro et al.	53 5-18 yo ♀ 32 controls	↑	Suspected under- reported
Morrow & Sorell	101 lower SES adolescent girls	↑ Graded response to trauma severity**	↓ self-esteem

Table A.4. Depression and Childhood Trauma *(continued)*

Year/Author	Study characteristics	Depression/ suicide	Other effects of trauma
1990 Hooper	60 CSA vs. 358 controls	2x	↑ neurosis
Knowles & Schroeder	199 ACoAs 601 controls	↑	↑ anger, poor health, somatization
Winfield et al.	1,157 women CTs v controls	↑	↑ SA/CD, PTSD, panic disorder
Greenwald et al.	54 CSA nurses 54 controls	↑	↑ anxiety, phobia, OC, paranoid, psychoticism, somatization
1991 Kiser et al.	40 CS/PA	↑	↑ anxiety, behavior problems
Saunders et al.	399 CSA 3,609 controls	↑	Final report in 1999
1992 Wind & Silvern, white collar women	122 CSA/PA vs. 137 controls	↑	↑ trauma Sx/PTSD like adult neg. experiences
Toth et al.	153 children lower SES 46 abused, 35 neglected, 72 controls	↑	↑ aggressive behavior ↓ self-esteem
Bushnell et al.	39 CSA ♀ 262 controls	2.1x (also prospective)	1.2x SA, 1.5x eating disorder
Scott	167 CSA survivors 2,964 controls	↑	SA 2.1-5.2x, phobia 3.4x, 2.4x any affective disorder
Yama et al.	139 college students: (46 CSA women vs. 93 controls)	↑	↑ anxiety and family dysfunction
Gross & Keller	260 college students, CT vs. controls	↑	↓ self esteem
Saunders et al.	131 CSA 260 controls	↑	
1994 Bagley et al.	116 men 18-27 CSA vs. 634 controls, random sample	↑	

Table A.4. Depression and Childhood Trauma *(continued)*

Year/Author	Study characteristics	Depression/ suicide	Other effects of trauma
Fox & Gilbert	253 college ♀ CT vs. controls	↑	↓ self esteem
1995 Elliott & Briere	113 CSA 385 controls	↑ depression Most Sx = recent recovered memories	↑ anxiety, anger/irritability, dissociation, sexual problems, tension reduction behavior, ↓ self-esteem
1996 Mullen et al.	107 abused (53 SA, 39 PA, EA 57) vs. 390 controls	3.7x 5-18x suicide attempt	2-3x SA, 3.2 ED, 3x sex prob & early pregnancy; 7.2x ever hospitalized
1994 Pelcovitz et al.	27 CPA teens vs. 27 controls	10 x depression	↑ behavior problems, thought disorders
1995 Mancini et al.	205 consec. anxiety disorder patients (23-45% CP/SA)	↑ depression	↑ anxiety
Andrews et al.	101 women CT vs. controls	2.9x	
1996 Davidson et al.	67 SA (1/3 < age 16) 2,851 controls	3/10 x depression/ suicide	3-4 x PTSD 2x panic attacks,
Duncan et al.	104 CPA 3,904 controls	2-4x	5-10x PTSD, 2-3.4x SA/CD, 4x legal problems
Fergusson et al.	106 CSA vs. 919 controls	5.5x for contact CSA 7x for intercourse	Anxiety 4x contact & 4.2x intercourse
Toth & Cicchetti	52 CT children 40 conrols	↑ (very ↑ if CSA and "confused" rel'n with mother)	Single types abuse (CSA, PA, N rare
Whitfield & Stock	100 CSA adults 88 women, 12 men	7 x (57%)	14 x DID, 40% ED, 1/3 self harm, 3 x psychosis, 7 x PTSD, 6 x SA
1997 Flisher et al.	665 9-17 YOs 26% (172) PA	↑	↑ anxiety, conduct, defiant & impairment

Table A.4. Depression and Childhood Trauma *(continued)*

Year/Author	Study characteristics	Depression/ suicide	Other effects of trauma
Fergusson & Lynskey	1,265 children surveyed; PA, some CSA	↑, & ↑ suicide	↑ anxiety in a graded fashion
Styron & Janoff-Bulman	232 CT college students	↑	↑ relationship difficulties Attachment problems in most
Moyer et al.	65 CSA teen girls 136 controls	↑	↓ self-esteem
Kessler et al.	5,877 people CT vs. controls	↑	↑ anxiety, SA/CD, behavior problems
1998 Ackerman et al.	127 CSA only, 43 CPA only, 34 both 7-13-year old	↑ depression and bipolar	↑ Anxiety, phobia, ADHD, operational defiant, conduct disorder, PTSD, OCD, avoident
1998 Alexander et al.	92 CSA women	↑	↑ PTSD; focus on attachment disorder
Blumenthal et al.	326 college students, CTs vs. controls	↑	↑ anxiety, ± PTSD
Kent & Waller	236 women CT vs. controls	↑	↑ anxiety, ED symptoms, dissociation
1999 Fondacaro & Holt	86 CSA vs. 125 controls, prison inmates	↑ (41% of CSA did not believe they were abused)	↑ anxiety, panic, SA/CD, PTSD, OCD, ASPD, psychosis
Liem & Boudewyn	145 CSA vs. 542 controls, college students	↑	↓ self-esteem
Bensley et al.	4,790 CT students vs. controls	↑	↑ SA & antisocial behavior
Armsworth et al.	36 women CSA vs. 35 controls	3-9x, + 2x suicide	1.9-5x anxiety 13x psy hospitalization 2-11x Eat Disorder
Zuravin & Fontanella	105 CSA 408 controls	About 3x depression	
2000 Kendler et al.	1,411 ♀ twins, 30% CSA	2 - 5.7x	↑ SA, anxiety, panic, bulimia; CSA *causal* of diverse psychiatric disorders

Table A.4. Depression and Childhood Trauma *(concluded)*

Year/Author	Ctudy characteristics	Depression/ suicide	Uther effects of trauma
Krantz & Ostergren	128 P/CSA ♀ 263 controls	↑	↑ anxiety & somatic symptoms, esp musculo-skeletal
Harter & Taylor	333 college students	↑	↑ anxiety, paranoia, psychosis, hostility
Neumark-Sztainer et al.	9,943 teens CTs vs. controls	1.6-2.4x	Co-morbid with eating disorders
2001 Cecil & Matson	57 CSA teens vs. 192 controls	↑	↑ family distress, physical & emotional abuse, ↓ self-esteem
MacMillan et al.	7,016 people, CTs vs. controls	1.8-3.3x	2x anxiety, 1.4-2.3x SA/CD, 2.5-5.3x antisocial behavior
Lipman et al.**	305 CT 1,166 controls	2.1x	2.1x anxiety 3.2x SA/CD
2002 Nelson et al.	1,991 twin pairs	1.9x	1.9x anxiety, 1.7-3x SA/CD, 2x nicotine, 2.5-6.6x conduct disorder, 3.6-26x revictimized
2003 Thompson et al.	97 women CT vs. controls	2.3x	↑ SA/CD, 7x PTSD, 3x anxiety
Community 70 Studies 1985 - 2003	**69,724 trauma survivors & controls**	**Depression ↑ to 10x** **Suicidality ↑ to 18x**	**↑ Co-Morbidity**

* Other family dysfunctions are factors that influence abuse. ** CT history was consistent & significant association with adult problems even when controlled for.
For abbreviations see key for Table A.3 on page 210.

Table A.5. Associations Among Depression and

Year/Author	Study Characteristics	Depression/suicide
1984 Bagley & McDonald	57 abused girls (20 CSA) separated from M. vs. 30 non-abused Followed 8 years	2x high correlated over 8 year follow-up
Bagley et al.	149 CSA women vs. 471 controls, prospective	↑ to 10x
1986 Bagley & Ramsey	82 CSA, 285 controls	↑
1989 Mechanic & Hansell	288 CT teens, 507 controls	↑
1991 Bifulco et al.	25 CSA, 261 controls	↑
1995 Stern et al.	84 CSA children, 84 controls	↑
1995 Leifer & Shipiro 1 year	64 CSA girls age 5–16	↑
1996–99 Widom et al.	1,575 children followed 20 yrs* Abuse count documented (5 reports)	↑ + suicide
1996 Fergusson et al.	1,000 children CSA followed yearly to 18 YO	↑ + suicide
1997 Fergusson et al.	1,265 children PA followed yearly to 18 YO	↑ + suicide
1996 Silverman et al.	375–519 children, 17 yr. follow-up ages 5, 9, 15, 18, 21; at 21, retrospective abuse assessment	
1998 Putnam et al.	164 girls: 77 CSA, 15 other abuse, 77 controls; followed ↑ 2 yrs x 20 yrs to young adulthood	↑

Childhood Trauma: 22 Prospective Studies

Other effects of trauma	Comments
2x ↓ self-esteem & sexual problems ↑ neurosis-related to separation from M, physical abuse & neglect	Vulnerable & hopeless, without recovery work became involved in repeated abusive relationships
70–80% of those with ↓ social support are depressed & often suicidal (cited in Bagley & Young 1989/90)	↑ childhood stress, CSA & ↓ self-esteem & social support = high-risk for depression & suicide
↑ anxiety, psychosis ↓ self-esteem	
↑ anxiety, somatization	
↑ anxiety, SA/CD	
↑ behavior problems ↓ self-esteem	
↑ anxiety, behavior problems	No difference between foster care vs. not
↑ anxiety, SA, aggression, violence, anti-social behavior	↑ PTSD (520 neglect, 110 PA, 96 CSA, 543 matched controls)
↑ anxiety, SA, aggression, violence, anti-social behavior	Effects had a graded relationship to severity of trauma
↑ anxiety, SA, aggression, violence, anti-social behavior	Effects had a graded relationship to severity of trauma
	↑ Co-Morbidity (multiple)
↑ anxiety, SA, dissociation, somatization, ADHD, hyper sexual, older partners, developmental problems**	See also Trickett et al. 1994

Table A.5. continued on next page

Table A.5. Prospective Studies *(concluded)*

Year/Author	Study Characteristics	Depression/Suicide
1997 Ellason & Ross	54/135 CT DID patients	↑
1997 Tebbutt et al.	84 children vs. controls (1/4 boys) CSA followed @ 0, 18 mos & 5 yrs	↑ (43%, i.e., 4.3x the adult incidence of 8%)
1996 Boney-McCoy & Finkelhor	1,433 10–16 YO, national, 15 month follow-up	↑
1999 Wozniak et al.	260 children & teens, CT vs. controls	↑
Swanston et al.	68 CSA children, 84 controls, 5 years follow-up	↑ anxiety, SA/CD, ED, somatization
Bagley et al. "Calgary study"	565 teens followed from birth	↑
2000 Cameron	72 women, 51 for the full 5 surveys over 12 years follow-up	7x (60%; 32% somewhat depressed; 47% suicidal)
2001 Johnson et al.	593 biological parents & their children were followed and assessed for 18 years	↑
2002 Kendler et al.	1,942 adult twin ♀ CT vs. controls, 9 year follow	↑, complex development (see Figure 5.2)
Lansford et al.	585 children, CSA vs. controls 12 year	↑

SUMMARY

22 Studies 1984–2002	**11,009 subjects ↑ to 7x & controls** followed from one to 20+ years	**Depression/suicide ↑ to 10x**

Other effects of trauma	Comments
↑ anxiety, psychotic symptoms	↑ other traumas during follow-up. Need for earlier & stronger treatment
↑ behavior problems (46%) ↓ self-esteem (43%)	Trauma appears causal of psychological symptoms.
↑ PTSD (other problems not screened for)	
↑ SA/CD anxiety	
↑ anxiety, conduct, behavior problems	
77% anxiety; 88% ↓ self-esteem; 82% CD; 78% sexual probs; 63% PTSD; 75% GYN; 67% headaches/jaw	With trauma-focused treatment there was substantial improvement in these disorders & symptoms over time
↑ other psychiatric disorders	Disorders were associated with parental maladaptive behavior, but not with parental psychiatric disorder
↑ anxiety, PTSD, dissoc; behavior, school & thought problems	
High & multiple Co-Morbidity	**Graded relationship to trauma severity. One: substantial improvement with trauma-focused treatment**

Table A.6. Depression/Suicide & Childhood Trauma:

Year/Author	Study Characteristics	Childhood Trauma
1979 Rosenfeld	18 ♀ psych pts. with mixed disorders, including personality disorders, chart review	6/18 (33%) reported incest. 5/6 (83%) dx'd hysterical personality disorder (3) & hysterical neurosis (2)
1987 Hallstrom	60 depressed ♀ vs. 400 controls	↑ physical abuse (PA)
Jacobson & Richardson	32 depressed inpatients.	↑ (81% of totals reported)
1989 Anales & Torgeson	298 psych. outpatients, most were depressed	↑ childhood trauma
Coons et al	14 depressed	↑ CT (36%)
Jabson	11 depressed	↑
Morrison	311 primary affective disordered patients	16% CSA
1992 Carlin & Ward	22 depressed, 11 bipolar psych. inpt. women vs. 89 controls	44% CSA, 46% CSA
Kuyken & Brewin	58 depressed women	60% (35/58) CT
1993 Wurr & Partridge	43 depressed	56% CSA
1998 Levitan et al.	653 depressed 8% of 8,116 surveyed	↑ CT
1975–1998 11 Studies	**8,931 subjects**	**↑ childhood trauma**

11 Index Case Studies

Other findings	Comments
No objective assessment beyond psychiatric clinical interactions	Published before PTSD became an accepted diagnosis in psychiatry
Felt misunderstood by parents, esp. mother	
	No controls. Compared with other psychiatric patients
20–93% had PTSD symptoms.	(be aware for dissociative amnesia)
↑ adult trauma (revictimization)	
Lowest % CSA to be reported in depression	
Used MMPI	Likely underestimated abuse %
Strong relationship with bipolar & physical abuse in all & CSA in ♀	

Miscellaneous findings, as above adult trauma

Some researchers have looked at the trauma-illness model from another angle: taking the person with an illness or condition as the index case and looking for clinical evidence, i.e., historical &/or laboratory findings, of childhood trauma. I summarize some of these reports in this table.

Table A.7. Depression and Childhood Trauma:

Year/Author	Study Characteristics	Depression/Suicide
1975 Benward & Densen-Gerber	Interview of 118 CD ♀ inpatients 52 CSA vs. 66 controls	1.5x depressed (CSA vs. non-CSA)
1996 Boney-McCoy & Finkelhor	1,433 10–16 YO, national, 15 month follow-up	↑ (most other problems not looked for)
1999 Kendler et al.	1,898 ♀ twins distressed vs. controls	3.5-4.5x
1999, 2000 Kendler et al.	1,411 ♀ twins, 30% CSA	2–5.7x
1975–2000 13 authors	**4,752 subjects. One prospective & one on twins by genetics research team**	**↑ to 5.7x**

CD = chemical dependent, ♀ = female

4 Studies Concluding That the Trauma Is *Causal*

Other Effects of Trauma	Comments
↑ antisocial behavior	One of earliest data-based reports CSA described as *causative*
↑ PTSD	Trauma appears *causal* of psychological symptoms
apparently not looked for	Recent distress is 2/3 *casual* of onset of depression
↑ SA, anxiety, panic, bulimia	CSA is *causal* of diverse psychiatric disorders
↑ SA, anxiety, panic, PTSD, bulimia, antisocial behavior	**All authors use *causal* in a clear & firm manner**

See also Brown & Harris (1978)[108] for trauma and causality

Table A.8. Depression and Childhood Trauma: Meta-Analysis/Literature Reviews of 110 Studies*

Year/Author	Study Characteristics	Depression/ Suicide	Other Effects of Trauma	Comments
1995 Jumper	18 study meta-analysis CSA 1978–81, 3,546 subjects	↑	Multiple co-morbidities & re-victimization	↓ self-esteem
1993 Bemporad & Romano	Summarizes 17 European literature reports*	Two suggest childhood trauma may be an important cause of adult depression	Other childhood relationship & circumstantial problems may be factors	Few assessed childhood trauma; 2 that did are summarized (1987, 1989)
1996 Newmann et al.	38 study meta-analysis CSA/ depression/ other disorders, 11,162 subjects	↑ association with co-morbidities	Symptoms were effects of trauma, not character defects	
2002 Paolucci et al.	37 study meta-analysis CSA/depression /suicide	↑	↑ association with co-morbidities	High difficulty to disprove these results

*Other literature reviews include references 50, 112, 263 and 421.

Table A.9. Suicide and Childhood Trauma:
22 Clinical Studies

Year/Author	Study characteristics	Childhood trauma/ or suicide	Other effects of trauma
1988 Briere	133 CSA vs. 61 controls	2 x (suicide lethality)	↑ dissoc (2x), Sa/CD (4-9x), revictimization
Caviola & Schiff	150 S/PA teens In a CD Tx center vs. 60 CDE & 60 controls	↑ suicide attempts & ideation	
1989 Langevin et al.	CSA Hx in sex offenders vs. nonabused	↑ ideation 2x attempts	
1989 Briere & Zaidi	35 CSA vs. 75 controls	↑ suicidality	
1990 Byne et al.	15 BPDs 14 Schizs, most with severe CT	↑ suicidality	↑ SA/CD, anxiety, behavior problems, bedwetting
1991 Brown & Anderson	166 patients PA & CSA vs. inpatient controls	↑ suicidality [control bias?]	2x eating disorders, ↑ SA/CD
1992 Wallen & Berman	217 SA/CDs CT vs. controls	↑ suicidality	↑ revictimization
1993 Mullen et al.	298 CSA 252 covert 191 overt	20-7 x	↑ revictimization
Shaunesey et al.	40 CT psych inpt teens, 77 non-abused psych inpatient controls	↑ attemps & ideation	[control bias?]
De Bellis et al.	20 girls SA vs. 22 controls	↑ suicide attempts & ideation	
Gould et al.	Of 292 med pts 73 CSA adults 218 controls	6.4x suicide attempts	
1994 Yellowlees & Kaushik	44 CSA women 88 controls	3.4x attempts	3-46x SA/CD 6.4x revictimized

Table A.9. Suicide and Childhood Trauma *(concluded)*

Year/Author	Study characteristics	Childhood trauma/ or suicide	Other effects of trauma
1995 Smith et al.	89 CSA adults 9 mos follow-up	↑ suicidality	↑ anxiety, doctor visits
1995 Bryant & Range	182 college students ♀ CT vs. controls	↑ suicidality	
1998 Molnar et al.	775 homeless & runaway 12-19 YO; abused vs. controls	1.9-4.3x suicide attempts among CSA	↑ CoAs &/or children of foster homes
Schrier et al. (community)	7,884 teens CT vs. controls	↑ suicidality	↑ sexual risking, bulimic & violent behavior
1999 Armsworth et al.	36 CSA (incest) vs. 35 controls	2x suicidal	↑ depression, EDs, anxiety
Lipshitz et al.	64 suicidality 35 controls	32-61% CT	Control bias possible
Gladstone et al.	40 CSA women 130 controls All depressed	↑ suicidality	↑ BPD, self-harm, psych visits, ↓ self-esteem
Grilo et al	70 CT teens 90 controls	↑ suicidality	↑ BPD-like symptoms
2001 Dube et al.	17,337 HMO members	2-5x suicidality Strong graded relationship	Depression & SA/CD strongly associated
Romans et al.	254 CSA 223 controls	↑ suicidality	↑ anxiety, panic disorder, ED
Molnar et al.	5,877 people CT vs. controls	2-11x	Strong link, especially with CSA
22 Studies 1983-2001	**34,911n CT people & controls**	**↑ to 74 times suicidality, including attempts and completions**	**↑ Co-Morbidity**

PA = physical abuse; SA = sexual abuse; EA = emotional abuse; ED = eating disorder

Table A.10. Suicide and Childhood Trauma: 7 Index Case Studies

Year/Author	Study characteristics	Childhood trauma/ or suicide	Other effects of trauma
1985 Deykin et al.	159 teen attempters 318 controls	3-6x CT reflected in DSS contacts	(DSS = Department of Social Services)
1989 Brent et al.	27 completers 19 YO & younger vs. 56 suicidal inpatients* (Close relatives interviewed)	All 27 completed suicide, & showed "no difference" vs. "controls"* (of whom over half have been abused)	*Most suicidal inpatients have the same high incidence of childhood trauma, so there would be no significant differ-ence expected here.
1993 Brent et al. Prospective	49 adolescents (attempts [13], ideation [36]) vs. 121 controls	Ideation group had more child sexual abuse	
1993 Van Egmond	150 ♀ suicide survivors	50% CSA survivors	CSA Hx: common re-attempts
1994 Brent et al.	67 completers 19 YO & less vs. 67 community controls	All who completed showed ↑ PA in past year	Parents, sibs & friends interviewed
Beautrais	85 attemptors vs. 90 random controls	Attempts 11.7x Contact CSA 35% 1.4% controls	Medically serious suicide attempts. Cited in M&F
1995 Shafi et al.	20 completers vs. 17 closest friends	All who completed showed ↑ PA, EA or neglect in past year	Suicide determined by coroner
1985-1995 7 Studies	**787 Suicidal People & Controls**	**↑ CT in 6 of 7 studies**	**Control bias in 1995 study**

Table A.11. Literature Reviews of Suicide & Trauma (Examples)

1997 Wagner	Analyzes 34 studies on suicide & family risk factors	Shows—"Consistent evidence that a history of PA or SA is a risk factor, and some evidence for poor communication, loss of caregiver, and psychopathol-ogy in first degree relatives." Says most claims in these studies are not justified due to faulty research designs.	
1998 Santa Mina & Gallop	Reviews 21 studies on suicidality and 12 on self harm	Shows there is a definite link between CT and suicidality and other self harm.	

Table A.12. SSRI Withdrawal Report Examples Published

(as of August 2002)* *Compiled from* http://www.socialaudit.org.uk/425ssritable.htm

Drug	Reports	Dates	"Warning" from Drug Company[†]
Fluoxetine (Prozac)	25 publ. /402 + (WHO reports)	1988–2002	"When dosing is stopped, active drug substances will persist in the body for weeks. This should be borne in mind when starting or stopping treatment."
Fluvoxamine (Luvox/ Faverin)	10	1992–2002	"Symptoms, including headache, nausea, dizziness and anxiety, have rarely been reported after abrupt discontinuation of [Luvox]/Faverin."
Nefazodone (Serzone/Dutonin)	6	1996–1999	None. [Note discrepency in reports and warnings for all].
Paroxetine** (Paxil/Seroxat)	45/2,003	1993–2002	"Symptoms, including dizziness, sensory disturbance (eg paraesthesia), anxiety, sleep disturbances, (including vivid dreams), agitation, tremor, nausea, sweating and confusion have been reported following abrupt discontinuation of [Paxil]/Seroxat. They are usually self-limiting and symptomatic treatment is seldom warranted. No particular patient group appears to be at higher risk of these symptoms; it is therefore recommended that when antidepressant treatment is no longer required, gradual discontinuation by dose-tapering or alternate day dosing be considered."
Sertraline (Zoloft/Lustral)	17/585+	1994–2002	"Rare cases of withdrawal reactions have been reported."

*There are countless more cases reported on the internet (e.g., search "SSRI [or specific drug name] withdrawal"). **SmithKline Beecham apparently knew in the 1980s that many *healthy* volunteers experienced

Table A.12. SSRI Withdrawal Report Examples Published *(concluded)*

Drug	Reports	Dates	"Warning" from Drug Company
Venlafaxine (Effexor/Efexor)	24/1,058	1996–2002	"Discontinuing Effexor: No definitive withdrawal syndrome has been observed with Effexor. During clinical trials, symptoms reported on abrupt discontinuation of Effexor from daily doses of 150mg or more included fatigue, nausea and dizziness and one episode of hypomania. Discontinuation effects are well known to occur with antidepressants; therefore, when Effexor has been administered for more than one week and is then stopped, it is generally recommended that the dose be reduced gradually over a few days and the patient monitored in order to minimise the risk of discontinuation symptoms. Patients who have received Effexor for six weeks or more should have their dose reduced gradually over at least a one-week period."
Citalopram (Celexa/Cipramil)	4	1998–2002	"Withdrawal reactions have been reported in association with selective serotonin reuptake inhibitors (SSRIs), including [Celexa] Cipramil. Common symptoms include dizziness, paraesthesia, headache, anxiety and nausea. Abrupt discontinuation of treatment with cipramil should be avoided. The majority of symptoms experienced on withdrawal of SSRIs are non-serious and self-limiting."
Total **7 SSRIs**	131 published	1988–2002	**In spite of their knowing of their drug's withdrawal syndrome existance, most drug companies delayed their warnings to patients and their physicians until the late 1990s. Only 2 (for paroxetine and venlafaxine) approached being appropriate or adequate, although delayed.**

withdrawal symptoms with paroxetine (Paxil).[523] *** Some individual reports are included with WHO, (World Health Organization) and others. †All from Data Sheet compendium 1998–2000.

Table A.13. Antidepressant Drugs, Trade Names, Some

Drug	Trade Name	Daily Dose	Sedation[†]	ACH[††] Effects
Tricyclics Desipramine	Norpramin Pertofrane	150–300 mg.	+	+
Protriptyline	Vivactil	15–40 mg.	+	++
Imipramine	Tofranil	150–300 mg.	++	++
Nortriptyline	Aventyl Pamelor	75–125 mg.	++	++
Trimipramine	Surmontil	100–300 mg.	+++	++
Doxepin	Sinequan Adapin	150–300 mg.	+++	++
Amitriptyline	Elavil	150–300 mg.	+++	+++
Chlomipramine	Anafranil	50–150 mg.	++	+++
Others Metprotaline	Ludiomil	150–125 mg.	++	+
Amoxapine	Asendin	150–400 mg.	++	+
Trazodone	Desyrel	150–400 mg.	++	0
Nefazodone	Serzone	100–600 mg.	++	+
Bupropion	Welbutrin	150–450 mg.	+	0
Mirtazapine	Remeron	15–60 mg.	++	+

Adverse Effects and Comments (See references for details 39)

Comments

Many people who are prescribed an ADP drug are helped by a lower dose than many of those recommended by the drug companies

Today tricyclic ADP drugs are prescribed much less often than SSRIs

Even so, SSRIs are no more efficacious than tricyclics or the "other" category

In UK called Allegron, Motival, Motripress. Multiple trade names may be confusing. For marketing, drug companies make up both generic and trade names.

Higher toxic "side effects" are said to cause less tricyclic use

But most SSRIs also have unacceptably high toxic effects, as others and I, and especially our patients, have observed (see text)

ADPs often vary in effectiveness & toxicity from person to person: They are unpredictable.

Clomipramine is marketed for OCD, although it may not be uniquely effective for it

This and the rest of the "others" category are no more effective than tricyclics or SSRIs

Most all of these ADP drugs can be viewed as chemical "clones" of one another

Used also for sleep in a single low dose (e.g., 50–100 mg. an hour before bedtime)

Anti-anxiety & ADP, less long-term toxic effects than most others. Liver toxicity rare

Marketed as Zyban for nicotine addiction. May cause seizures in high doses. Limited anti-anxiety effects.

Taken at bedtime. As for other ADPs, weight gain & sedation can be problems. Zispin in UK.

Table A.13. continued on next page

Table A.13. Antidepressant Drugs, Trade Names, Adverse Effects and Comments *(concluded)*

Drug	Trade Name	Daily Dose	Sedation*	ACH** Effects
SSRIs				
Fluoxetine	Prozac	5–40 mg.	+	0
Sertraline	Zoloft	12–200 mg.	+	0
Paroxetine	Paxil	5–40 mg.	+	0
Venlafaxine (an SNRI)	Effexor	20–375 mg.	+	0
Fluvoxamine	Luvox	12–300 mg.	+	+
Citalopram Escitalopram	Celexa Lexapro	10–60 mg.	+	+
You name it	**New ADPs coming**		**Similar effects will be likely**	

* Sedation can work to advantage for some. Variable occurrence and degree. May also cause overstimulation, the severest from being akathisia, described in Table 10.2 on page 126.
**ACH (anticholinergic) effects include dry mouth, constipation, difficulty urinating and blurred vision.

In part, from Hales RE: Clinical challenges, clinical solutions: a customized approach to depression management. Continuing education teleconference, Nov. 7, 2000, sponsored by Bristol-Myers Squibb Company and continuing education of SC, Inc., and Stahl SM: Selecting an antidepressant by using mechanism of action to enhance efficacy & avoid side effects. Journal of Clinical Psychiatry 59 (suppl 18): 23–9, 1998, and Baldessarini.[39]

Comments

Marketed as Serafem for severe PMS. I list lower-than-standard doses for all the SSRIs. These lower doses are often effective in all ages, especially in elderly

Lustral in UK. FDA-approved for panic disorder, OCD and PTSD. Other ADPs are approved for these and other disorders, but as for depression, their efficacy for them may be low.

Seroxat in UK. Commonly has one of the more painful withdrawal syndromes

May help in hypersomnia & weight gain. Dose-related hypertension. May have lower toxic side effects than others.

Faverin in UK. Marketed mostly for OCD & social anxiety, though may not be specific for these.

Cipramil in UK. Sedation can be a problem.
Escitalopram is a clone ("active part") of citalopram with claimed less toxic effects

Caution: Continued toxic effects for most ADPs. Most have disabling withdrawal symptoms (see Table A.12). More are being marketed for other disorders, even though efficacy may be as low as for depression. Most ADPs have "shotgun" effects, and it is unlikely than an effective "single bullet" ADP drug will be developed any time soon.

References

A

1. Ackerman PT, Newton JE, McPherson WB, Jones JG, Dykman RA (1998). Prevalence of post-traumatic stress disorder and other psychiatric diagnoses in three groups of abused children (sexual, physical, and both) Child Abuse & Neglect 22:759–74

2. Ackerson J, Scogin F, McKendree-Smith N, Lyman RD (1998). Cognitive bibliotherapy for mild and moderate adolescent depressive symptomatology. J Consult Clin Psychol 66(4):685–90

3. Ageton SS (1983). Sexual assault among adolescents. Lexington Books, Lexington MA

4. Alexander P, Lupfer S (1987). Family characteristics and long term consequences associated with sexual abuse. Archives of Sexual Behavior 16: 235–245

5. Alexander PC, Anderson CL, Brand B, Schaeffer CM, Grelling BZ, Kretz L (1998). Adult attachment and longterm effects in survivors of incest. Child Abuse & Neglect 22:45–61

6. American Medical Association, Council on Scientific Affairs (1993). Mental health consequences of interpersonal and family violence: implications for the practitioner. CSA Report (BCA-93). Chicago

7. American Psychiatric Association. (1980). Diagnostic and statistical manual of mental disorders (DSM-III) Washington, DC

8. American Psychiatric Association (1994). Diagnostic and Statistical Manual of Mental Disorders (DSM-IV) Washington DC

9. Ammerman RT, Cassisi JE, Hersen M, Van Hasselt VB (1986). Consequences of physical abuse and neglect in children. Clinical Psychology Review 6:291–310

10.   Anda RF, Whitfield CL, Felitti VJ, Chapman D, Edwards VJ, Dube SR, Williamson DF (2002). Adverse childhood experiences, alcoholic parents, and later risk of alcoholosm and depression. Psychiatric Services 53: 1001–9

11.   Anderson SC, Bach CM, Griffith S (1981). Psychosocial sequelae in intrafamilial victims of sexual assault and abuse. Paper presented at the 3rd annual conf on child abuse & neglect, Amsterdam, Netherlands; cited in Elliott DJ, Tarnowski KJ (1990). Depressive characteristics of sexually abused children. Child Psychiatry Hum Dev 21(1):37–48

12.   Anderson CM, Teicher MH, Polcari A, Renshaw PF (2002). Abnormal T2 relaxation time in the cerebellar vermis of adults sexually abused in childhood: potential role of the vermis in stress-enhanced risk for drug abuse. Psychoneuroendocrinology 27(1–2):231–44

13.   Anderson G, Yasenik L & Ross CA (1993). Dissociative experiences and disorders among women who identify themselves as sexual abuse survivors. Child Abuse & Neglect 17 (5): 677–686

14.   Andrews B, Valentine R, Valentine JD (1995). Depression and eating disorders following abuse in childhood in two generations of women. British Journal of Clinical Psychology 34: 37–52

15.   Angell M, Relman AS (2001). Prescription for Profit. The Washington Post June 20

16.   Angell M (2000). Is academic medicine for sale? New England Journal of Medicine 342:1516–8

17.   Anonymous (1976) A Course in Miracles. Viking, NY

18.   Anthenelli RM, Schuckit MA (1997). Chapter 5. Genetics. In Lowinson JH et al (eds). Substance Abuse: A comprehensive textbook. 3rd ed, Williams & Wilkins, Baltimore, p 41–51

19.   Armsworth MW, Stronck K, Carlson C (1999). Body image and self perceptions of women with histories of incest. In J. Goodwin, & R. Attias, Eds., Splintered Reflections: Images of the body in trauma. New York: Basic Behavioral Science

B
_____

20.   Bachman G et al (1988). Childhood sexual abuse and the consequences in adult women. Obstetrics and Gynecology 71:631–42

21.   Bagley C (1988). Daycare, mental health, and child development: evidence from a longitudinal study. Early Child Development and Care 39:134–61

22. Bagley C, McDonald M (1984) Adult mental health sequelae of sexual abuse, physical abuse and neglect in maternally separated children. Canadian Journal of Community Mental Health. 3(1): 15–26

23. Bagley C (1989). Prevalence and correlates of unwanted sexual acts in childhood: evidence from a national Canadian survey. Canadian Journal of Public Health 80:295–6

24. Bagley C (1991). The prevalence and mental health sequels of child sexual abuse in a community sample of women age 18–27. Canadian Journal of Community Mental Health 10:103–16

25. Bagley C, Shewchuk-Dann D (1991). Characteristics of 60 children & adolescents who have a history of sexual assault against others: evidence from a controlled study. Journal of Child and Youth Care special issue: 43–52

26. Bagley C (1992). Psychological dimensions of poverty and parenthood. International Journal of Marriage and the Family 1:37–49

27. Bagley C (1992). The urban setting of juvenile pedestrian injuries: a study of behavioral ecology and social disadvantage. Accident Analysis and Prevention 24:673–8

28. Bagley C, Wood M, Young L (1994). Victim to abuser: mental health and behavioral sequels of the sexual abuse of males in childhood. Child Abuse and Neglect 18:683–97

29. Bagley C (1996). A typology of sexual abuse: the interaction of emotional, physical, and sexual abuse as predictors of adult psychiatric sequelae in women. Canadian Journal of Human Sexuality 5:101–112

30. Bagley C, Bolitho F, Bertrand L (1995). Mental health profiles, suicidal behavior, and community sexual assault in 2112 Canadian adolescents. Crisis: Journal of Crisis Intervention and Suicide Prevention 16:126–31

31. Bagley C, Mallick K (1997). Temperament, CNS problems, and maternal stressors: interactive predictors of conduct disorder in 9-year-olds. Perceptual and Motor Skills 72:287–8

32. Bagley C, Mallick K (2000). Prediction of sexual, emotional, and physical maltreatment and mental health outcomes in a longitudinal cohort of 290 adolescent women. Child Maltreatment 5 (3): 218–226

33. Bagley C, Young L (1998). Long-term evaluation of group counseling for women with a history of child sexual abuse: focus on depression, self-esteem, suicidal behaviors, and social support. Social Work with Groups 21:63–74

34. Bagley C, Young L (1999). Chapter 5. Long-term evaluation of group

counseling for women with a history of child sexual abuse In Bagley C, Mallick K (eds.) Child Sexual Abuse in Adult Offenders: New Theory and Research (pp 143–158). Brookfield, VT: Ashgate International

35. Bagley C, Young L (1989/90). Depression, self-esteem, and suicidal behavior as sequels of sexual abuse in childhood: research and therapy. In M. Rothery, G. Cameron (eds.), Child Maltreatment: Expanding Our Concept of Healing. (pp 183–209) Hillsdale, NJ Earlbaum

36. Bagley C, Young L, Mallick K (1999). The interactive effects of physical, emotional, and sexual abuse on adjustment in a longitudinal study of 565 children from birth to 17. In Bagley C, Mallick K (eds.) Child Sexual Abuse in Adult Offenders: New Theory and Research (pp 143–158). Brookfield, VT: Ashgate International

37. Bagley C, Ramsay R (1986). Sexual abuse in child hood: Psycho-social outcomes and implications for social work practice. Journal of Social Work and Human Sexuality 4(1–2): 33–47

38. Bailey JM, Shriver A (1999). Does childhood sexual abuse cause borderline personality disorder? J Sex Marital Ther. 25:45–57

39. Baldessarini RJ (1996). Chapters 18 & 19. Drugs and the treatment of psychiatric disorders. (p 399–459). In Hardman JG & Limbird LE (eds.) Goodman and Gilman's The Pharmacologic Basis of Therapeutics 9th ed., McGraw Hill, NY

40. Banyard V (1999). Childhood maltreatment in the mental health of low-income women. American Journal of Orthopsychiatry 69:161–71

41. Barker LR, Whitfield CL (1991). Chapter 21. Alcoholism. In Barker LR, Burton JR, Zieve PD (eds): Principles of Ambulatory Medicine, 3rd Edition, Williams & Wilkins, Baltimore

42. Barnes GM, Reifman AS, Farrell MP, Dintcheff BA (2000). The effects of parenting on the development of adolescent alcohol misuse: A six-wave latent growth model. Journal of Marriage and the Family 62:175–86

43. Barondes, S. et al (1999) An agenda for psychiatric genetics. Arch. Gen. Psych. 56: 549–552

44. Bauer MS, Shea N, McBride L, Gavin C (1997). Predictors of service utilization in veterans with bipolar disorder: a prospective study. J Affect Disord 44(2–3):159–68

45. Bauer MS, Kirk GF, Gavin C, Williford WO (2001). Determinants of functional outcome and health care costs in bi-polar disorder: A high-intensity follow-up study. Journal of Affective Disorders 65:231–41

46. Beautrais AL, Joyce PR, Mulder RT. Childhood sexual abuse and risks of suicidal behaviour. In: Joyce PR, Mulder RT, Oakley-Browne MA, Sellman JD, Watkins WGA. (eds.). Development, Personality and Psychopathology. Department of Psychological Medicine, Christchurch School of Medicine, Christchurch, New Zealand. 1994; pp. 141–148

47. Beck JC, van der Kolk B (1987). Reports of childhood incest and current behavior of chronically hospitalized women. American Journal of Psychiatry 144 (11): 1474–76

47a. Bekelman JE, Lily, Gross CP (2003). Scope and impact of financial conflicts of interest in biomedical research: a systematic review. Journal of the American Medical Association 289: 454–65

48. Becker-Lausen E, Sanders B, Chinsky JM (1995). Mediation of abusive childhood experiences: depression, dissociation, and negative life outcomes. Am J Orthopsychiatry. 65(4):560–73

49. Beers SR, De Bellis MD (2002). Neuropsychological function in children with maltreatment-related posttraumatic stress disorder. Am J Psychiatry 159(3):483–6

49a. Beilke R (1986). Behavioral problems in sexually abused young children. J Pediatr Psychol 11:47–57

50. Beitchman JH, Zucker KJ, Hood JE, daCosta GA, Akman D, Cassivia E (1992). A review of the long-term effects of child sexual abuse. Child Abuse & Neglect 16:101–118

51. Belkin DS, Greene AE, Rodrigue JR, Boggs SR (1994). Psychopathology and history of sexual abuse. Journal of Interpersonal Violence 9:535–47

52. Bemporand JR, Romano S (1993). Childhood experience and adult depression: a review of 17 European studies. American Journal of Psychoanalysis 53(4):301–315

53. Bender L, Blau A (1937). The reaction of children to sexual relations with adults American Journal of Orthopsychiatry 7:500–18

54. Bensley LB, Speiker SJ, van Eenwyck J, Schoder J. (1999). Self-reported abuse history and adolescent problem behaviors. I. Antisocial and suicidal behaviors. Journal of Adolescent Health, 24, 163–172

55. Berger AM, Knutson JF, Mehm JG, Perkins KA (1988). The self-report of punitive childhood experiences of young adults and adolescents. Child Abuse Negl 12(2):251–62

56. Benward J, Densen-Gerber J (1975). Incest as a causative factor in anti-social behavior: an explorative study. Contemporary Drug Problems 4: 322–340

57.   Berkowitz CD (1998). Medical consequences of child sexual abuse. Child Abuse & Neglect 22:541–50

58.   Bernstein DP, Cohen P, Velez CN, Schwab-Stone M, Siever LJ, Shinsato L (1993). Prevalence and stability of the DSM-III-R personality disorders in a community-based survey of adolescents. Am J Psychiatry 150(8):1237–43

59.   Bernstein DP, Stein JA, Handelsman L (1998). Predicting personality pathology among adult patients with substance use disorders: effects of childhood maltreatment. Addictive behaviors 23:855–68

60.   Biederman J, Faraone SV, Hirshfield-Becker DR, Friedman D, Robin JA, Rosenbaum JF (2001). Patterns of psychopathology and dysfunction in high-risk children of parents with panic disorder and major depression. Am J Psychiatry 158(1): 49–57

61.   Bifulco A, Brown GW, Adler Z (1991). Early sexual abuse and clinical depression in adult life. British Journal of Psychiatry 159: 115–122

62.   Bifulco A, Brown GW, Lillie A, Jarvis J (1997). Memories of childhood neglect and abuse: corroboration in a series of sisters. J Child Psychol Psychiatry 38(3):365–74

63.   Blount HR, Chandler TZ (1979). Relationship between childhood abuse and assaultive behavior in adolescent male psychiatric patients. Psychological Reports 44:1126

64.   Bliss EL (1984). A symptom profile of patients with multiple personalities, including MMPI results. J Nerv Ment Dis.172(4):197–202

65.   Blumenthal DR, Neeman J, Murphy CM (1998). Lifetime exposure to interparental physical and verbal aggression and symptom expression in college students. Violence Vict 13:175–181

66.   Boney-McCoy S, Finkelhor D (1995). Prior victimization: a risk factor for child sexual abuse and for PTSD-related symptomatology among sexually abused youth. Child Abuse Negl. 19(12):1401–21

67.   Boney-McCoy S, Finkelhor D (1996). Is youth victimization related to trauma symptoms and depression after controlling for prior symptoms and family relationships? A longitudinal, prospective study. J Consult Clin Psychol. 64(6):1406–16

68.   Bower P, Richards D, Lovell K (2001).The clinical and cost-effectiveness of self-help treatments for anxiety and depressive disorders in primary care: a systematic review. Br J Gen Pract 51(471):838–45

69.   Boyer AM (2001) Treating substance abuse in women with untreated childhood sexual abuse: are we treating the symptom but not the cause? Presented

at the 32nd Annual Medical-Scientific Conference of ASAM, Los Angeles, 20 April, published in meeting abstracts

69a. Boyle M (1990). Schizophrenia: a scientific delusion? Rontledge, London

70. Boudewyn AC, Liem JH (1995). Childhood sexual abuse as a precursor to depression and self-destructive behavior in adulthood. Journal of Traumatic Stress 8:445–59

71. Bousha DM, Twentyman CT (1984). Mother-child interactional style in abuse, neglect, and control groups: naturalistic observation in the home. Journal of abvnormal Psychology 93:106–14

72. Bradley RH, Caldwell BM, Fitzgerald JA, Morgan AG, Rock SL (1986). Experiences in day care and social competence among maltreated children. Child Abuse & Neglect 10:181–9

73. Bradley RG, Follingstad DR (2001). Utilizing disclosure in the treatment of the sequelae of childhood sexual abuse: A theoretical and empirical review. Clin Psychol Rev 21(1):1–32

74. Breggin PR, Cohen D (1999). Your Drug May Be Your Problem: How and why to stop taking psychiatric drugs. Perscus Publishing, Cambridge MA

75. Breggin PR (1998). Electroshock: scientific, ethical, and political issues The International Journal of Risk and Safety in Medicine 11(1): 5–40

76. Bremner JD, Licinio J, Darnell A, Krystal JH, Owens MJ, Southwick SM, Nemeroff CB, Charney DS (1997). Elevated CSF corticotropin-releasing factor concentrations in posttraumatic stress disorder. American Journal of Psychiatry 154:624–9

77. Bremner JD, Randall P, Scott TM, Bronen RA, Delaney RC, Seibyl JP, Southwick SM, McCarthy G, Charney DS, Innis, RB (1995). MRI-based measurement of hippocampal volume in posttraumatic stress disorder. Am. J. Psychiatry; 152:973–981

78. Bremner JD, Southwick SM, Darnell A, Charney DS (1996). Chronic PTSD in Vietnam combat veterans: Course of illness and substance abuse. Am. J. Psychiatry 153:369–375

79. Bremner JD, Randall P, Vermetten E, Staib L, Bronen RA, Capelli S, Mazure CM, McCarthy G, Innis RB, Charney DS (1997). MRI-based measurement of hippocampal volume in posttraumatic stress disorder related to childhood physical and sexual abuse: A preliminary report. Biol. Psychiatry 41:23–32

80. Bremner JD (1999). Does stress damage the brain? (review article). Biological Psychiatry 45:797–805

81. Bremner JD, Narayan M, Anderson ER, Staib LH, Miller H, Charney DS

(2000). Hippocampal volume reduction in major depression. Am J Psychiatry 157:115–117

82.   Bremner JD (2002). Does stress damage the brain? Understanding trauma based disorders from a neurological perspective. Norton, NY

82a. Bremner JD (2002). Structural changes in the brain in depression and relationship to symptom recurrance. CNS spectrums 7(2):129–139

83.   Bremner JD, Southwick SM, Johnson DR, Yehuda R, Charney DS (1993). Childhood physical abuse and combat related posttraumatic stress disorder in Vietnam Veterans. American Journal of Psychiatry 150:235–9

84.   Bremner JD, Vythilingam M, Vermetten E, Nazeer A, Adil J, Khan S, Staib L, Charney D (2002). Reduced Volume of Orbitofrontal Cortex in Major Depression Biological Psychiatry 51(4):273–9

85.   Brent DA, Perper JA, Goldstein CE, Kolko DJ, Allan MJ, Allman CJ, Zelenak JP (1988). Risk factors for adolescent suicide. A comparison of adolescent suicide victims with suicidal inpatients. Arch Gen Psychiatry 45(6):581–8

86.   Brent DA, Kolko DJ, Wartella ME, Boylan MB, Moritz G, Baugher M, Zelenak JP (1993). Adolescent psychiatric inpatients' risk of suicide attempt at 6-month follow-up. J Am Acad Child Adolesc Psychiatry 32(1):95–105

87.   Brent DA, Perper JA, Moritz G, Schweers J, Balach L, Roth C (1994). Familial risk factors for adolescent suicide: a case-control study. Acta Psychiatr Scand 89:52–58

88.   Brewin CR, Andrews B, Gotlib IH (1993). Psychopathology and early experience: A reappraisal of retrospective reports. Psychological Bulletin, 113, 82–89

89.   Bridges KW, Goldberg DP (1985). Somatic presentation of DSM III psychiatric disorders in primary care. Journal of Psychosomatic Research 29:563–9

90.   Briere J (1988). The long-term clinical correlates of childhood sexual victimization. Journal of the New York Academy of Sciences 528:327–334

91.   Briere J, Runtz M (1988). Symptomatology associated with childhood sexual victirnization in a non clinical adult sample. Child Abuse and Neglect, 12, 51–59

92.   Briere J, Evans D, Runtz M, Wall T (1988). Symptomatology in men who were molested as children: a comparison study. American Journal of Orthopsychiatry 58:457–61

93.   Briere J, Runtz M (1990). Differential adult symptomatology associated

with three types of child abuse histories. Child Abuse & Negect 14:357–64

94. Briere J, Runtz M (1991). The long-term effects of sexual abuse: A review and synthesis. New Directions for Mental Health Services 51:3–13

95. Briere J, Woo R, McRae B, Foltz J, and Sitzman (1997). Lifetime victimization history, demographics, and clinical status in female psychiatric emergency room patients. Journal of Nervous and Mental Disease 185:95–101

96. Briere JN (1996). Treatment of adults sexually molested as children: Beyond survival (Rev. 2nd ed.). New York: Springer

97. Briere JN, Elliot DM (1994). Immediate and long-term impacts of child sexual abuse. The Future of Children, 4, 54–69

98. Briere J, Runtz M (1987). Post sexual abuse trauma. Journal of Interpersonal Violence, 2(4): 367–379

99. Briere J, Zaidi L (1989). Sexual abuse histories and sequelae in female psychiatric emergency room patients. American Journal of Psychiatry, 146, 1602–1606

100. Brodsky BS, Cloitre M, Dulit RA (1995). Relationship of dissociation to self-mutilation and childhood abuse in borderline personality disorder. American Journal of Psychiatry 152:1788–1792

101. Brown B (1999) Soul Without Shame: A guide to liberating yourself from the judge within. Shambhala Boston, MA

102. Brown BE, Garrison CJ (1990). Patterns of symptomatology of adult women incest survivors. Western Journal of Nursing Research 12(5):587–600

103. Brown D, Scheflin A, Whitfield CL (1999): Recovered memories: the current weight of the evidence in science and in the courts. The Journal of Psychiatry and Law 26:5–156, Spring

104. Brown D, Scheflin AW, Hammond C (1997). Trauma, Memory, Treatment & Law. WW Norton, NY

105. Brown D (2001). (Mis) reprensations of the long-term effects of childhood sexual abuse in the courts. Journal of Child Sexual Abuse 9:79–107

106. Brown GR, Anderson (1991). Psychiatric morbidity in adult inpatients with childhood histories of sexual and physical abuse. American Journal of Psychiatry 148 (1) 55–61

107. Brown GR, Anderson B (1991): Psychiatric Morbidity in adult inpatients with childhood histories of sexual and physical abuse. American Journal of Psychiatry 148 (1) 55–61

108. Brown GW, Harris T (1978). Social Origins of Depression: A study of psychiatric disorder in women. The Free Press/Mac Millan NY

109. Brown J, Cohen P, Johnson JG, Salzinger S (1998). A longitudinal analysis of risk factors for child maltreatment: Findings of a 17-year prospective study of officially recorded and self-reported child abuse and neglect. Child Abuse and Neglect 22(11):1065–1078

110. Brown J, Cohen P, Johnson JG, Smailes EM (1999). Childhood abuse and neglect specificity of effects on adolescent and young adult depression and suicidality. Journal of the American Academy of Child & Adolescent Psychiatry 38 (12): 1490–1496

111. Brown GW, Moran P (1994). Clinical and psychosocial origins of chronic depressive episodes. I: a community survey. British Journal of Psychiatry 165:447–56

112. Browne A, Finkelhor D (1986). Impact of child sexual abuse: a review of the research. Psychological Bulletin 99(1):66–77

113. Browne KD, Hamilton CE (1999). Police recognition of the links between spouse abuse and child abuse. Child Maltreatment 4(2): 136–147

114. Browning DH, Boatman B (1977). Incest: children at risk. American Journal of Psychiatry 134:69–72

115. Brunngraber LS (1986). Father-daughter incest: immediate and long-term effects of sexual abuse. ANS Adv Nurs Sci 8(4):15–35

116. Bryer JB, Nelson BA, Miller JB, Kroll PA (1987). Childhood sexual and physical abuse as factors in adult psychiatric illness. American Journal of Psychiatry 144: 1426–1430

117. Buist A, Barnett B (1995). Childhood sexual abuse: a risk factor for postpartum depression? Australian and New Zealand Journal of Psychiatry 29:604–8

118. Bulik CM, Sullivan PF, Rorty M (1989). Childhood sexual abuse in women with bulimia. J Clin Psychiatry Dec;50(12):460–4

119. Burgess AW, Hartman CR, McCausland MP, Powers P (1984). Response patterns in children and adolescence exploited through sex rings and pornography. American Journal of Psychiatry 141: 656–662

120. Burgess AW, Hartman CR, McCormack A (1987). Abused to abuser: Antecedents of social deviant behaviors. American Journal of Psychiatry, 144:1431–6

121. Burgess A, Hartman CR, Baker T (1995). Memory presentations of childhood sexual abuse. Journal of Psychosocial Nursing, 33(9), 9–16

122. Burgess RL, Conger RD (1977). Family interaction patterns related to child abuse and neglect: some preliminary findings. Child Abuse & Neglect 1:267–77

123. Burgess RL, Conger RD (1978). Family interaction in abusive, neglectful, and normal families. Child Development 49:1163–73

124. Burnam MA, Stein JA, Golding JM, Siegel JM, Sorenson SB, Forsythe AB, Telles CA (1988). Sexual assault and medical disorders in a community population. J Consult Clin Psychol 56:843–850

125. Bushnell JA, Wells JE, Oakley-Brown MA (1992). Long-term effects of intrafamilial sexual abuse in childhood. Acta Psychiatria Scandavia 85: 136–142

126. Byrne CP, Velamoor VR, Sernovsky ZZ, Cortese L, Losztyn S (1990). A comparison of borderline and schizophrenic for childhood life events and parent-child relationships Canadian Journal of Psychiatry 35:590–5

C

127. Cadoret RJ, Winokur G, Langbehn D, Troughton E, Yates WR, Stewart MA (1996). Depression spectrum disease, I: The role of gene-environment interaction. Am J Psychiatry. 153(7):892–9

128. Caffaro-Rouget A, Lang RA, van Santen V (1989). The impact of child sexual abuse on victims' adjustment. Annals of Sex Research 2: 29–47

129. Calam, RM, Slade, PD (1989). Sexual experience and eating problems in female undergraduates. International Journal of Eating Disorders, 8, 391–397

130. Calam RM, Horne L, Glasgow D, Cox A (1998). Psychological disturbance in child sexual abuse: a follow-up study. Child Abuse & Neglect 22:901–13

131. Cameron, C (1994). Women survivors confronting their abusers: issues, decisions and outcomes. Journal of Child Sexual Abuse, 3(1), 7–35

132. Cameron C (2000). Resolving Childhood Trauma: a long-term study of abuse survivors. Sage Publications, Thousand Oaks, CA

133. Caplan PJ (1995). They Say You're Crazy: How the World's Most Powerful Psychiatrists Decide Who's Normal. Addison-Wesley, NY

134. Carlin AS, Ward NG (1992). Subtypes of psychiatric in-patient women who have been sexually abused Journal of Nervous and Mental Disease 180:392–7

135. Carlin AS, Kemper K, Ward WG, Sowell H, Gustafson B, Stevens N (1994). The effect of differences in objective and subjective definitions of childhood

physical abuse on estimates of its incidence and relationship to psychopathology. Child Abuse & Neglect 18:393–399

136. Carlson B (1984). Children's observations of interparental violence. In AR Roberts (ed.), Battered women and their families (pp. 147–167). NY: Springer

137. Carlson M, Earls F (1997). Psychological and neuroendocrinological sequelae of early social deprivation in institutionalized children in Romania. Ann N Y Acad Sci 807:419–28

138. Carlson EB, Dalenberg C (2000). A conceptual framework for the impact of traumatic experiences. Trauma, Violence & Abuse 1:4–28

139. Carmen E, Rieker PP, Mills T (1984). Victims of violence and psychiatric illness. American Journal of Psychiatry 141:378–383

140. Carrion VG, Weems CF, Eliez S, Patwardhan A, Brown W, Ray RD, Reiss AL (2001). Attenuation of frontal asymmetry in pediatric posttraumatic stress disorder. Biol Psychiatry 15;50(12):943–51

141. Carrion VG, Weems CF, Ray RD, Glaser B, Hessl D, Reiss AL (2002). Diurnal salivary cortisol in pediatric posttraumatic stress disorder. Biol Psychiatry 51(7):575–82

142. Carrion VG, Steiner H (2000). Trauma and dissociation in delinquent adolescents. J Am Acad Child Adolesc Psychiatry 39(3):353–9

143. Cashden S (1988). Object Relations Therapy: Using the Relationship. WW Norton, NY

144. Cavaiola AA, Schiff M (1988). Behavioral sequelae of physical and/or sexual abuse in adolescence. Child Abuse & Neglect 12:181–8

145. Cecil H, Matson SC (2001). Psychological functioning and family discord among African-American adolescent females with and without a history of childhood sexual abuse. Child Abuse Negl 2001 Jul;25(7):973–88

146. Chaffin M, Kelleher K, Hollenberg J (1996). Onset of physical abuse and neglect: psychiatric, substance abuse, and social risk factors from prospective community data. Child Abuse Negl 20(3):191–203

147. Chalmers I (1990). Underreporting research is scientific misconduct. Journal of the American Medical Association 263:1405–8

148. Cheasty M, Clare AW, Collins C (1998). Relation between sexual abuse in childhood and adult depression: case control study. British Medical Journal 316: 198–201

149. Choudhry NK, Stelfox HT, Detsky AS (2002). Relationships between authors of clinical practice guidelines and the pharmaceutical industry. JAMA 287: 612

150. Chu, JA, Dill DL (1990). Dissociative symptoms in relation to childhood physical and sexual abuse. American Journal of Psychiatry, 147, 887–892

151. Chu JA (1998). Rebuilding Shattered Lives: The Responsible Treatment of Complex Post-Traumatic and Dissociative Disorders. John Wiley, NY

152. Cicchetti D, Rogosch FA (2001a). Diverse patterns of neuroendocrine activity in maltreated children. Development and Psychopathology 13: 677–93

153. Cicchetti D, Rogosch FA (2001b). The impact of child maltreatment and psychopathology on neuroendocrine functioning. Development and Psychopathology 13: 783–804

154. Clark DB, Lesnick L, Hegedus A (1997). Traumas and other adverse life events in adolescents with alcohol abuse and dependence. Journal of the American Academy of Child and Adolescent Psychiatry 36:1744–51

155. Clark AH, Foy DW (2000). Trauma exposure and alcohol use in battered women. Violence Against Women, January vol. 6(1):37–48(12)

156. Classen C, Field NP, Atkinson A, Spiegel D (1998). Representations of self in women sexually abused in childhood. Child Abuse & Neglect 22:997–1004

157. Clayton P, Ernst C, Angst J (1994). Pre-morbid personality traits of men who develop unipolar or bipolar disorders. Eur. Arch. Clin. Neurosci. 243, pp. 340–346

158. Cohen FS, Densen-Gerber J (1982). A study of the relationship between child abuse and drug addiction in 178 patients: preliminary studies. Child Abuse & Neglect 6:383–7

159. Cohen AJ, Adler N, Kaplan SJ, Pelcovitz D, Mandel FS (2002). Interactional effects of marital status and physical abuse on adolescent psychopathology. Child Abuse Negl 26(3):277–88

160. Cold J, Petruckevitch A, Feder G, Chung W, Richardson J, Moorey S (2001). Relation between childhood sexual and physical abuse and risk of revictimization in women: a cross-sectional survey. Lancet, 258:450–454

161. Cole C (1988). Routine comprehensive inquiry for abuse: A justifiable clinical asessment procedure. Clinical Social Work Journal 16:33–42

162. Cole CE, Paterson RM, Craig JB, Thomas WE, Ristine LP, Stahly M, Pasamanick B (1959). A controlled study of efficacy of ipronazid in treatment of depression. Archives of General Psychiatry 1:513–8

163. Cole P, Putnam FW (1992). Effect of incest on self and social functioning:

a developmental psychopathology perspective. Journal of Consulting and Clinical Psychology, 60, 174–184

164. Conaway LP, Hansen DJ (1989). Social behavior of physically abused and neglected children: a critical review. Clinical Psychology Review 9:627–52

165. Connors ME, Morse W (1993). Sexual abuse and the eating disorders: A review. International Journal of Eating Disorders, 13:141

165a. Consumer Reports (2003). Free rein for drug ads? February, pages 33–7

166. Conte JR (1996) [Reliability of self reports of abuse] Presented at the National Conference on Trauma & Memory, Univ. of New Hampshire.

167. Coons PM, Millstein V (1986). Psychosexual disturbances in multiple personality: characteristics, etiology, and treatment. J Clin Psychiatry. 47(3):106–10

168. Coons, PM, Bowman, ES, Milstein V. (1988). Multiple personality disorder. Journal of Nervous and Mental Diseases, 176, 519–527

169. Coons, PM, Bowman, ES, Pellow, TA, Schneider, P (1989). Posttraumatic aspects of the treatment of victims of sexual abuse and incest. Psychiatric Clinics of North America, 12, 335–338

170. Copeland ME (1992). The Depression Workbook: A guide for living with depression and manic depression. New Harbinger, Oakland Ca

171. Copeland ME (1994). Living without Depression and Manic Depression. New Harbinger, Oakland Ca

172. Courtois C (1991). Theory, sequencing, and strategy in treating adult survivors. In. J. Briere, ed., Treating Victims of Child Sexual Abuse. Jossey-Bass

173. Courtois C (1979). The incest experience and its aftermath. Victimology: An International Journal 4:337–47

174. Courtois, CA (1998). Recollections of sexual abuse. New York: Norton

175. Coxell A, King M, Mezey G, Gordon D (1999). Lifetime prevalence, characteristics, and associated problems of non-consensual sex in men: cross sectional survey. British Medical Journal 318:846–50

176. Craine LS, Henson CE, Colliver JA and MacLean DG (1988). Prevalence of a history of sexual abuse among female psychiatric patients in a state hospital system. Hospital and Community Psychiatry 39 (3) 300–304

177. Culhane C (2002). Favor of the month—Did the Whitehouse give the drug industry veto power over FDA appointments? The New Republic, March

178. Curtis D: Genetics of functional psychiatric disorders. Lecture notes, Royal London School of Medicine, July 2002, posted at website: *www.mds.qmw.ac.uk/statgen/dcurtis/lectures/pgenfunc.html*

179. Curtiss AB (2001). Depression Is a Choice: Winning the Fight Without Drugs. Hyperion, NY

D

180. Dallam SJ (2001). The long-term medical consequences of childhood trauma. In K Franey, R Geffner, R Falconer (eds.), The cost of child maltreatment: Who pays? We all do. (pp. 1–14). San Diego, CA: Family Violence & Sexual Assault Institute

181. Darves-Bornoz JM, Lemperiere T, Degiovanni A & Gaillard P (1995). Sexual victimization in women with schizophrenia and bi-polar disorder. Social Psychiatry and Psychiatric Epidemiology 30:78–84

182. Davidoff F et al (2001). Sponsorship, authorship, and accountability. Lancet 325:854–856 (published simultaneously in 12 other medical journals)

183. Davidson S, Smith R (1990). Traumatic experiences in psychiatric outpatients. Journal of Traumatic Stress Studies 3:459–75

184. Davidson J, Foa EB, Blank AS, Brett EA, Fairbank J, Green BL, Herman JL, Keane TM, Kilpatrick, D, March JS, McNally RJ, Pitman RK, Resnick HS, Rothbaum BO: Posttraumatic stress disorder. In DSM IV Sourcebook, vol. 2. Washington, D.C., American Psychiatric Press, 1994; 577–605

185. Davidson JR, Hughes DC, George LK, Blazer DG (1996). The association of sexual assault and attempted suicide within the community. Arch Gen Psychiatry 53(6):550–5

186. Davies JM, Frawley MG (1994). Treating the Adult Survivor of Childhood Sexual Abuse: A psychoanalytic perspective. Basic Books, San Francisco

187. DeAngelis CD (2000). Conflict of interest and the public trust. Journal of the American Medical Association 284:2237–8

188. De Bellis M., Lefter L., Trickett P, and Putnam F (1994a) Urinary catecholamine excretion in sexually abused girls. Journal of the American Academy of Child and Adolescent Psychiatry 33:320–27

189. De Bellis MD, Chrousos GP, Dorn LD, Burke L, Helmers MA, Kling MA, Trickett PK, Putnam FW (1994b). Hypothalamic-pituitary-adrenal axis dysregulation in sexually abused girls. Journal of Clinical Endocrinology and Metabolism 78:249–55

190. De Bellis MD (1997). PTSD and acute stress disorder. In RT Ammerman & M Hersen (eds). Handbook of prevention and treatment with children and adolescents. (p 455–94) Wiley, NY

191. De Bellis MD, Keshavan MS, Shifflett H, Iyengar S, Dahl RE, Axelson DA, Birmaher B, Hall J, Moritz G, Ryan ND (2002). Superior temporal gyrus

volumes in pediatric generalized anxiety disorder. Biol Psychiatry 1;51(7):553–62

192. De Bellis MD, Keshavan MS, Frustaci K, Shifflett H, Iyengar S, Beers SR, Hall J (2002). Superior temporal gyrus volumes in maltreated children and adolescents with PTSD. Biol Psychiatry Apr 1;51(7):544–52

193. De Bellis MD (2002). Abuse and ACTH response to corticotropin-releasing factor. Am J Psychiatry 159(1):157–8

194. De Bellis MD (2002). Developmental traumatology: a contributory mechanism for alcohol and substance use disorders. Psychoneuroendocrinology 27(1–2):155–70

195. De Bellis MD, Keshavan MS, Harenski KA (2001). Anterior cingulate N-acetylaspartate/creatine ratios during clonidine treatment in a maltreated child with posttraumatic stress disorder. J Child Adolesc Psychopharmacol 11(3):311–6

196. De Bellis MD (2002). Personal communication, Pittsburgh, PA, June

197. De Bellis MD, Broussard ER, Herring DJ, Wexler S, Moritz G, Benitez JG (2001). Psychiatric co-morbidity in caregivers and children involved in maltreatment: a pilot research study with policy implications. Child Abuse Negl 25(7):923–44

198. De Bellis MD (2001). Developmental traumatology: the psychobiological development of maltreated children and its implications for research, treatment, and policy. Dev Psychopathol 200113(3):539–64

199. De Bellis MD, Hall J, Boring AM, Frustaci K, Moritz G (2001). A pilot longitudinal study of hippocampal volumes in pediatric maltreatment-related posttraumatic stress disorder. Biol Psychiatry 2001 50(4):305–9

200. De Bellis MD, Casey BJ, Dahl RE, Birmaher B, Williamson DE, Thomas KM, Axelson DA, Frustaci K, Boring AM, Hall J, Ryan ND (2001). A pilot study of amygdala volumes in pediatric generalized anxiety disorder. Biol Psychiatry 1;48(1):51–7

201. De Bellis MD, Keshavan MS, Spencer S, Hall J (2000). N-Acetylaspartate concentration in the anterior cingulate of maltreated children and adolescents with PTSD. Am J Psychiatry 157(7):1175–7

202. De Bellis MD, Clark DB, Beers SR, Soloff PH, Boring AM, Hall J, Kersh A, Keshavan MS (2000). Hippocampal volume in adolescent-onset alcohol use disorders. Am J Psychiatry 157(5):737–44

203. De Bellis MD, Keshavan MS, Clark DB, Casey BJ, Giedd JN, Boring AM, Frustaci K, Ryan ND (1999). A.E. Bennett Research Award.

Developmental traumatology. Part II: Brain development. Biol Psychiatry 15;45(10):1271–84

204. De Bellis MD, Baum AS, Birmaher B, Keshavan MS, Eccard CH, Boring AM, Jenkins FJ, Ryan ND (1999). A.E. Bennett Research Award. Developmental traumatology. Part I: Biological stress systems. Biol Psychiatry 15;45(10):1259–70

205. De Bellis MD, Baum AS, Birmaher B, Ryan ND (1997). Urinary catecholamine excretion in childhood overanxious and posttraumatic stress disorders. Ann N Y Acad Sci 1997 Jun 21;821:451–5

206. Deblinger E, Lippman J, Stauffer L, Finkel M (1994). Personal vs. professional responses to child sexual abuse allegations. Child Abuse & Neglect 18:679–82

207. Deblinger E, McLeer SV, Atkins MS, Ralphe D, Foa E (1989). Posttraumatic stress in sexually abused, physically abused and non-abused children. Child Abuse & Neglect 13:1403–8

208. Dembo R, Dertke M, Borders S, Washburn M, Schmeidler J (1988). The relation between physical and sexual abuse and tobacco, alcohol, and illicit drug use among youths in a juvenile detention center. The International Journal of the Addictions 23:351–78

209. Dembo R, Wothke W, Seeberger W, Shemwell M, Pacheco K, Rollie M, Schmeidler J, Klein L, Hartsfield A, Livingston S. (2000). Testing a model of the influence of family problem factors on high-risk youths' troubled behavior: a three-wave longitudinal study. Journal of Psychoactive Drugs 32(1):55–65

210. Dembo R, Williams L, Wothke W, Schmeidler J (1994). The relationships among family problems, friends' troubled behavior, and high risk youths' alcohol/other drug use and delinquent behavior: a longitudinal study. International Journal of the Addictions 29(11):1419–42

211. Dembo R, Williams L, Wothke W, Schmeidler J, Brown CH (1992). The role of family factors, physical abuse, and sexual victimization experiences in high-risk youths' alcohol and other drug use and delinquency: a longitudinal model. Violence and Victims 7(3):245–66

211a. *DepressionReliefNaturally.com*: since 1988, among the pioneers in photobiology (the clinical science of light therapy for reducing depression and other problems) (800-234-3724) An example study: Nakazawa T, Okubo Y, Suwazono Y, Kobayash E, Komine S, Kato N, Nogawa K (2002). Association between duration of daily VDT (video display terminal [computer monitor screen]) use and subjective symptoms. American Journal of Industrial Medicine 42:421–426

212. Deykin EY, Alpert JJ, McNamarra JJ (1985). A pilot study of the effect of exposure to child abuse or neglect on adolescent suicidal behavior. Am J Psychiatry 142(11):1299–303

213. Dhaliwal GK, Gauzas L, Atonowicz DH, Ross RR (1996). Adult male survivors of childhood sexual abuse: prevalence, sexual abuse characteristics, and long-terms effects. Clinical Psychology Review 16(7):619–39

214. Diaz A, Simantov E, Rickert VI (2002). Effect of abuse on health: results of a national survey. Arch Pediatr Adolesc Med 156(8):811–7

215. Dickinson LM, deGruy FV, Dickinson WP, Candib LM (1999). Health-related quality of life and symptom profiles of female survivors of sexual abuse. Archives of Family Medicine 8:35–43

216. Dierker LC, Avenevoli S, Stolar, Merikangas KR (2002). Smoking and depression: an examination of mechanisms of comorbidity. American Journal of Psychiatry 159:947–53 Add

217. Dimock PT (1988). Adult males sexually abused as children: characteristics and implications for treatment. Journal of Interpersonal Violence 3:203–21

218. Donaldson MA & Gardner R, Jr. (1985). Diagnosis and treatment of traumatic stress among women after childhood incest. In CR Figley (ed), Trauma and Its Wake: the study and treatment of Post-traumatic Stress Disorder. Brunner/ Mazel, NY

219. Dossey L (1997). Healing Words: The power of prayer and the practice of medicine. Harper, NY

220. Downs WR, Miller BA, Gondoli DM (1987). Childhood experience of parental physical violence for alcoholic women as compared with a randomly selected household sample of women. Violence and Victims 2:225–40

221. Driessen M, Hermann J, Stahl K, Zwaan M, Meier S, Hill A, Osterheider M, Petersen D (2000). Magnetic resonance imaging volumes of the hippocampus and the amygadala in women with borderline personality disorder and early traumatization. Archives of General Psychiatry 57:1115–22

222. Drossman DA, Leserman J, Nachman G, Li Z, Gluck H, Toomey TC and Mitchell M (1990): Sexual and physical and sexual abuse in women with functional or organic gastrointestinal disorders. Annals of Internal Medicine 113: 828–833

223. Dube SR, Anda RF, Felitti VJ, Chapman DP, Williamson DF, Giles WH

(2001). Childhood abuse, household dysfunction, and the risk of attempted suicide throughout the life span: findings from the Adverse Childhood Experiences Study. JAMA 286(24):3089–96

224. Dubowitz H, Black M, Harrington D, Verschoore A (1993). A follow up study of behavior problems associated with child sexual abuse. Child Abuse & Neglect 17:743–54

225. Duncan RD, Saunders BE, Kilpatrick DG, Hanson RF, Resnick HS (1996). Childhood physical assault as a risk factor for PTSD, depression, and substance abuse: findings from a national survey. American Journal of Orthopsychiatry 66:437–48

E

226. Ehrle LH (2002). Partnerships between universities and industry. JAMA 287(11):1398–9; discussion 1399–400

227. Einbender AJ, Friedrich WN (1989). Psychological functioning and behavior of sexually abused girls. Journal of Consulting and Clinical Psychology 57(1):155–7

228. Ellason J, Ross C (1997). Childhood trauma and psychiatric symptoms. Psychological Reports 80:447–50

229. Ellason J, Ross C, and Fuchs D (1996). Lifetime axis I and II comorbidity and childhood trauma history in dissociative identity disorder. Psychiatry 59:255–66

230. Ellason J, Ross C (1995). Positive and negative symptoms in dissociative identity disorder and schizophrenia: A comparative analysis. Journal of Nervous and Mental Disease 183:236–41

231. Ellason JW, Ross CA, Sainton K, Mayran LW (1996). Axis I and II Comorbidity and Childhood Trauma History in Chemical Dependency. Bulletin of the Menninger Clinic. 60:39–51

232. Ellason JW, Ross CA (1997). Two year follow-up of inpatients with dissociative identity disorder. American Journal of Psychiatry 154, 832–839, 1997

233. Ellenson G (1985). Detecting a history of incest: A predictive syndrome. Social Casework Nov.:525–32

234. Elliott DJ, Tarnowski KJ (1990). Depressive characteristics of sexually abused children. Child Psychiatry Hum Dev 21(1):37–48

235. Elliott DM, Briere J (1995). Posttraumatic stress associated with delayed

recall of sexual abuse: A general population study. Journal of Traumatic Stress 8, 629–647

236. Ensink B (1992). Confusing Realities: A study on child sexual abuse and psychiatric symptoms. Amsterdam: Vu University Press.

237. Epstein JN, Saunders BE, Kilpatrick DG, Resnick HS: PTSD as a mediator between etiology, and treatment. Journal of Clinical Psychiatry 47:106–10

238. Erickson MF (2000). Attachment theory (presented at the Annual Conference of the Georgia Council on Child Abuse), Atlanta, Ga, August 1

239. Everill JT, Waller G (1995). Reported sexual abuse and eating psychopathology: a review of the evidence for a causal link. Int J Eat Disord 18(1):1–11

F

240. Famularo R, Kinscherff R, Fenton T (1991).Posttraumatic stress disorder among children clinically diagnosed as borderline personality disorder. J Nerv Ment Dis 179(7):428–31

241. Famularo R, Kinscherff, R., and Fenton, T (1992). Psychiatric diagnoses of maltreated children: Preliminary findings. Journal of the American Academy of Child and Adolescent Psychiatry (1992) 31:863–67

242. Famularo R, Kinscherff R, Fenton T (1992 a) Parental substance abuse and the nature of child maltreatment. Child Abuse & Neglect 16: 475–83

243. Famularo R, Kinscherff R, Fenton T (1992). Psychiatric diagnoses of abusive mothers. A preliminary report. J Nerv Ment Dis 180(10):658–61

244. Famularo R, Kinscherff R, Fenton T (1992). Psychiatric diagnoses of maltreated children: preliminary findings. J Am Acad Child Adolesc Psychiatry 31(5):863–7

245. Famularo R, Fenton T, Kinscherff R, Ayoub C, Barnum R (1994). Maternal and child posttraumatic stress disorder in cases of child maltreatment. Child Abuse Negl 18(1):27–36

246. Famularo R, Fenton T, Augustyn M, Zuckerman B (1996). Persistence of pediatric post traumatic stress disorder after 2 years. Child Abuse Negl. 1996 Dec;20(12):1245–8.

247. Fava GA, Tomba E (1998). The use of antidepressant drugs: some reasons for concern. The International Journal of Risk and Safety in Medicine 11(4): 271–274

248. Fava GA (2002). Long-term treatment with antidepressant drugs: the

spectacular achievements of propaganda. Psychotherapy and Psychosomatics 71:3:2002, 127–132

249. Feifel D (2002). Advances in the treatment of depression: moving beyond the SSRIs. Talk given at Peachford Hospital, Atlanta, Ga, April 9

250. Felitti VJ, Williams SA (1998) Long-term follow-up and analysis of more than 100 patients who each lost more than 100 pounds. The Permanente Journal 2 (3): 17–21

251. Felitti V (1991). Long-term medical consequences of incest, rape, and molestation. Southern Medical Journal 84 (3) 328–331

252. Felitti VJ (1993). Childhood sexual abuse, depression, and family dysfunction in adult obese patients: a case control study. Southern Medical Journal 86 (7): 732–736

253. Felitti VJ (2000). Adverse childhood experiences and the leading causes of death in America. Videotape presentation from Kaiser Permanente, San Diego

254. Felitti VJ, Anda, RF, Nordenberg D, Williamson DF, Spitz A M, Edwards V, Koss MP, Marks JS (1998). Relationship of childhood abuse and household dysfunction to many of the leading causes of death in adults. American Journal of Preventive Medicine 14:245–258.

255. Femina DD, Yeager CA, Lewis DO (1990). Child abuse: adolescent records vs adult recall. Child abuse & neglect 14:227–231

256. Fergusson DM, Horwood LI (1998). Exposure to interparental violence in childhood and psychological adjustment in young adulthood. Child Abuse & Neglect 22:339–57

257. Fergusson DM, Horwood LI, Lynskey MT (1996). Childhood sexual abuse and psychiatric disorder in young adulthood: II. Psychiatric outcomes of childhood sexual abuse. Journal of the American Academy of Child and Adolescent Psychiatry 34(10):1365–74

258. Fergusson DM, Lynskey MT (1997). Physical punishment/maltreatment during childhood and adjustment in young adulthood. Child Abuse & Neglect, 21, 617–630

259. Fergusson DM, Horwood LI, Woodward LJ (2000). The stability of child abuse reports: a longitudinal study of the reporting behavior of young adults. Psychological Medicine 30:529–44

260. Ferguson KS, Dacey CN (1997). Anxiety, depression and dissociation in women health care providers reporting a history of childhood psychological abuse. Child Abuse & Neglect 21 (10) 9410952

261. Figley CR (1999). Traumatology of Grieving: Conceptual, theoretical, and treatment foundations. Brunner-Routlege, London

261a. Fink PJ (2003). Discussion on treatment of depression (personal communication), Philadelphia, Pa, February 2

262. Finlay-Jones R, Brown GW (1981). Types of stressful life events and the onset of anxiety and depressive disorders. Psychological Medicine 11:803–15

263. Finkelhor D (1984). Child Sexual Abuse: New theory & research. Free Press, NY

264. Finkelhor D, Hotaling G, Lewis IA., & Smith C (1990). Sexual abuse in a national survey of adult men and women: prevalence, characteristics, and risk factors. Child Abuse & Neglect, 14, 19–28

265. Finn S, Hartinan, M, Leon G, Lawson L (1986). Eating disorders and sexual abuse: Lack of confirmation for a clinical hypothesis. International Journal of Eating Disorders, 5, 10:1060

266. Flisher AJ, Kramer RA, Hoven CW, Greenwald S, Alegria M, Bird HR, Canino G, Connell R, Moore RE (1997). Psychosocial characteristics of physically abused children in adolescence. Journal of the American Academy of Child and Adolescent Psychiatry 36:123–31

267. Fleming J, Mullen P, Sibthorpe B, and Bammer G, The long-term impact of childhood sexual abuse in Australian women. Child Abuse & Neglect (1999) 23:145–59

268. Folsom V, Krahn D, Nairn K, Gold, L, Demitrack M, Silk K (1993). The impact of sexual and physical abuse on eating disordered and psychiatric symptoms: A comparison of eating disordered and psychiatric inpatients. International Journal of Eating Disorders, 13, 249–257

269. Fondacaro KM, Holt JC, Powell TA (1999). Psychological impact of childhood sexual abuse on male inmates: the importance of perception. Child Abuse & Neglect 23: 361–9

270. Ford JD, Racusin R, Davis WB, Ellis CG, Thomas J, Rogers K, Reiser J, Schiffman J, Sengupta A (1999a). Trauma exposure among children with oppositional defiant disorder and attention deficit-hyperactivity disorder. J Consult Clin Psychol 67(5):786–9

271. Ford JD, Racusin R, Ellis CG, Daviss WB, Reiser J, Fleischer A, Thomas J (2000). Child maltreatment, other trauma exposure, and posttraumatic symptomatology among children with oppositional defiant and attention deficit hyperactivity disorders. Child Maltreatment 5: 205–217

271a. Forward S, Buck C (1989). Toxic Parents. Bantam, NY

272. Fossum MA, Mason MJ (1986). Facing Shame: Families in recovery. WW Norton, NY

273. Frank E, Turner SM, Stewart BD, Jacob M, West D (1981). Past psychiatric symptoms and the response to sexual assault. Comprehensive Psychiatry 22:479–87

274. Frank E, Kupfer DJ, Perel JN, Comes C, Jarrett DB, Mallinger AG, Thase ME, McEachran AB, Grochocinski VJ (1990). 3-year outcomes for maintenance therapies in recurrent depression. Archives of General Psychiatry 47:1093–9

275. Frazier PA, Cohen BB (1992). Research on the sexual victimization of women: implications for counselor training. The Counseling Psychologist 20(1): 141–58

275a. Frias-Armenta M (2002). Long-term effects of child punishment on Mexican women: a structural model. Child Abuse & Neglect 26:371–86

276. Friedrich WN (1998) Behavioral manifestations of child sexual abuse. Child Abuse & Neglect 22 (6): 523–31

277. Friedrich WN, Luecke WJ, Beilke RL, Place V (1992). Psychotherapy outcome of sexually abused boys: an agency study. Journal of Interpersonal Violence 7(3):396–409

278. Friedrich WN, Schafer LC (1995). Somatic symptoms in sexually abused children. J Pediatric Psychol 20(5): 661–70

279. Fromuth ME (1986). The relationship of childhood sexual abuse with later psychological and sexual adjustment in a sample of college women. Child Abuse & Neglect 10: 5–15

280. Fromuth ME, Burkhart BR (1989). Long-term psychological correlates of childhood sexual abuse in two samples of college men. Child Abuse & Neglect 13:533–42

281. Frothingham TE, Hobbs CJ, Wynne JM, Yee L, Goya A, Wadsworth DJ (2000). Follow up study eight years after diagnosis of sexual abuse Archives of Diseases of Childhood 83:132–134

282. Fukuyama F (2002). Our Post Human Future. Farrar Straus & Giroux, NY

283. Fullilove MT, Fullilove RE, Smith M, Winkler K, Michael C, Panzer PG, Wallace R (1993). Violence, trauma, and posttraumatic stress disorder among women drug users. Journal of Traumatic Stress 6:533–43

284. Fullilove MT (2002). Social and economic causes of depression. J Gend Specif Med 5(2):38–41

G

285. Galenberg AJ (2002). Out of the box. Archives of General Psychiatry 59:281

286. Gara MA, Allen LA, Herzog EP, Woolfolk RL (2000). The abused child as parent: the structure and content of physically abused mothers' perceptions of their babies. Child Abuse & Neglect 24(5)627–39

287. Garland A, Scott J (2002). Using homework in therapy for depression. J Clin Psychol 58(5):489–98

288. Gelijns AC, Their SO (2002). Medical innovation and institutional interdependence: Rethinking university-industry connections. Journal of the American Medical Association 287:72–7

288a. Gelinas DJ (1983). The persisting negative effects of incest. Psychiatry 46: 312–32

289. George C, Main M (1979). Social interaction of young abused children: approach, avoidance, and aggression. Child Development 50:306–18

289a. Gershuny BS, Thayer JF (1999). Relations among psychological trauma, dissociative phenomena, and trauma-related distress: a review and integration. Clinical psychology review 19: 631–57

290. Gladstone G, Parker G, Wilhelm K, Mitchell P, Austin MP (1999). Characteristics of depressed patients who report childhood sexual abuse. American Journal of Psychiatry 156(3):431–7

291. Glod CA, Teicher MH (1996). Relationship between early abuse, posttraumatic stress disorder, and activity levels in prepubertal children. Journal of the American Academy of Child and Adolescent Psychiatry 35:1384–1393

292. Glod CA, Teicher MH, Hartman CR, Harakal T, McGreenery CE (1997). Enduring effects of early abuse on locomotor activity, sleep and circadian rhythms. Annals New York Academy of Science 821:465–467

293. Gold ER (1986). Long-term effects of sexual victimization in childhood: An attributional approach. Journal of Consulting and Clinical Psychology 54: 471–475

294. Gold SN, Lucenko BA, Elhai JD, Swingle JM, Sellers AH (1999). A comparison of psychological/psychiatric symptomatology of women and men sexually abused as children. Child Abuse Negl 23(7):683–92

295. Gold SN, Hill EL, Swingle JM, Elfant AS (1999). Relationship between childhood sexual abuse characteristics and dissociation among women in therapy. Journal of Family Violence, 14, 157–171

296. Gold SN (2000). Not Trauma Alone: Therapy for Child Abuse Survivors in Family and Social Context. Brunner-Routledge Philadelphia

297. Goldberg D (2001). Vulnerability factors for common mental illnesses. British Journal of Psychiatry 178:69–71

298. Goldberg T, Gold J, Greenberg R, Griffin S, Schulz C, Pickar D, Kleinman J, Weinberger D (1993). Contrasts between patients with affective disorders and patients with schizophrenia on a neuropsychological test battery. American Journal of Psychiatry, 150:1355–62

299. Goldberg RT (1994). Childhood abuse, depression, and chronic pain. Clinical Journal of Pain 10:277–281

299a. Goldstein DJ, Mallinckrodt C, Lu Y, Demitrack MA (2002). Duloxetine in the treatment of major depressive disorder: a double-blond clinical trial. Journal G of Clinical Psychiatry 63(3):225–31

300. Gomes-Schwartz B, Horowitz J, Sauzier M (1984). The aftermath of sexual abuse: 18-month follow-up. In:Tufts New England Medical Center, Child Psychiatry Division. Sexually Exploited Children: Service and Research Project. Final Report of the Office of Juvenile Justice and Delinquency Prevention. Washington, DC, US Department of Justice

301. Gomes-Schwartz B, Horowitz JM, Sauzier M (1985). Severity of emotional distress among sexually abused preschool, school-age, and adolescent children. Hosp Community Psychiatry 36(5):503–8

301a. Goodkin K, Visser AP (2000). Psychoneuroimmunology: stress, mental disorders, and health. American psychiatric Press, Washington, DC

302. Goodman L, Rosenberg S, Mueser T, Drake R (1997). Physical and sexual assault history in women with serious mental illness: Prevalence, correlates, treatment and future research directions. Schizophrenia Bulletin 23:685–96

303. Goodman LA, Thompson KM, Weinfurt K, Corl S, Acker P, Mueser KT, Rosenberg SD (1999). Reliability of reports of violent victimization and posttraumatic stress disorder among men and women with serious mental illness. J Trauma Stress 12(4):587–99

304. Goodsitt A (1997). Chapter 11. Eating disorders: a self-psychological perspective. In Garner D., Garfinkle P (eds) Handbook of Eating Disorders, Guilford Press

305. Goodwin J, McCarthy T, Divasto P (1981). Prior incest in mothers of abused children. Child Abuse & Neglect 5:87–96

306. Goodwin J, Attias R, McCarty T, Chandler S, Romanik R (1988). Reporting by adult psychiatric patients of childhood sexual abuse. Am J Psychiatry 145(9):1183–4

307. Gorcey M, Santiago JM, McCall PF (1986) Psychological consequences for women sexually abused in childhood. Social Psychiatry 21(3): 129–33

308. Gorner P (2002). Top medical journal [NEJM] eases ethics policy. Chicago Tribune, June 13

309. Gottman IM, Katz LF (1989). Effects of marital discord on young children's peer interaction and health. Developmental Psychology 3:373–81

310. Gould DA, Stevens NG, Ward NG, Carlin AS, Sowell HE, & Gufstavson B (1994) Self-reported childhood abuse in an adult population in a primary care setting: prevalence, correlates and associated suicide attempts. Archives of Family Medicine 3:252–6

311. Grayston AD, De Luca RV, Boyes DA (1992). Self-esteem, anxiety, and loneliness in preadolescent girls who have experienced sexual abuse. Child Psychiatry Hum Dev 22(4):277–86

312. Grayston AD, De Luca RV (1999). Female perpetrators of child sexual abuse: a review of the clinical and empirical literature. 4:93–106

313. Greden JF (2001). Statement in (BW HealthWire) Eli Lilly and Company: in two trials duloxetine significantly reduced symptoms of depression. Business, Editors, Health/Medical Writers, Anne Griffin, May 7

314. Greden JF (2002). Unmet need: What justifies the search for a new antidpressant? Journal of Clinical Psychiatry 63 (suppl2):3–7

315. Green B: Problem-based psychiatry. Churchill Livingston, NY 1996

316. Greenwald E, Leitenberg OH, Cado S, Tarran MJ (1990). Childhood sexual abuse: long-term effects on psychological and sexual functioning in a non-clinical and non-student sample of adult women. Child Abuse & Neglect 14 (4): 503–514

317. Greyson CB (1999). Personal communication. Atlanta, Ga, June 15

317a. Greyson B (1986). Incidence of near-death experiences following attempted suicide. Suicide and Life-threatening Behavior 16:40–5

318. Grice DE, Brady KT, Dustan LR, Malcolm R (1995). Sexual and physical assault history and post-traumatic stress disorder in substance-dependent individuals. American Journal of Addictions 4:297–305

319. Grilo CM, Sanislow C, Fehon DC, Martino S, Mc Glashan TH (1999). Psychological and behavioral functioning in adolescent psychiatric inpatients who report histories of childhood abuse. American Journal of Psychiatry 156 (4) 538–543

320. Guntrip H (1973). Psychoanalytical Theory, Therapy and the Self. Basic Books/Harper Torch Books, NY.

321. Gurvits TV, Shenton ME, Hokama H, Ohta H, Laskow NB, Gilbertson MW, Orr SP, Kikinis R, Jolez FA, Mc Carley RW, Pittman RK, (1996). Magnetic

resonance imaging study of hippocampal volume in chronic, combat related posttraumatic stress disorder. Biological Psychiatry 40:1091–9

H

322. Hallstrom, T. (1987). Major depression, parental mental disorder and early family relationships. Acta Psychiatr. Scand. 75: 259–263

323. Hanson RF, Spratt EG (2000). Reactive attachment disorder: what we know about the disorder and implications for treatment. Child Maltreatment 5:137–145

324. Handwerker WP (1999). Childhood origins of depression: evidence from native and non-native women in Alaska and the Russian far-east. Journal of Women's Health 8 (1) 87–94

325. Hardman JG, Limbird LE (eds.) (1996). Goodman and Gilman's The Pharmacologic Basis of Therapeutics 9th ed., McGraw Hill, NY

326. Harkness KL, Wildes JE (2002). Childhood adversity and anxiety versus dysthymia co-morbidity in major depression. Psychol Med 32(7):1239–49

327. Hart LE, Mader L, Griffith K, deMendonca M (1989). Effects of sexual and physical abuse: a comparison of adolescent in-patients. Child Psychiatry and Human Development 20:49–57

328. Hart J, Gunnar M, Cicchetti D (1995). Salivary cortisol in maltreated children: Evidence of relations between neuroendicrone activity and social competence. Development and Psychopathology 7:11–26

329. Hart J, Gunnar M, Cicchetti D (1996). Altered neuroendicrine activity in maltreated children related to symptoms of depression. Development and Psychopathology 8:201–14

330. Harter S, Alexander PC, Neimeyer RA (1988). Long-term effects of incestuous child abuse in college women: social adjustment, social cognition and family characteristics. Journal of Consulting and Clinical Psychology 56:5–8

331. Harter SL, Taylor TL (2000). Parental alcoholism, child abuse, and adult adjustment. Journal of Substance Abuse 11(1):31–44

332. Hasin D, Liu X, Nunes E, McCloud S, Samet S, Endicott J (2002). Effects of major depression on remission and relapse of substance dependence. Arch Gen Psychiatry 59(4):375–80

333. Hasin DS, Grant BF (2002a). Major depression in 6,050 former drinkers: association with past alcohol dependence. Arch Gen Psychiatry 59(9):794–800 Alcs 4x depressed even long sober

334. Hazell P, O'Connell D, Heathcote D, Henry D (2000). Tricyclic drugs for

depression in children and adolescents (Cochrane Review). In: The Cochrane Library, Issue 3

335. Healy D (1987). The structure of psychopharmacological revolutions. Psychiatr. Dev. 1987. 5, 349–376.

336. Healy D (1991). The Marketing of 5-Hydroxytryptamine: Depression or Anxiety? Br J Psychiatry 1991, 158, 737–742.

337. Healy D (1996). The Psychopharmacologists, London: Chapman & Hall (Altman)

338. Healy D (1998). The Psychopharmacologists II, London: Chapman & Hall (Altman)

339. Healy D (1998). The Antidepressant Era, Cambridge, Mass., Harvard University Press

340. Healy D (2000). Good science or good business?, Hastings Center Report, 2000, 30 No 2, 19–22

341. Healy DR, Tranter R (1991). Pharmacological stress diathesis syndromes, J Psychopharmacol 13(3), 287–290. And: In the shadow of the benzodiazepines (Responses to commentaries on the above paper), Ibid, p. 299

342. Healy D (1998). Commentary on J. Moncrieff et al, Meta-analysis of trials comparing antidepressants with active placebos, Brit J Psychiatry, 1998, 172, 232–234.

343. Healy D (1993). Images of trauma: from hysteria to PTSD. Faber & Faber, London (Chapter 10)

344. Healy D (1999). The three faces of antidepressants. Journal of Mental and Nervous Disease187:174–180

345. Healy D (2002). The [antidepressant] drugs don't work (also titled "Drug Story"). Documentary on Channel 4, London, UK, May 19

346. Heim C, Newport DJ, Bonsall R, Miller AH, Nemeroff CB (2001). Altered pituitary-adrenal axis responses to provocative challenge tests in adult survivors of childhood abuse. Am J Psychiatry 158(4):575–81

347. Heim C, Nemeroff CB (2001). The role of childhood trauma in the neurobiology of mood and anxiety disorders: preclinical and clinical studies. Biol Psychiatry 49(12):1023–39

348. Heim C, Nemeroff CB (2002). Neurobiology of early life stress: Clinical studies. Seminars in Clinical Neuropsychiatry 7(2):147–59

349. Heim C, Newport DJ, Heit S, Graham YP, Wilcox M, Bonsall R, Miller AH, Nemeroff CB (2000). Pituitary-adrenal and autonomic responses to stress in

women after sexual and physical abuse in childhood. Journal of the American Medical Association 284:592–7

350. Heins T, Gray A, Tennant M (1990). Persisting hallucinations following childhood sexual abuse. Australian and New Zealand Journal of Psychiatry 24:561–5

351. Henton J, Cate R, Koval J, Lloyd S, Christopher S (1993). Romance and violence in dating relationships. Journal of Family Issues 4:467–82

352. Herman JL, Schatzow E (1984). Time-limited group therapy for women with a history of incest. International Journal of group psychotherapy 34:605–16

353. Herman JL, Russell DEH, Trocki K (1986). Long-term effects of incestuous abuse in childhood. American Journal of Psychiatry 143:1293–6

354. Herman JL: Histories of violence in an outpatient population. Am J Orthopsychiatry 1986; 56:137–141

355. Herman JL, Russell DEH, Trocki K: Long-term effects of incestuous abuse in childhood. Am J Psychiatry 1986; 143:1293–1296

356. Herman JL, Schatzow E (1987). Recovery and verification of memories of childhood sexual trauma. Psychoanalytic Psychology 4:1–14

357. Herman JL, van der Kolk BA (1987). Traumatic antecedents of borderline personality disorder. In van der Kolk BA (Ed.), Psychological trauma. Washington, DC, American Psychiatric Press p 111–26

358. Herman JL (1988). Histories of violence in an outpatient population. In Burgess AW (Ed.) Rape and sexual assault, Vol. 2. New York: Garland, p 41–49

359. Herman JL, Perry JC, van der Kolk BA (1989). Childhood trauma in borderline personality disorder. American Journal of Psychiatry 146:490–5

360. Herman JL (1992). Trauma and Recovery. Basic Books, NY, Second Edition 1997

361. Herman JL (1992). Sequelae of prolonged and repeated trauma: Evidence for a complex post-traumatic syndrome. In Davidson JR, Foa EB (Eds), Post-traumatic stress disorder: DSM-IV and beyond. Washington, DC: American Psychiatric Press 213–228

362. Herman JL (1992). Complex PTSD: A syndrome in survivors of prolonged and repeated trauma. J. Traumatic Stress 5:377–391

363. Herman JL (1998). Recovery from psychological trauma. Psychiatry and Clinical Neurosciences 52

364. Herrenkohl RC, Russo MJ (2000). Abusive early child rearing and early childhood aggression. Child Maltreatment, February 2001, vol. 6, no. 1, pp. 3–16(14)

365. Higgins DJ, McCabe MP (1994). The relationship of child sexual abuse and family violence to adult adjustment: Toward an integrated risk-sequelae model. Journal of Sex Research 31(4):255–66

366. Hill SY, De Bellis MD, Keshavan MS, Lowers L, Shen S, Hall J, Pitts T (2001). Right amygdala volume in adolescent and young adult offspring from families at high risk for developing alcoholism. Biol Psychiatry 1;49(11):894–905

367. Hjorth CW, Ostrov E (1982). The self image of physically abused adolescents. Journal of Youth and Adolescence 11:71–6

368. Hoffman-Plotkin D, Twentyman CT (1984). A multimodal assessment of behavioral and cognitive deficits in abused and neglected preschoolers. Child Dev 1984 Jun;55(3):794–802

369. Hooper PD (1990) Psychological sequelae of sexual abuse in childhood British Journal of General Practice 40:29–31

370. Horney K (1950). The Neurotic Personality of Our Time. Norton, NY

371. Houston TK, Cooper LA, Ford DE (2002). Internet support groups for depression: a 1-year prospective cohort study. Am J Psychiatry 2002 Dec;159(12):2062–8

372. Hull AM (2002). Neuroimaging findings in post-traumatic stress disorder: Systematic review. Br J Psychiatry 181(2):102–110

373. Hulme PA (2000). Symptomatology and health care utilization of women primary care patients who experienced childhood sexual abuse. Child Abuse & Neglect 24:1471–84

374. Hunter JA (1991). A comparison of the psychosocial maladjustment of adult males and females sexually molested as children. Journal of Interpersonal Violence 6(2): 205–17

375. Huntoon JL (1994). The relationship of serotonin uptake in blood platelets to a self-reported history of childhood trauma. Unpublished doctoral dissertation, Lawrence, Kansas: University of Kansas

376. Hurt H, Malmud E, Brodsky NL, Giannetta J (2001). Exposure to violence psychological and academic correlates in child witnesses Archives of Pediatric and Adolescent Medicine.;155:1351–1356.

377. Hussey DL, Singer M (1993). Psychological distress, problem behaviors, and family functioning of sexually abused adolescent inpatients. Journal of

the American Academy of Child and Adolescent Psychiatry 32 (5) 954–960

I

378. Irwin, H., Green, M., Marlsh P (1999). Dysfunction in smooth pursuit eye movements and history of childhood trauma. Perceptual and Motor Skills 89:1230–1236.

379. Ito Y, Teicher M, Glod C, and Ackerman E (1998). Peliminary evidence for aberrant cortical development in abused children: A quantitative EEG study. Journal of Neuropsychiatry and Clinical Neurosciences 10:298–307

380. Ito Y, Teicher MH, Glod CA, Harper D, Magnus E, Gelbard HA (1993). Increased prevalence of electrophysiological abnormalities in children with psychological, physical, and sexual abuse. Journal of Neuropsychiatry and Clinical Neurosciences 5:401–408

J

381. Jackson SW (1986). Melancholia and Depression: From Hippocratic times to modern times. Yale University press, New Haven

382. Jacobson, A, Richardson B (1987). Assault experiences of 100 psychiatric inpatients: evidence of the need for routine inquiry. American Journal of Psychiatry, 144: 908–913

383. Jacobson A, Kohler JE, Jones-Brown C (1987). The failure of routine assessment to detect histories of assault experienced by psychiatric patients. Hospital and Community Psychiatry 38: 386–89

384. Jacobson A (1989). Physical and sexual assault histories among psychiatric outpatients. American Journal of Psychiatry 146(6):755–8

385. Jacobson A, Herald C (1990). The relevance of childhood sexual abuse to adult psychiatric inpatient care. Hospital and Community Psychiatry 41:15

386. Jacobs D, Cohen D (1999). What is really known about psychological alterations produced by psychiatric drugs? The International Journal of Risk and Safety in Medicine Volume 12, Number 1/: 37–47

387. Jacobson, A (1989). Physical and sexual assault histories among psychiatric outpatients. American Journal of Psychiatry, 146, 751–758

388. Jacobson, A, Richardson B (1987). Assault experiences of 100 psychiatric inpatients: evidence of the need for routine inquiry. American Journal of Psychiatry, 144: 908–913

389. Jacobson A, Herald C (1990). The relevance of childhood sexual abuse to

adult psychiatric inpatient care. Hospital and Community Psychiatry 41:154–8 40% CSA

390. Jacobson NS, Dobson KS, Truax PA, Addis ME, Koerner K, Gollan JK, Gortner E, Prince SE (1996). A component analysis of cognitive behavioral treatment for depression. Journal of Consulting & Clinical Psychology 64:295–304

391. Jaffe P, Wolfe D, Wilson S, Zak L (1986). Similarities in behavioral and social maladjustment among child victims and witnesses to family violence. American Journal of Orthopsychiatry 56:142–6

392. Joffe R, Sokolov S, & Streiner D (1996). Antidepressant treatment of depression: A metaanalysis. Canadian Journal of Psychiatry, 41, 613–616

393. James K (1977). Incest: the teenager's perspective. Psychotherapy: Theory, Research & Practice 14(2): 144–6

394. James J, Meyerding J (1977). Early sexual experiences and prostitution. American Journal of Psychiatry 134:1381–5

395. Jellen LK, McCarroll JE, Thayer LE (2001). Child emotional maltreatment: a 2-year study of US Army cases. Child Abuse Negl 25(5):623–39

396. Jicks SS, Dean AD, Jicks H (1995). Antidepressants and suicide. British Medical Journal 311:215–8

397. Johnson RL, Shrier DK (1985). Sexual victimization of boys. Journal of Adolescent Health Care 6:372–6

398. Johnson JG, Cohen P, Brown J, Smailes EM, Bernstein DP (1999). Childhood maltreatment increases risk for personality disorders during early adulthood. Archives of General Psychiatry, 56, 600–606

399. Johnson JG, Smailes EM, Cohen P, Brown J, Bernstein DP (2000). Associations between four types of childhood neglect and personality disorder symptoms during adolescence and early adulthood: findings of a community-based longitudinal study. J Personal Disord 14(2):171–87

400. Johnson DM, Pike JL, Chard KM (2001). Factors predicting PTSD, depression, and dissociative severity in female treatment-seeking childhood sexual abuse survivors. Child Abuse Negl. 2001 Jan;25(1):179–98

401. Johnson J, Weissman MM, Klerman GL (1992). Service utilization and social morbidity associated with depressive symptoms in the community. Journal of the American Medical Association 267 (11): 1478–1483

402. Jones P, Rodgers B, Murray R, Marmont M (1994). Child developmental risk factors for adult schizophrenia in the British 1946 birth cohort. Lancet 344:1398–1402

403. Jones L, Hughes M, Unterstaller U (2001). Post-traumatic stress disorder (PTSD) in victims of domestic violence. Trauma, Violence & Abuse 2:99–119

404. Joseph, J (1998). The equal environment assumption of the classical twin method: A critical analysis. Journal of Mind and Behavior, 19, 325–358

405. Joseph J (1999). A critique of the Finnish Adoptive Family Study of Schizophrenia. Journal of Mind and Behavior, 20, 133–154

406. Joseph J (1999a). The genetic theory of schizophrenia: A critical overview. Ethical Human Sciences and Services, 1, 119–145

407. Joseph J (2001). Don Jackson's "A critique of the literature on the genetics of schizophrenia": A reappraisal after 40 years. Genetic, Social, & General Psychology Monographs 127:27–57

408. Jumper S (1995). A meta-analysis of the relationship of child sexual abuse to adult psychological adjustment. Child Abuse & Neglect, 19: 715–728

K

409. Kaiser D (1996). Against Biologic psychiatry (commentary) Psychiatric Times, December (Web site *www.mhsource.com* in 2001)

410. Kalb PE, Koehler KG (2002). Legal issues in scientific research. Journal of The American Medical Association 287:85–91

411. Kaplan SJ, Pelcovitz D, Salzinger S, Weiner M, Mandel FS, Lesser ML, Labruna VE (1998). Adolescent physical abuse: risk for adolescent psychiatric disorders. Am J Psychiatry 155(7):954–9; more at Pediatrics 1999 Jul;104(1 Pt 1):43–9; and J Trauma Stress 2000 Jan;13(1):77–88

412. Kashani JH, Carlson GA (1987). Seriously depressed preschoolers. American Journal of Psychiatry 144:348–50

413. Katz LF, Gottman JM (1997). Buffering children from marital conflict and dissolution. J Clin Child Psychol 26(2):157–71

413a. Kaufman G (1989). The Psychology of Shame. Springer NY

414. Kaufman G (1980). Shame: The Power of Caring. Schenkman Publishing Company, Cambridge, MA

414a. Kaufman J (1991). Depressive disorders in maltreated children. Journal of the American Academy of Child and Adolescent Psychiatry, 30(2), 257–265.

415. Kaufman J, Birmaher B, Perel J, Dahl RE, Stull S, Brent D, Trubnick L, Al-Shabbout M, Ryan ND (1998) Serotonergic functioning in depressed abused children: clinical and familial correlates. Biological Psychiatry 44:973–8

416. Kaufman J, Charney DS (1999). Neurobiological correlates of child abuse. Biological Psychiatry 45:1235–6

417. Kaufman J (1991). Depressive disorders in maltreated children. J Am Acad Child Adolesc Psychiatry 30:257–265.

418. Kaufman J, Plotsky PM, Nemeroff CB, Charney DS (2000). Effects of early adverse experiences on brain structure and function. Biological Psychiatry 48:778–90

419. Kazdin AE, Mosher J, Colbus D, Bell R (1985). Depressive symptoms among physically abused and psychiatrically disturbed children. Journal of Abnormal Psychology 94(3): 298–307

420. Keeler MH (1982). Chapter 47. Alcoholism and affective disorder (p 618) In: Pattison EM & Kaufman R (eds): Encyclopedic Handbook of Alcoholism, Gardner Press, NY

421. Kendall-Tackett C, Williams LM, Finkelhor D (1993). Impact of sexual abuse on children: A review and synthesis of recent empirical studies. Psychological Bulletin, 113, 164–180

422. Kendall-Tackett KA, Simon AF (1988). Molestation and the onset of puberty: Data from 365 adults molested as children. Child Abuse & Neglect 12:73–81

423. Kendall-Tackett KA (2000). Physiological correlates of childhood abuse: chronic hyperarousal in PTSD, depression, and irritable bowel syndrome. Child Abuse & Neglect 24(6):799–810

424. Kendler K, Karkowski LM, Prescott CA (1999). Causal relationship between stressful life events and the onset on major depression. American Journal of Psychiatry 156:837–841

425. Kendler K, Bulik C, Silberg J, Hettema J, Myers J, Prescott C, (2000). Childhood sexual abuse and adult psychiatric and substance use disorders in women: An epidemiological and co-twin control analysis. Arch Gen Psychiatry 57:953–959

426. Kendler KS, Gardner CO, Prescott CA (2002). Toward a comprehensive developmental model for major depression in women. Am J Psychiatry 159(7):1133–45

427. Kennedy BL, Dhaliwal N, Pedley L, Sahner C, Greenberg R, Manshadi MS (2002). Post-Traumatic Stress Disorder in subjects with schizophrenia and bipolar disorder. J Ky Med Assoc 100(9):395–9

428. Kent JT (1976). A follow-up study of abused children. Journal of Pediatric Psychology 1:25–31

429. Kent P (2001). Personal communication, Atlanta, GA, March

430. Kent A, Waller G, Dagnan D (1999). A greater role of emotional than

physical or sexual abuse in predicting disordered eating attitudes: the role of mediating variables. International Journal of Eating Disorders 25:159–67

431. Kent A, Waller G (1998). The impact of childhood emotional abuse: and extension of the child abuse and trauma scale. Child Abuse & Neglect 22:393–9

432. Kerig PK, Fedorowicz AE (1999): Assessing maltreatment of children of battered women: methodological and ethical considerations. Child Maltreatment 4(2): 103–115.

433. Kessler R, Magee W (1993). Childhood adversities and adult depression: Basic patterns of association in a US National Survey. Psychol. Med. 23, pp. 679–690

434. Kessler R., Davis C, Kendler R (1997). Childhood adversity and adult psychiatric disorder in the US National Comorbidity Survey. Psychol. Med. 27:1101–1119

435. Kiesler CA (1982b) Public and professional myths about mental hospitalization: An empirical reassessment of policy-related beliefs. American Psychologist, 37, 1323–1339

435a. Khan A, Khan S, Brown WA (2002). Are placebo controls necessary to test new antidepressants and anxiolytics? International Journal of Neuropsychophamacology 5(3):193–7

436. Kilpatrick KL, Williams LM (1998). Potential mediators of post-traumatic stress disorder in child witnesses to domestic violence. Child Abuse & Neglect 22:319–30

437. Kilpatrick AC (1986). Some correlates of women's childhood sexual experiences: a retrospective study. Journal of Sex Research 22(2): 221–42

438. Kilpatrick DG, Best CL, Veronen LJ, Amick AE, Villeponteaux LA, Ruff GA (1985). Mental health correlates of criminal victimization: a random community survey. J Consult Clin Psychol 1985 Dec;53(6):866–73

439. Kinard EM (1994). Methodological issues and practical problems in conducting research on maltreated children. Child Abuse Negl 18(8):645–5 Add

440. Kinard EM (1995). Mother and teacher assessments of behavior problems in abused children. Journal of the American Academy of Child and Adolescent Psychiatry 34 (8): 1043–53

441. Kinard EM (1998). Depressive symptoms in maltreated children from mother, teacher, and child perspectives. Violence and Victims 13:131–47

442. Kinderman, Cooke, Bentall R (2000). Recent Advances in Understanding Mental Illness and Psychotic Experiences. Leicester, UK: British Psychological Society

443. King CH (1975). The ego and the integration of violence in homicidal youth. American Journal of Orthopsychiatry 45(1):134–45

444. King M, Coxell A, Mezey G (2002). Sexual molestation of males: associations with psychological disturbance. Br J Psychiatry 181(2):153–157

445. Kirkengen AL (2001). Inscribed Bodies: Health Impact of Childhood Sexual Abuse. Kluwer Academic Publishers, Boston

446. Kirsch I, Sapirstein G (1998). Listening to Prozac but hearing placebo—A meta-analysis of antidepressant medication, June, Prevention and Treatment, vol. One, http://www.journals.apa.org/prevention

447. Kirsch I (1998). Reducing noise and hearing placebo more clearly: Rejoinder to comments on Listening to Prozac but hearing placebo. Prevention & Treatment, Volume 1, Article 0007r, posted June 26

448. Kirsch I, Moore TJ, Scoboria A, Nicholls SS (2002). The Emperor's new drugs: An analysis of antidepressant medication data submitted to the FDA. Prevention and Treatment, American Psychological Association, www.journals.apa.org/prevention

449. Kiser LJ, Heston J, Millsap PA, Pruitt DB (1991). Physical and sexual abuse in childhood: relationship with post-traumatic stress disorder. J Am Acad Child Adolesc Psychiatry. 30(5):776–83

450. Kitchens JA (1990). Beyond the Shame: Understanding and treating the child molester ADS-CO, Dallas, TX

451. Kitzinger J (1996). Media representations of sexual abuse risks. Child Abuse Review 5:319–333

452. Kluft RP (Ed) (1990). Incest-Related Syndromes of Adult Psychopathology. American Psychiatric Press, NY

453. Kluft ES (1993). Expressive and Functional Therapies in the Treatment of Multiple Personality Disorder. Charles C Thomas, Springfield, Il

454. Klump KL, Wonderlich S, Lehoux P, Lilenfeld LR, Bulik CM (2002). Does environment matter? A review of nonshared environment and eating disorders. Int J Eat Disord 31(2):118–35

455. Kolko, DJ (1996). Child physical abuse. In J. Briere, L. Berliner, J.A. Bulkley, C. Jenny, & T. Reid, (eds): The APSAC handbook on child maltreatment. (pp. 21–50), Chicago: APSAC

456. Knowles EE, Schroeder DA (1990). Personality characteristics of sons of alcohol abusers. Journal of Studies of Alcohol 142–147

457. Krantz G, Ostergren PO (2000). The association between violence victimization and common symptoms in Swedish women. Journal of Epidemiology and Community Health 54:815–821

458. Kripke DF (1998). Light treatment for nonseasonal depression: speed, effi-
      cacy, and combined treatment. Journal of Affective Disorders 49:109–17

459. Kroll PD, Stock DF, James ME (1985). The behavior of adult alcoholic men
      abused as children. Journal of Nervous and Mental Disease 173:689–93

460. Krug RS (1989). Adult male report of childhood sexual abuse by mothers:
      case descriptions, motivations and long-term consequences. Child Abuse
      Negl 13(1):111–9

461. Kuhn TS (1970). The Structure of Scientific Revolutions. Univ Chicago Press

462. Kumar G, Steer RA, Deblinger E (1996). Problems in differentiating sexu-
      ally from non-sexually abused adolescent psychiatric inpatients by self-
      reported anxiety, depression, internalization, and externalization. Child
      Abuse & Neglect 20 (11): 1079–1086

463. Kunitz SJ, Levy JE, McCloskey J, Gabriel KR (1998). Alcohol dependence
      and domestic violence as sequelae of abuse and conduct disorder in child-
      hood. Child Abuse Negl 22(11):1079–91

464. Kutchins H, Kirk SA (1997). Making Us Crazy—DSM: The Psychiatric
      Bible and the creation of mental disorders. The Free Press, NY

465. Kuyken W, Brewin CR (1994). Intrusive memories of childhood abuse dur-
      ing depressive episodes. Behav Res Ther 32(5):525–8

L

466. Ladwig GB, Anderson MD (1989). Substance abuse in women: relationship
      between chemical dependency in women and past reports of physical and
      sexual abuse. International Journal of the Addictions, 24: 739–744

467. Lake-White J, Kline CM (1985). Treating the dissociative process in adult
      victims of childhood incest. Social Case Work 66:394–402

468. Lam RW (ed) (1998). Seasonal Affective Disorder and Beyond: Light treat-
      ment for SAD and non-SAD conditions. American Psychiatric Press, p 167–9

469. Lancet (2001). Editorial 358:854–6

470. Lancet (2002). Just how tainted has medicine become? Editorial 359:1167
      and 9313

471. Langeland W, Hartgers C (1998). Child sexual and physical abuse and alco-
      holism: a review. Journal of Studies on Alcoholism 59:336–48

472. Langevin R Wright P, Handy L (1989). Characteristics of sex offenders who
      were sexually victimized as chidlren. Annals of Sex Research (now Journal
      of Sexual Abuse) 3:187–204

473. Langevin R, Paitich D, Orchard B, Handy L, Russon A (1983). Childhood

and family background of killers seen for psychiatric assessment: a controlled study. Bull Am Acad Psychiatry Law.11(4):331–41

474. Lansford JE, Dodge KA, Pettit GS, Bates JE, Crozier J, Kaplow J (2002). A 12-year prospective study of the long-term effects of early child physical maltreatment on psychological, behavioral, and academic problems in adolescence. Archives of Pediatric and Adolescent Medicine 156:824–830

475. Lanz JB (1995). Psychological, behavioral, and social characteristics associated with early forced sexual intercourse among pregnant adolescents. Journal of Interpersonal Violence 10 (2): 188–200

476. Laplanche J, Pontalis JB (1973). The Language of Psycho-analysis. WW Norton, NY

477. Lawlor DA, Hopker SW (2001). The effectiveness of exercise as an intervention in the management of depression: systematic review and meta-regression analysis of randomised controlled trials BMJ 322:763

478. The Leadership Council for Mental Health, Justice & the Media (2002). *www.leadershipcouncil.org/*

479. Lebowitz L, Harvey M, Herman JL (1993). A stage-by-dimension model of recovery from psychological trauma. J. Interpersonal Violence, 8:378–391

480. Lechner ME, Vogel ME, Garcia-Shelton LM, Leichter JL, Steibel KR (1993). Self-reported medical problems of adult female survivors of childhood sexual abuse. J Fam Pract 36(6):633–8

481. Lecklitner GL, Malik NM, Aaron SM, Lederman CS (1999). Promoting safety for abused children and battered mothers: Miami-Dade County's modeled dependency court intervention program. Child Maltreatment 4(2): 175–182

482. Lecrubier Y, Clerc G, Didi R, et al. (2002). Efficacy of St. John's wort extract WS 5570 in major depression: a double-blind, placebo-controlled trial. American Journal of Psychiatry 159:1361–1366

483. Lee JKP, Jackson HJ, Pattison P, Ward T (2002). Developmental risk factors for sexual offending. Child Abuse & Neglect 26:73–92

484. Lehrman NS (2002). Dead Wrong: The drug treatment of depression is one of the great fallacies in the history of medicine. Redflagsweekly.com, August 15

485. Leifer M, Shapiro JP, Kassem L (1993). The impact of maternal history and behavior upon foster placement and adjustment in sexually abused girls. Child Abuse & Neglect, 17, 755–766

486. Leifer M, Shapiro JP (1995). Longitudinal study of the psychological effects

of sexual abuse in African-American girls in foster care and those who remain at home. Journal of Child Sexual Abuse, 4, 27–44

487. Leuchter AF, Cook IA, Witte EA, Morgan M, Abrams M (2002). Changes in brain function of depressed subjects during treatment with placebo. Am J Psychiatry 159:122–129

488. Levitan RD, Parikh SV, Lesage AD, Hegadoren KM, Adams M, Kennedy SH & Goering PN (1998). Major depression in individuals with a history of childhood physical or sexual abuse: relationship to neurovegetative features, mania and gender. American Journal of Psychiatry 155 (12) 1746–52

489. Leverich GS, McElroy SL, Suppes T, Keck PE Jr, Denicoff KD, Nolen WA, Altshuler LL, Rush AJ, Kupka R, Frye MA, Autio KA, Post RM (2002). Early physical and sexual abuse associated with an adverse course of bipolar illness. Biol Psychiatry 2002 Feb 15;51(4):288–97

490. Lewontin R, Rose S, Kamin L (1984) Not in our genes: biology, ideology, and human nature. NY: Pantheon

491. Lewis DO, Moy E, Jackson LD (1985). Biopsychosocial characteristics of children who later murder: a prospective study. American Journal of Psychiatry, 142:1161–7

492. Liem JH, Boudewyn AC (1999). Contextualizing the effects of childhood sexual abuse on adult self- and social-functioning: an attachment theory perspective. Child Abuse Negl Nov;23(11):1141–57

493. Lindberg FH, Distad LJ (1985). Post-traumatic Stress Disorders in Women who Experienced Childhood incest. Child Abuse & Neglect 9:329

494. Lipman EL, McMillan HL, Boyle MH (2001). Childhood abuse and psychiatric disorders among single and married mothers. Am J Psychiatry 158:73–77

495. Lipschitz D, Kaplan M, Sorkenn J, Faedda G, Chorney P, Asnis G (1996). Prevalence and characteristics of physical and sexual abuse among psychiatric outpatients. Psychiatric Services 47:189–91

496. Lipschitz D, Winegar R, Nicolaou A, Hartnick, E, Wolfson M, Southwick S (1999). Perceived abuse and neglect as risk factors for suicidal behavior in adolescent inpatients. Journal of Nervous and Mental Disease 187:32–39

497. Livingston R (1987). Sexually and physically abused children. Journal of the American Academy of Child and Adolescent Psychiatry 26 (3):413–5

498. Lo B, Wolf LE, Berkeley A (2000). Conflict-of-interest policies for investigators in clinical trials. New England Journal of Medicine 343:1616–20

499. Ludolph PS, Westen D, Misle B, Jackson A, Wixom J, Wiss FC (1990). The

borderline diagnosis in adolescents: symptoms and developmental history. Am J Psychiatry 147(4):470–6

500. Lukianowicz N (1972). Incest. British Journal of Psychiatry 120:301–13

501. Lundberg O (1993). The impact of childhood living conditions on illness and mortality in adulthood. Soc Sci Med 36(8):1047–52

502. Lundberg-Love PK, Marmion S, Ford K, Geffner R & Peacock L (1992). The long-term consequences of childhood incestuous victimization upon adult women's psychological symptomatology Journal of Child Sexual Abuse 1:81–102

503. Luntz BK, Widom CS (1994). Antisocial personality disorder in abused and neglected children grown up. American Journal of Psychiatry, 151: 670–674.

504. Lynskey MT, Fergusson DM (1997). Factors protecting against the development of adjustment difficulties in young adults exposed to childhood sexual abuse. Child Abuse & Neglect 21(12): 1177–90

505. Lyons-Ruth K, Jacobvitz D. (1999). Attachment disorganization: Unresolved loss, relational violence, and lapses in behavioral and attentional strategies, In J. Cassidy & P.R. Shaver (Eds.). Handbook of attachment: theory, research, and clinical applications (pp. 520–554). New York: Guilford.

506. Lysaker PH, Meyer PS, Evans JD, Clements CA, Marks KA (2001). Childhood sexual trauma and psychosocial functioning in adults with schizophrenia. Psychiatric Services 52:1485–8

M

507. MacEwen KE (1994). Refining the intergenerational transmission hypothesis. Journal of Interpersonal Violence, 9, 350–365

508. MacMillan HL, Fleming JE, Trocme N, Boyle MH, Wong M, Racine YA, Beardslee WR, Offord, D R (1997). Prevalence of child physical and sexual abuse in the community: Results from the Ontario Health Supplement. Journal of the American Medical Association, 278, 131–135

509. Malarcher A, Sharp D (2002). Sexual abuse as a risk factor for smoking, substance abuse, and attempted suicides for boys and girls. (in submission)

510. Malinosky-Rummell R & Hansen D (1993). Long-term consequences of childhood physical abuse. Psychological Bulletin 114.68–79

511. Mancini C, Van Ameringen M, MacMillan H (1995). Relationship of chi]dhood sexual and physical abuse to anxiety disorders. Journal of Nervous and Mental Disease. 183. 309–314

512. Manly J, Cichetti D, Barnett D (1994). The impact of subtype, frequency, chronicity, and severity of child maltreatment on social competency and behavior problems. Development and Psychopathology 6:121–4.

513. Mann SJ (1999). Healing Hypertension: A Revolutionary New Approach. John Wiley & Sons

514. Marks IM (1989). The gap between research and policy in mental health care. Journal of the Royal Society of Medicine 82:514–7

515. Masterson JF (1988). The Search for the Real Self: Unmasking the Personality Disorders of Our Age. Free Press/MacMillan NY

516. Mazure C, Bruce M, Maciejewski P, Jacobs S (2000). Adverse life events in major depression. American Journal of Psychiatry 157: 896–903

517. McCann IL, Pearlman LA (1990). Psychological Trauma and the Adult Survivor: Theory, Therapy, and Transformation. Brunner/Mazel, NY

518. McCauley J, Kern DE, Kolodner K, Dill L., Schroeder AF, DeChant HK, Ryden J, Derogatis L, Bass EB (1997). Clinical characteristics of women with a history of childhood abuse: unhealed wounds. Journal of the American Medical Association 277 (17): 1362–1368, 1997

519. McEwen, BS (2000). Allostasis and allostatic load: implications for neuropsychopharmacology. Neuropsychopharmacology, 22(2), 108–124

520. McGee D, Wolfe D, Wilson S (1997). Multiple maltreatment experience and adolescent behavior problems; adolescent's perspectives. Development and Psychopathology 9:131–49

521. McLeer SV, Deblinger E, Atkins MS, Foa EB & Ralphe DL (1988) Post-traumatic stress disorder in sexually abused children. Journal of the American Academy of Child and Adolescent Psychiatry. 27:650–4

522. Mechanic D, Hansell S (1989). Divorce, family conflict, and adolescents' well-being. J Health Soc Behav 30(1):105–16

523. Medawar C (2002). The antidepressant web—Marketing depression and making medicines work. The current version can be viewed and downloaded from this site (www.socialaudit.org.uk). The original printed version, published in International Journal of Risk & Safety in Medicine (1997) can also be ordered either from Social Audit or from the publishers.

524. Medawar C (1996). Drug education materials for children—are they good enough? in Proc. USP Open Conference, Reston, Va., Sep 29–Oct 1; Children & Medicines: Information isn't just for grown-ups, available from US Pharmacopeia, 12601 Twinbrook Parkway, Rockville, Md 20852, USA

525. Medawar C (1996a). Secrecy and medicines. Int J Risk & Safety in Medicine, 9, 133–141

526. Medawar C (1994). Defining risk and patients' perceptions of risk, in Proc. USP Open Conference, Communicating risks to patients, Washington DC, available from US Pharmacopeia, 12601 Twinbrook Parkway, Rockville, Md 20852, USA.

527. Medawar C (1994a). Through the doors of deception? Nature 24 March 368, 369–370.

528. Medawar C (1993). Drugs, secrecy and society (editorial), BMJ, 9 Jan 306:6870, 81–82.

529. Mennen FE, Meadow D (1995): The relationship of abuse characteristics to symptoms in sexually abused girls. Journal of Interpersonal Violence 10(3): 259–74

530. Merrill LL, Thomsen CJ, Gold SR, Milner, JS (2001). Childhood abuse and premilitary sexual assault in male Navy recruits. Journal of Consulting and Clinical Psychology, 69, 252–261

531. Merrill LL, Thomsen CJ, Sinclair BB, Gold SR, Milner JS (2001). Predicting the impact of child sexual abuse on women: the role of abuse severity, parental support, and coping strategies. J Consult Clin Psychol 69(6):992–1006

532. Merikangas KR, Stolar M, Stevens DE, Goulet J, Presig MA, Fenton B, Zhang H, O'Malley SS, Rounsaville BJ (1998). Familial transmission of substance abuse disorders. Archives of General Psychiatry 55: 973–979, 1998

533. Metcalfe M, Oppenheimer R, Dignon A, Palmer RL (1990). Child sexual experiences reported by male psychiatric patients. Psychological Medicine 20:925–9

534. Miller BA, Downs WR, Gondoli DM, Keil A (1987). The role of childhood sexual abuse in the development of alcoholism in women. Violence and Victims 2:157–172

535. Miller BA, Downs WR, Testa M (1993). Interrelationships between victimization experiences and women's alcohol use. Journal of Studies on Alcohol, Supplement no.11, pp. 109–117

536. Miller J, Moeller D, Kaufman A, Divasto P, Fitzsimmons P, Prather D, Christi J (1978). Recidivism among sexual assault victims. American Journal of Psychiatry 135:1003–4

537. Moeller TP, Bachman GL, Moeller JR (1993). The combined effects of physical. sexual. and emotional abuse during childhood: Long term health consequences for women. Child Abuse & Neglect. 17, 623–640

538. Moisan PA, Sanders-Phillips K, Moisan PM (1997). Ethnic differences in circumstances of abuse and symptoms of depression and anger among sexually abused black and Latino boys. Child Abuse and Neglect 21 (5) 473–488

539. Molnar BE, Shade SB, Kral AH, Booth RE, Watters JK (1998). Suicidal behavior and sexual/physical abuse among street youth. Child Abuse & Neglect 22:213–22

540. Molnar BE, Berkman LF, Buka SL (2001). Psychopathology, childhood sexual abuse and other childhood adversities: relative links to subsequent suicidal behaviour in the US. Psychol Med 31(6):965–77

541. Moncrieff J, Drummond D, Candy B, Checinski K, Farmer, R (1996). Sexual abuse in people with alcohol problems. A study of the prevalence of sexual abuse and its relationship to drinking behavior. British Journal of Psychiatry 169:355–360

542. Moncrieff J, Wessely S, Hardy R (1998). Meta-analysis of trials comparing antidepressants with active placebos British Journal of Psychiatry 172: 227–231

543. Morin K, Rakatansky H, Riddick FA, Morse LJ, O'Bannon JM, Goldrich MS, Ray P, Weiss M, Sade RM, Spillman MA (2002). Managing conflicts of interest in the conduct of clinical trials. Journal of The American Medical Association 287:78–84

544. Morrison J (1989). Childhood sexual histories of women with somatization disorder American Journal of Psychiatry 146:239–41

545. Morrow KB, Sorell GT (1989). Factors effecting self-esteem, depression, and negative behaviors in sexually abused female adolescents. Journal of Marriage and the Family 51:677–86

546. Morton N, Browne KD (1998). Theory and observation of attachment and its relation to child maltreatment: a review. Child Abuse Negl 1998 Nov; 22 (11):1093–104

547. Moyer D (1997). Childhood sexual abuse and precursors of binge eating in an adolescent female population. International Journal of Eating Disorders 21:23–30

548. Muenzenmaier K, Meyer I, Struening E, Ferber J (1993). Childhood abuse and neglect among women outpatients with chronic mental illness. Hospital and Community Psychiatry 44:666–70

549. Mueser KT, Goodman LB, Trumbetta SL, Rosenberg SD, Osher C, Vidaver R, Auciello P, Foy DW (1998). Trauma and posttraumatic stress disorder in

severe mental illness. J Consult Clin Psychol 66(3):493–9

550. Mullen PE, Linsell CR, Parker D (1986). Influence of sleep disruption and calorie restriction on biological markers for depression. Lancet Nov 8; 2(8515):1051–5

551. Mullen PE, Martin JL, Anderson JC, Romans SE, Herbison GP (1993). Childhood sexual abuse and mental health in adult life. British Journal of Psychiatry 163:721–32

552. Mullen PE, Romans-Clarkson SE, Walton VA, Herbison GP (1998). Impact of sexual and physical abuse on women's mental health. Lancet 1: 841–845

553. Mullen PE, Martin JL, Anderson JC, Romans SE, Herbison GP (1993). Childhood sexual abuse and mental health in adult life. British Journal of Psychiatry 163: 721–732

554. Mullen PE, Martin JL, Anderson JC et al. (1996). The long-term impact of the physical, emotional, and sexual abuse of children: a community study. Child Abuse & Neglect, 20:7–21.

555. Muller RT, Lemieux KE. (2000). Social support, attachment, and psychopathology in high risk formerly maltreated adults. Child Abuse Negl 24(7):883–900

556. Murphy WD, Coleman E, Hoon E, Scott C (1980). Sexual dysfunction and treatment in alcoholic women. Sexuality and Disability 3:240–55

557. Murphy SM, Kilpatrick DG, Amick-McMullan A, Veronen LJ, Paduhovich J, Best CL, Villeponteaux LA, Saunders BE (1988). Current psychological functioning of child sexual assault survivors. Journal of Interpersonal Violence 3:55–79

N _____

558. Nash M, Hulsey T, Sexton M, Harralson T & Lambert W (1993). Long-term sequelae of childhood sexual abuse: perceived family environment, psychopathology, and dissociation. Journal of Consulting and Clinical Psychology 61: 276–283

559. Nelson EC, Heath AC, Madden PA, Cooper ML, Dinwiddie SH, Bucholz KK, Glowinski A, McLaughlin T, Dunne MP, Statham DJ, Martin NG (2002). Association between self-reported childhood sexual abuse and adverse psychosocial outcomes: results from a twin study. Arch Gen Psychiatry 59(2):139–45

560. Neumann DA, Houseamp BM, Poilace VE, Briere J (1996). The long term sequelae of childhood sexual abuse in women: a meta-analysis review. Child Maltreatment 1:6–16

560a. Newcomer JW, Selke, Melson AK, Hershey T, Craft S, Richards K, Anderson AL (1999). Decreased memory performance in healthy humans induced by stress-level cortisol treatment. Archives of General Psychiatry 56:527-33.

561. NIAAA (1974). National Institute on Alcohol and Alcohol Abuse: An Assessment of the Needs of and Resources for Children of Alcoholic Parents. (An extensive interview study of 50 CoAs) Commissioned study by Booz, Allen and Hamilton, Rockville, Md

562. Nierenberg AN (2001). Treatment resistant depression. Grand Rounds on the Internet, Harvard University, Boston, MA

563. Noblitt R (2000). Cult and Ritual Abuse: Its history, anthropology, and recent discovery in contemporary America, Revised Edition. with Pamela Sue Perskin. pp. 7–14. Westport, CT: Praeger Publishing

564. Norden MJ (1995). Beyond Prozac: Brain—toxic life styles, natural antidotes & new generation antidepressants. Regan Books/ HarperCollins NY

O _____

565. Oakley-Browne MA, Joyce PR, Wells JE, Bushnell JA, Hornblow AR (1995). Adverse parenting and other childhood experience as risk factors for depression in women aged 18-44 years. Journal of Affective Disorders 34:13-23

566. Oakley-Browne MA, Joyce PR, Wells JE, Bushnell JA, Hornblow AR (1995a). Disruptions in childhood parental care as risk factors for major depression in adult women. Australian and New Zealand Journal of Psychiatry 29:437–48

567. Ogata SN, Silk KR, Goodrich S, Lohr NE, Western D, Hill EM (1990). Childhood sexual and physical abuse in adult psychiatric patients with borderline personality disorder. American Journal of Psychiatry, 147, 100–1013

568. OReilly W (2002). Television and violence effect on children. Fox Channel documentary, April

P _____

569. Palmer RL, Oppenheimer R, Dignon A, Chaloner DA, Howells K (1990). Childhood sexual experiences with adults reported by women with eating disorders: an extended series. Br J Psychiatry 156:699-703

570. Palmer RL, Chaloner DA, Oppenheimer R (1992). Childhood sexual experiences with adults reported by female psychiatric patients. British Journal of Psychiatry 160:261-5

571. Palmer RL, Bramble D, Metcalfe M, Oppenheimer R & Smith J (1994). Childhood sexual experiences with adults: adult male psychiatric patients and general practice attenders. British Journal of Psychiatry 165:675–9

572. Pam A (1995). Chapter 1. Biological psychiatry: science or pseudoscience? In Ross CA & Pam A: Pseudoscience in Biological Psychiatry. John Wiley, NY

573. Pam A (1990): A critique of the scientific status of biological psychiatry. Acta Psychiatrica Scandinavica 82:1–35 (Supp l362)

574. Paolucci EO, Genuis ML, Violato C (2001). A meta-analysis of the published research on the effects of child sexual abuse. J Psychol 135(1):17–36

575. Parker G (1983). Parental affectionless control as an antecedent to adult depression. Archives of General Psychiatry 40:956–60

576. Paykel ES, Myers JK, Dienelt MN, Klerman GL, Lindenthal JJ, Pepper MP (1969). Life events and depression. A controlled study. Arch Gen Psychiatry 21(6):753–60

577. Pearlman LA (2001). Chapter 9. Treatment of persons with complex PTSD and other trauma-related disruptions of the self. In Wilson JP, Friedman MJ, Lindey JD (eds). Treating Psychological Trauma and PTSD. Guilford, New York

578. Pears KC, Capaldi DM (2001). Intergenerational transmission of abuse: a two-generational prospective study of an at-risk sample. Child Abuse Negl 25(11):1439–61

579. Pelcovitz D, Kaplan S, Goldenberg B, Mandel F, Lehane J, Guarrera J (1994). Post-traumatic stress disorder in physically abused adolescents. J Am Acad Child Adolesc Psychiatry 33(3):305–12

580. Pelcovitz D, Kaplan SJ, DeRosa RR, Mandel FS, Salzinger S (2000). Psychiatric disorders in adolescents exposed to domestic violence and physical abuse. Am J Orthopsychiatry 70(3):360–9

581. Pelletier G, Handy L (1999). Chapter 3. Is family dysfunction more harmful than child sexual abuse? A controlled study. In Bagley C, Mallick K (eds.) Child Sexual Abuse in Adult Offenders: New Theory and Research (pp 143–158). Brookfield, VT: Ashgate International

582. Pennebaker JW (1999). The effects of traumatic disclosure on physical and mental health: the values of writing and talking about upsetting events. Int J Emerg Ment Health 1(1):9–18

583. Pennebaker JW (2000). Telling stories: the health benefits of narrative. Literature and Medecine 19(1):3–18

584. Perry BD (2000). The neurodevelopmental impact of violence in childhood. In D. Schetky & E. Benedek (Eds.), Textbook of Child and Adolescent

Forensic Psychiatry. Washington, D.C.: American Psychiatric Press, Inc. (available on the Internet)

585. Perry BD (1994). Neurobiological sequelae of childhood trauma: post-traumatic stress disorders in children. In M. Murberg (Ed.), Catecholamines in Post-traumatic Stress Disorder: Emerging Concepts. (pp. 253–276). Washington, D.C.: American Psychiatric Press

586. Perry BD (1999). The memories of states: how the brain stores and retrieves traumatic experience. In J.M. Goodwin & R. Attias (Eds.), Splintered Reflections: Images of the Body In Trauma. (pp. 9–38). New York: Basic Books

587. Perry BD (2000). The neurodevelopmental impact of violence in childhood. In D. Schetky & E. Benedek (Eds.), Textbook of Child and Adolescent Forensic Psychiatry. Washington, D.C.: American Psychiatric Press, Inc.

588. Perry BD & Pollard R (1998). Homeostasis, stress, trauma, and adaptation: A neurodevelopmental view of childhood trauma. Child and Adolescent Psychiatric Clinics of North America, 7, 33–51

589. Perry BD, Pollard RA, Blakley TL, Daker WL, Vigilante D (1995). Childhood trauma, the neurobiology of adaptation and use-dependent development of the brain: How states become traits. Infant Mental Health Journal, 16, 271–291

590. Perry BD, Azad I (1999). Posttraumatic stress disorders in children and adolescents. Current Opinion in Pediatrics 11: 310–16

591. Perry JC, Herman JL (1992). Trauma and defense in the etiology of borderline personality disorder. In Paris J (Ed.), Etiology of borderline personality disorder. Washington DC: American Psychiatric Press, 123–140

592. Peters SD (1988) Child sexual abuse and later psychological problems in G. Wyatt & G. Powell (eds) The Lasting Effects of Child Sexual Abuse (pp119–123). Sage, 1000 Oaks, CA

593. Pharris MD, Resnick MD, Blum RW (1997). Protecting against hopelessness and suicidality in sexually abused American Indian adolescents, Journal of Adolescent Health, vol. 21, no. 6, pp. 400–406

594. Pillay AL, van der Venn MBW (1997). Depression, developmental level and disclosure in sexually abused children. South African Medical Journal 87 (12): 1688–91

595. Pollock VE, Briere J, Schneider L, Knop J, Mednick SA, Goodwin DW (1990). Childhood antecedents of antisocial behavior: parental alcoholism and physical abusiveness. Am J Psychiatry 147(10):1290–3

596. Pollak SD, Cicchetti D, Klorman R, Brumaghim JT (1997). Cognitive brain

event-related potentials and emotion processing in maltreated Children. Child Development 68(3):773–87

597. Pollak SD, Klorman R, Thatcher JE, Cicchetti D (2001). P3b reflects maltreated children's reactions to facial displays of emotion. Psychophysiology 38:267–74

598. Portegijs PJM, Jueken FMH, van der Horst FG, Kraan HF, Knotterus JA (1996). A troubled youth: Relations with somatization, depression and anxiety in adulthood. Family Practice 13:1–11

599. Post RM, Leverich GS, Xing G, Weiss RB (2001). Developmental vulnerabilities to the onset and course of bipolar disorder. Dev Psychopathol 13(3):581–98

600. Potter-Efron R, Potter-Efron P (1989). Letting Go of Shame: Understanding how shame affects your life. Hazelden, Center City Mn

601. Potter-Efron R & Potter-Efron P (1999). The Secret Message of Shame: Pathways to hope and healing. New Harbinger Publications, Oakland CA

602. Prevent Child Abuse America (2001). Data available on http://www.preventchildabuse.org/learn_more/research_docs/cost_analysis.pdf

603. Pribor EF, Dinwiddie SH (1992): Psychiatric correlates of incest in childhood. American Journal of Psychiatry 149 (1) 52–56

604. Putman FW, Trickett PK, Helmers K, Dorn L, Everett B (1991). Cortisol abnormalities in sexually abused girls. Paper presented at 144th Annual Meeting, Washington DC (Cited in De Bellis 2001)

605. Putnam FW (1998) Developmental pathways in sexually abused girls. Presented at Psychological Trauma: Maturational Processes and Psychotherapeutic interventions. Harvard Medical School, Boston MA. March 20.

Q _____

606. Queiroz EA, Lombardi AB, Furtado S, Peixoto CRH, Soares CCD, Fabre TA, Basquies ZL, Fernandes JC, Lippi JRS, (1991). Biochemical correlate of depression in children. Arquivos de Neuro-Psiquiatra 49:4125

607. Quick J (2001). Maintaining the integrity of the clinical evidence base. Bulletin of The World Health Organization 79(12):1093

608. Quitkin FM (1999). Placebos, Drug Effects, and Study Design: A Clinician's Guide. Am. J. Psychiatry 156: 829–836

608a. Ramsay R, Bagley C (1985). The prevalence of suicidal behaviors and associated experiences in an urban population. Suicide and life threatening behavior 15(2): 151–60

R

609. Rasmussen A (1934). Die bedeutung sexualler attentate auf kinder unter 14. Acta Psychiat et Neurlog 9:351; summarized in Bender & Blau 1937

610. Read JP, Stern AL, Wolfe J, Ouimette PC (1997a). Use of a screening instrument in women's health care: detecting relationships among victimization history, psychological distress, and medical complaints. Women Health 25(3):1–17

611. Read J, Fraser A (1998a) Abuse histories of psychiatric inpatients: To ask or not to ask. Psychiatric Services 49:355–59

612. Read J, Fraser A (1998b) Staff response to abuse histories of psychiatric inpatients. Australian and New Zealand Journal of Psychiatry 32:206–13

613. Read J (1998c). Child abuse and severity of disturbance among adult psychiatric inpatients. Child Abuse & Neglect 22:359–68

613a. Read J, Perry BD, Moskowitz A, Connolly J (2001). The contribution of early traumatic events to schizophrenia in some patients: a traumagenic neurodevelopmental model. Psychiatry 64:319–45

614. Reece RM (1998) Behavioral manifestations of child sexual abuse: response. Child Abuse & Neglect 22(6): 533–5

615. Regier DA, Farmer ME, Rae DS, Locke BZ, Keith SJ, Judd LL, & Goodwin FK (1990). Comorbidity of mental disorders with alcohol and other drug abuse: Results from the epidemeologic catchment area (ECA) study JAMA 264(19): 2511–2518

617. Regush N (2002). Prescribing untested drugs to children. NY Times April 3

618. Relman A (2001). Trust me, I'm a scientist. New Scientist 22 Sept. page 46–7

619. Rew L (1989): Childhood sexual exploitation: long-term effects among a group of nursing students. Issues in Mental Health Nursing 10: 181–191

620. Reynolds MW, Wallace, Hill, Weist MD, Nabors LA (2001). The relationship between gender, depression, and self-esteem in children who have witnessed domestic violence. Child Abuse & Neglect 25:1201–6

621. Roberts GL, Lawrence JM, Williams GM, Raphael B (1998). The impact of domestic violence on women's mental health. Australian and New Zealand of Public Health 22:796–801

622. Robins LN, Schoenberg SP, Holmes SJ, Ratcliff KS, Benham A, Works J (1985). Early home environment and retrospective recall: A test for concordance between siblings with and without psychiatric disorders. American Journal of Orthopsychiatry, 55, 27–41.

623. Robin RW, Chester B, Rasmussen JK, Jaranson JM, Goldman D (1997). Prevalence, characteristics and impact of childhood sexual abuse in a southwestern American Indian tribe. Child Abuse & Neglect 21(8):769–87

624. Robins L (1966). Deviant Children Grown Up. Williams and Wilkins, NY

625. Rodgers B (1994). Pathways between parental divorce and adult depression. Journal of Child Psychology and Psychiatry and Allied Disciplines 35:1289–1308

626. Rodriguez N, Ryan SW, Rowan AB, Foy DW (1996). Posttraumatic stress disorder in a clinical sample of adult survivors of childhood sexual abuse. Child Abuse Negl 1996 Oct;20(10):943–52

627. Roesler TA, McKenzie N (1994). Effects of childhood trauma on psychological functioning in adults sexually abused as children Journal of Nervous and Mental Disease 182:145–150

628. Roesler T (1994). Reactions to disclosure of childhood sexual abuse: The effect on adult symptoms. Journal of Nervous and Mental Diseases, 182, 618–624

629. Rohsenow DJ, Corbett R, Devine D (1988). Molested as children: a hidden contribution to substance abuse? Journal of Substance Abuse Treatment 5:13–18

630. Romans SE, Martin JL, Anderson JC, Herbison GP, Mullen PE (1995). Sexual abuse in childhood and deliberate self-harm. Am J Psychiatry. Sep; 152(9):1336–42

631. Romans SE, Martin JL, Anderson JC, O'Shea ML, Mullen PE (1995a). Factors that mediate between child sexual abuse and adult psychological outcome. Psychol Med. 25(1):127–42

632. Romans SE, Martin J, Mullen P (1996). Women's self-esteem a community study of women who report and do not report childhood sexual abuse. British Journal of Psychiatry 169: 696–704

633. Rorty M, Yager J, Rossotto E (1994a). Childhood sexual, physical, and psychological abuse and their relationship to comorbid psychopathology in bulimia nervosa. Int J Eat Disord 16(4):317–34

634. Rose S (2001). Moving on from old dichotomies: Beyond nature-nurture towards a lifetime perspective. British Journal of Psychiatry s3–s7.

635. Rose S, Peabody C, Stratigeas B (1991). Undetected abuse among intensive case management clients. Hospital and Community Psychiatry 42:499–50

635a. Rosen DH (1976). Suicide survivors: Psychotherapeutic implications of egocide. Suicide and Life-threatening Behavior 6:209–215

635b. Rosen DH (1976). Suicide survivors: a follow-up study of persons who survived jumping from the Golden Gate & San Francisco-Oakland Bay bridges. Western Journal of Medicine 122: 289

636. Rosenfeld AA (1979). Incidence of a history of incest among 18 female psychiatric patients American Journal of Psychiatry 136(6):791–5

637. Rosenthal PA, Rosenthal S (1984). Suicidal behavior by preschool children. American Journal of Psychiatry 141:520–5

638. Ross C, Pam A (eds) (1995). Pseudoscience in Biological Psychiatry: Blaming the Body. John Wiley, NY

639. Ross CA, Norton GR, Wozney K (1989). Multiple Personality Disorder: An Analysis of 236 Cases. Canadian Journal of Psychiatry 34(5):413–418

640. Ross CA, Miller SD, Reagor P, Bjornson L, Fraser GA, Anderson G (1990). Structured Interview Data on 102 Cases of Multiple Personality Disorder from Four Centers. American Journal of Psychiatry, 147(5):596–601

640a. Ross CA (1986). biological tests for mental illness: their use and misuse. Biological psychiatry 21:431–5

641. Ross CA, Kronson J, Koensgen S, Barkman K, Clark P, Rockman G (1992). Dissociative Comorbity in 100 Chemically Dependent Patients. Hospital and Community Psychiatry, 43:840–842

642. Ross CA, Anderson G, Clark P (1994). Childhood Abuse and the Positive Symptoms of Schizophrenia, Child and AdolescentPsychiatric Clinics of North America, 45 (5): May

643. Ross CA (2000). The Trauma Model: A solution to the problem of co-morbidity in psychiatry. Manitou publications, Richardson, TX

644. Ross CA (1995). Chapter 2. Errors of logic in biological psychiatry. In Ross CA & Pam A: Pseudoscience in Biological Psychiatry. John Wiley, NY

645. Ross CA (1995). Chapter 3. Pseudoscience in The American Journal of Psychiatry. In Ross CA & Pam A: Pseudoscience in Biological Psychiatry. John Wiley, NY

646. Rowan AB, Foy DW (1993). PTSD in child sexual abuse. Journal of Traumatic Stress 6:3–20

647. Rowan AB, Foy DW, Rodriguez N, Ryan S (1994). Post-traumatic stress

disorder in a clinical sample of adults sexually abused as children. Child Abuse Neglect 18: 51–61

648. Roy A (1985). Early parental separation and adult depression. Archives of General Psychiatry, 42:987–91

649. Roy A, 1990. Personality variables in depressed patients and normal controls. Neuropsychobiology 23, pp. 119–123

650. Roy A, 1996. Aetiology of secondary depression in male alcoholics. Br. J. Psychiatry 169, pp. 753–757

651. Roy A, DeJong J, Lamparski D and Linnoila M (1991). Mental disorders among alcoholics. Arch. Gen. Psychiatry 48, pp. 423–427

652. Roy A (1999). Childhood trauma and depression in alcoholics: Relationship to hostility. Journal of Affective Disorders 56(2–3);215–8

653. Ruggiero KJ, Mc Leer SV, Dickson JF (2000). Sexual abuse characteristics associated with survivor psychopathology. Child Abuse & Neglect 24(7): 951–64

S

654. Sacco ML, Farber BA (1999). Reality testing in adult women who report childhood sexual and physical abuse. Child Abuse Negl. 23(11):1193–203

655. Saigh PA, Yasik AE, Oberfield RA, Halamandaris PV, McHugh M (2002). An analysis of the internalizing and externalizing behaviors of traumatized urban youth with and without PTSD. J Abnorm Psychol 111(3):462–70

655a. Saigh PA, Bremner JD (1999). Posttraumatic Stress Disorder: a comprehensive text. Allyn & Bacon, NY

656. Salter A (1995). Transforming Trauma: A guide to understanding and treating adult survivors of child sexual abuse. Sage, Thousand Oaks, CA

657. Salzinger S, Kaplan S, Pelcovitz D, Samit C, Krieger R (1984). Parent and teacher assessment of children's behavior in child maltreating families. J Am Acad Child Psychiatry 23(4):458–64

658. Sanders B, Giolas MH (1991). Dissociation and childhood trauma in psychologically disturbed adolescents. American Journal of Psychiatry 148:50–4

559. Sanford M, Offord D, Boyle M, Pearce A (1992). Ontario child health study: social and school impairment in children age 6–16. Journal of the American Academy of Child and Adolescent Psychiatry 199:60–7

660. Sarno J (1982). Mind Over Back Pain: A Radically New Approach to Diagnosis and Treatment of Back Pain. Berkley Books, New York

661. Sarno JE (1991). Healing Back Pain. Warner Books, NY

662. Sansone RA, Gaither GA, Songer DA (2002). The relationships among childhood abuse, borderline personality, and self-harm behavior in psychiatric in-patients. Violence and Victims 17(1):49–55

663. Sansonnet-Hayden H, Haley G, Marriage K, Fine S (1987). Sexual abuse and psychopathology in hospitalized adolescents. J Am Acad Child Adolesc Psychiatry 26(5):753–7

664. Santa Mina EE, Gallop RM (1998). Childhood sexual and physical abuse and adult self-harm and suicidal behaviour: a literature review. Can J Psychiatry 43(8):793–800

665. Sapolsky RM (2000). Glucocorticoids and hippocampal atrophy in neuropsychiatric disorders. Arch Gen Psychiatry 57(10):925–35

666. Saunders BE, Villeponteaux LA, Lipovsky JA, Kilpatrick DG, Veronen IJ (1992). Child sexual assault as a risk factor for mental disorders among women: a community survey. Journal of Interpersonal Violence 7:189–204

667. Saunders BE, Hanson RF, Kilpatrick DG, Resnick H, Best CL (1991). Prevalence, case characteristics, & long-term psychological correlates of child rape among women: a national survey. Paper presented at the American Orthopsychiatric Association, Toronto, Canada

668. Saunders BE, Kilpatrick DG, Hanson RF, Resnick HS, Walker, ME (1999). Prevalence, case characteristics, and long-term psychological correlates of child rape among women: A national survey. Child Maltreatment, 4(3), 187–200

669. Schaaf KK, McCanne TR (1998). Relationship of childhood sexual, physical and combined sexual and physical abuse to adult victimization and PTSD. Child Abuse & Neglect 22:1119–33

670. Schaefer MR, Sobieraj K, Hollyfield RL (1988). Prevalence of childhood physical abuse in adult male veteran alcoholics. Child Abuse and Neglect 12:141–9

671. Schetky DH (1988). A review of the literature of the long-term effects of child sexual abuse. In RP Kluft (ed), Incest Related Syndromes of Adult Psychopathology (pp35–54). American Psychiatric Press, Washington, DC

672. Schiffer F, Teicher MH, Papanicolaou AC (1995). Evoked potential evidence for right brain activity during recall of traumatic memories. Journal of Neuropsychiatry and Clinical Neurosciences 7:169–175

673. Schiraldi GR (2000). The PTSD Sourcebook. Lowell House, Los Angeles

674. Schmidt U, Tiller J, Treasure J (1993). Setting the scene for eating disorders: Childhood care, classification and course of illness. Psychological Medicine 23: 663–672

675. Schuck AM, Widom CS (2001). Childhood victimization and alcohol symptoms in females: causal inferences and hypothesized mediators. Child Abuse & Neglect 25:1069–92

676. Schuckit M (1983). Alcoholic patients with secondary depression. American Journal of Psychiatry 140 (6): 711–714, 1983

677. Schuckit M, Tipp J, Bergman M, Reich W, Hesselbrock V, Smith T (1997). Comparison of induced and independent major depressive disorders in 2,945 alcoholics. Am. J. Psychiatry 154, pp. 948–957

678. Schuckit MA (1999). New findings in the genetics of alcoholism. JAMA 281:1875–1876

678a. Scott KD (1992). Childhood sexual abuse impact on a community's mental health status. Child Abuse & Neglect, 16:285–95

679. Sedney MA, Brooks B (1984). Factors associated with a history of childhood sexual experience in a non-clinical female population. Journal of The American academy of Child Psychiatry 23:215–8

680. Seligman MEP (1995). The effectiveness of psychotherapy: The Consumer Reports study. American Psychologist, 50, 965–974. Available www.apa.org/journals/seligman.html

681. Sendi IB, Blomgren PG (1975). A comparative study of predictive criteria in the predisposition of homicidal adolescents. American Journal of Psychiatry 132:423–7

682. Seng MJ (1989). Child sexual abuse and adolescent prostitution: A comparative analysis Adolescence xxiv (95) 24:665–75

683. Shaunesey K, Cohen JL, Plummer B, Berman A (1993).Suicidality in hospitalized adolescents: relationship to prior abuse. Am J Orthopsychiatry 63(1):113–9

684. Shapiro JP, Leifer M, Martone MW, Kassen L (1990). Multi-method assessment of depression in sexually abused girls. Journal of Personality Assessment 55:234–48

685. Shapiro F, Forrest MS (1997) E.M.D.R. Basic Books, NY

686. Sharav VH (2002) conflicts of interest: 14th tri-service clinical investigation symposium, US army medical department and the Henry Jackson foundation for the advancment of military medicine May 5–7

687. Shea MT, Zlotnick C, Weisberg RB (1999). Commonality and specificity of personality disorder profiles in subjects with trauma histories. J Personal Disord 13(3):199–210

688. Shea MT, Zlotnick C, Dolan R, Warshaw MG, Phillips KA, Brown P, Keller

MB (2000). Personality disorders, history of trauma, and posttraumatic stress disorder in subjects with anxiety disorders. Compr Psychiatry 41(5):315–25

689. Shearer SL, Peters CP, Quaytman MS, Ogden RL (1990). Frequency and correlates of childhood sexual and physical abuse histories in adult female borderline in-patients. American Journal of Psychiatry, 147: 214–16

690. Sheldrick C (1991). Adult sequelae of child sexual abuse. British Journal of Psychiatry 158 (10): 55–62

691. Shepard M, Raschick M (1999). How child welfare workers assess and intervene around issues of domestic violence. Child Maltreatment 4(2): 148–156

692. Shepherd M (1993). The placebo: from specificity to the non-specific and back. Psychological Medicine 23:569–78

693. Sher KJ, Gershuny BS, Peterson L, Raskin G (1997). The role of childhood stressors in intergenerational transmission of alcohol use disorders. Journal of Studies on Alcohol 58:414–27

694. Shetky DH (1990). Chapter 3 A review of the long-term effects of childhood sexual abuse. In Kluft RP (ed) Incest-Related Syndromes of Adult Psychopathology. American Psychiatric Press, NY

695. Shields A, Cicchetti D (1998). Reactive aggression among maltreated children: the contributions of attention and emotion dysregulation. Journal of Clinical Child Psychology 27:381–95

696. Shields A, Cicchetti D (2001). Parental maltreatment and emotion dysregulation as risk factors for bullying and victimization in middle childhood. Clinical Child Psychology 30(3):349–63

697. Shorter E (1997). A History of Psychiatry—From the Era of the Asylum to the Age of Prozac. Toronto, John Wiley & Son

698. Shrier LA, Pierce JD, Emans SJ, DuRant RH (1998).Gender differences in risk behaviors associated with forced or pressured sex. Arch Pediatr Adolesc Med 152(1):57–63

699. Schultz RK, Braun BG, Kluft RP (1989). Multiple personality disorder: Phenomenology of selected variables in comparison to major depression. Dissociation, 2, 45–51

700. Sidebotham P, Golding J (2001). Child maltreatment in the "children of the nineties" a longitudinal study of parental risk factors. Child Abuse & Neglect 25(9):1177–200

701. Siebert A (1999) Brain disease hypothesis disconfirmed by all evidence. J. of Ethical Human Sciences and Services. 1(2) 179–199

702. Siegel JM, Burham MA, Stein JA, Golding JM, Sorenson SB (1986). Sexual assault and psychiatric disorder: a preliminary investigation. A Report to the National Institute of Mental Health [no other data given]

703. Silberg JL (2000). Fifteen years of dissociation in maltreated children: where do we go from here? Child Maltreatment 5:119–136(18)

704. Silverman AB, Reinherz HZ & Giaconia RM (1996). The long-term sequelae of child and adolescent abuse: A longitudinal community study. Child Abuse and Neglect, 20: 709–723

705. Simos BG (1979). A Time To Grieve: Loss as a universal human experience. Family Services Association of America NY (One of the best books on grieving that I have read)

706. Simpson TL, Westerberg VS, Little LM, Trujillo M, 1994. Screening for childhood physical and sexual abuse among outpatient substance abusers. J. Subst. Abuse Treat. 11: 347–58

707. Sloane P, Karpenski E (1942). Effects of incest on the participants. American Journal of Orthopsychiatry 12:666–73

708. Stahl SM (1998). Selecting an anti-depressant by using mechanism of action to enhance efficacy & avoid side effects. Journal of Clinical Psychiatry 59 (suppl 18): 23–9

709. Smith D, Pearce L, Pringle M, Caplan R (1995). Adults with a history of child sexual abuse: Evaluation of a pilot therapy service. British Medical Journal 310:1175–78

709a. Smith A, Traganza E, Harrison G (1969). Studiues on the effectiveness of antidepressant drugs. Psychophamacology Bulletin (special issue), March, pages 1–53

710. Steiger H, Zanko M (1990). Sexual traumata among eating disordered, psychiatric, and normal female groups: Comparison of prevalences and defense styles. Journal of Interpersonal Violence, 5:74–86

711. Stein D, Baldwin S (2000). Toward an operational definition of disease in psychiatry and psychology: Implications for diagnosis and treatment. The International Journal of Risk and Safety in Medicine Volume 13 (1):29–46

712. Stein JA, Golding JM, Siegel JM, Burnam MA, Sorenson SB (1988). Long-term psychological sequelae of child sexual abuse: the Los Angeles Epidemologic Catchment Area Study. In Wyatt GE & Powell GJ (eds): Lasting Effects of Child Sexual Abuse (pp 135–154) Sage, 1000 Oaks CA

713. Stein MB, Yehuda R, Koverola C, Hanna C (1997). Enhanced dexamethasone suppression of plasma cortisol in adult women traumatized by childhood sexual abuse. Biol Psychiatry. 1997 Oct 15;42(8):680–6

714. Stein MB, Koverola C, Hanna C, Torchia MG, McClarty B (1997a). Hippocampal volume in women victimized by childhood sexual abuse. Psychological Medicine 27: 1–9

715. Stein P, Kendall J (2002). Stress, Trauma and the Developing Brain: How the new neurobiology is leading to more effective interventions for troubled children. Binghamton, NY: Haworth Press

716. Stein MB, Walker JR, Anderson G, Hazen A, Ross CA, Eldridge G, Forde, D (1996). Childhood physical and sexual abuse in patients with anxiety disorders and in a community sample. American Journal of Psychiatry, 153(2):275–277

717. Steinhausen H (1995) Children of alcoholic parents. A review. European Child and Adolescent Psychiatry 4:1430–152

718. Stermac L, Reist D, Addison M, Miller GM (2002). childhood risk factors for women's sexual victimization. Journal of Interpersonal Violence, 2002 17(6):647–670

719. Stern AE, Lynch DL, Oates RK, O'Toole BI, Cooney G (1995). Self-esteem, depression, behavior and family functioning in sexually abused girls. Journal of Child Psychology and Psychiatry 36:1077–1089

720. Stevenson J (1999). The treatment of the long-term sequelae of child abuse. J Child Psychol Psychiatry 1999 Jan;40(1):89–111

721. Storosum JG, Elferink AJA, van Zwieten BJ, van der Vrink W, Gersons BPR, van Strik R, Broekmans AW (2001). Short-term efficacy of tricyclic antidepressants revisited: a meta-analytic study. European Neuropsychopharmacology. 11:173–80

722. Styron T, Janoff-Bulman R (1997). Childhood attachment and abuse: long-term effects on adult attachment, depression and conflict resolution. Child Abuse & Neglect 21(10)1015–23

723. Sullivan EV, Fama R, Rosenbloom MJ, Pfefferbaum A (2002). A profile of neuropsychological deficits in alcoholic women. Neuropsychology 16(1):74–83

724. Surtees PG, Ingham JG (1980). Life stress and depressive outcome: Application of a dissipation model to life events. Social Psychiatry 15:21–31

725. Sussman N (2002). Depression and anxiety: remission as a goal. Ga Psychiatric CME symposium. Peachford Hospital, Astlanta, Ga March 16

726. Swanston HY, Tebbutt JS, O'Toole BI, Oates RK (1997). Sexually abused children 5 years after presentation: a case-control study. Pediatrics 100(4):600–8

727. Swanston HY, Parkinson PN, Oates RK, O'Toole BI, Plunkett AM, Shrimpton S (2002). Further abuse of sexually abused children. Child Abuse & Neglect 26:115–27

728. Swett C, Cohen C, Surrey J, Compaine A, Chavez R (1991). High rates of alcohol use and history of physical and sexual abuse among women out-patients. American Journal of Drug and Alcohol Abuse 17:49–60

729. Swett C, Halpert M (1993). Reported history of physical and sexual abuse in relation to dissociation and other symptomatology in women psychiatric inpatients. Journal of Interpersonal Violence 8(4):345–55, 1993

730. Swett C, Surrey J, Cohen C (1990). Sexual and physical abuse histories and psychiatric symptoms among male psychiatric out-patients. American Journal of Psychiatry 147(5):632–6

T

731. Talbot N, Houghtalen R, Duberstein P, Cox C, Giles D, & Wynne L (1999). Effects of group treatment for women with a history of childhood sexual abuse. Psychiatric Services 50:686–692. group Tx Add

732. Taylor RR, Jason LA (2001). Sexual abuse, physical abuse, chronic fatigue, and chronic fatigue syndrome: a community-based study. Journal of Nervous and Mental Disease 189:709–715

733. Tebbutt J, Swanston H, Oates RK, O'Toole BI (1997). Five years after child sexual abuse: persisting dysfunction and problems of prediction. J Am Acad Child Adolesc Psychiatry 36 (3): 330–9

734. Teicher MH (2000). Wounds that time wouldn't heal: the neurobiology of childhood abuse. Cerebrum 2, 50–67

735. Teicher, MH, Glod CA, Surrey J, Swett C Jr (1993). Early childhood abuse and limbic system ratings in adult psychiatric outpatients. Journal of Neuropsychiatry and Clinical Neurosciences 5:301–306.

736. Teicher MH, Ito YN, Glod CA, Schiffer F, Gelbard HA (1994). Early abuse, limbic system dysfunction, and borderline personality disorder. In K. Silk (Ed.), Biological and Neurobehavioral Studies of Borderline Personality Disorder, American Psychiatric Association Press, 177–207

737. Teicher MH, Ito YN, Glod CA, Andersen SL, Dumont N, Ackerman E (1997). Preliminary evidence for abnormal cortical development in physically and sexually abused children using EEG coherence and MRI. Annals New York Academy of Science 821:160–175

738. Teicher MH, Ito Y, Glod CA, Schiffer F, Ackerman E (1994). Possible

effects of early abuse on human brain development, as assessed by EEG coherence. Am. J. Neuropsychopharmacol. 33, 52

739. Terr LC (1991). Childhood traumas: an outline and overview American Journal of Psychiatry 148:10–20

740. The Kept University (2000). Atlantic Monthly, March 285 (Part 1–4):3954

741. Thompson A, Kaplan C (1999). Emotionally abused children presenting to child psychiatry clinics. Child Abuse & Neglect 23:191–196

742. Thompson KM, Braaten-Antrim R (1998). Youth maltreatment and gang involvement. Journal of Interpersonal Violence 13:328–45

743. Thompson KM, Wonderlich SA, Crosby RD, Mitchell JE (2001a). Sexual victimization and adolescent weight regulation practices: a test across three community based samples. Child Abuse Negl 2001 Feb;25(2):291–305

744. Thompson KM, Wonderlich SA, Crosby RD, Mitchell JE (2001b). Sexual violence and weight control techniques among adolescent girls. Int J Eat Disord 2001 Mar;29(2):166–76

745. Thompson KM, Crosby RD, Wonderlich SA, Mitchell JE, Redland J, Demuth G, Smyth J, Haseltine B (in press for 2002/3). Psychopathology and sexual trauma in childhood and adulthood. Journal of Traumatic Stress

746. Tienari P (1991). Interaction between genetic vulnerability and family environment. Acta Psychiatrica Scandinavica 84:460–65

746a. Tong L, Oates K, McDowell M (1987) Personality development following sexual abuse. Child Abuse & Neglect 11:371–83

747. Toth SL, Manly JT, Cicchetti D (1992). Child maltreatment and vulnerability to depression. Development and Psychopathology 4:97–112

748. Toth SL, Cicchetti D (1996). Patterns of relatedness, depressive symptomatology and perceived competence in maltreated children. Journal of Consultant and Clinical Psychology 64 (1): 32–41

749. Toth SL, Cicchetti D, Macfie J, Rogosch FA, Maughan A (2000). Narrative representations of moral-affiliative and conflictual themes and behavioral problems in maltreated preschoolers. J Clin Child Psychol 29(3):307–18

750. Trickett PK, Susman EJ (1988). Parental perceptions of child-rearing practices in physically abusive and nonabusive families. Developmental Psychology, 24, 270–276

751. Trickett PK, McBride-Chang C, Putnam FW (1994). The class room performance and behavior of sexually abused females. Development and Psychopathology 6:183–194

752. Triffelman EG, Marmar CR, Delucci KI, Ronfeldt H (1995). Childhood trauma and post-traumatic stress disorder in substance abuse in patients. Journal of Nervous and Mental Disease 183:172–6

753. Trowell J, Kolvin I, Weeramanthri T, Sadowski H, Berelowitz M, Glasser, D, Leitch I (2002). Psychotherapy for sexually abused girls: psychopathological outcome findings and patterns of change. British Journal of Psychiatry, 180:234–47

754. Tsai M, Feldman-Summers S, Edgar M (1979). Childhood molestation: variables related to differential impacts on psychosexual functioning in adult women. Journal of Abnormal Psychology 88 (4): 407–417

755. Tufts New England Medical Center, Child Psychiatry Division (1984). Sexually Exploited Children: Service and Research Project. Final Report of the Office of Juvenile Justice and Delinquency Prevention. Washington, DC, US Department of Justice

756. Turkheimer E (1998). Heritability and biological explanation. Psychological Review 105:782–91

U

757. Ullman SE, Siegel JM (1995). Sexual assault, social reactions, and physical health. Women's Health:Research on Gender, Behavior, and Policy 1(4):289–308

758. U.S. Dept. of Health and Human Services (1999). A Report of the Surgeon General—executive summary. Rockville, MD

V

759. Valenstein ES (1998). Blaming the Brain: the truth about drugs and mental health. Basic Books, NY

760. Van Buskirk SS Cole CF (1983). Characteristics of 8 women seeking therapy for effects of incest. Psychotherapy: Theory, Research, and Practice 20: 503–514, 1983

761. van der Kolk BA (1994).The body keeps the score: memory and the evolving psychobiology of posttraumatic stress. Harv Review of Psychiatry. Jan-Feb 1(5):253–65

762. van derKolk BA, Fisler RE (1994). Childhood abuse and neglect and loss of self-regulation. Bulletin of the Menninger Clinic 58:145–68

763. van der Kolk B, Fisler R (1995). Dissociation and the fragmentary nature of

traumatic memories: Overview and exploratory study. Journal of Traumatic Stress, 8:505–52

764. van Egmond M, Garnefski N, Jonker D, Kerkhof A (1993).The relationship between sexual abuse and female suicidal behavior. Crisis 14(3):129–39

765. Van Etten ME, Taylor S (1998). Comparative efficacy of treatments for posttraumatic stress disorder: A meta-analysis. Clinical Psychology & Psychotherapy, 5, 126–144

766. Van Praag, H (1993). "Make-believes" in psychiatry, or the perils of progress. Clinical and Experimental Psychiatry Monograph No. 7. New York: Brunner/Mazel

766a. Vedantam S (2000). Against depression, a sugar pill is hard to beat. Washington Post, May 7

767. Vize CM, Cooper PJ (1995). Sexual abuse in patients with eating disorders, patients with depression and normal controls: a comparitive study. British Journal of Psychiatry. 167: 80–85

768. Vythilingam M, Heim C, Newport J, Miller AH, Anderson E, Bronen R, Brummer M, Staib L, Vermetten E, Charney DS, Nemeroff CB, Bremner JD (2002). Childhood trauma associated with smaller hippocampal volume in women with major depression. Am J Psychiatry 159(12):2072–80

W _____

769. Wade N (2002). A dim view of "post human future" New York Times April 2

770. Wagner BM (1997). Family risk factors for child and adolescent suicidal behavior. Psychol Bull 121(2):246–98

771. Waldinger RJ, Swett C Jr, Frank A, Miller K.Levels of dissociation and histories of reported abuse among women outpatients

772. Walker E, Cudeck R, Mednick S, Schulsinger F (1981). Effects of parental absence and institutionalization on the development of clinical symptoms in high-risk children. Acta Psychiatrica Scandiavica 63:95–109

773. Walker EA, Katon WJ, Hansom J, Harrop-Griffiths J, Holm L, Jones ML, Hickok L, Jemelka RP (1992). Medical and psychiatric symptoms in women with childhood sexual abuse. Psychosom Med 54(6):658–64

774. Walker E, Diforio D, Baum, K (1998) Developmental neuropathology and the precursors of schizophrenia. Acta Psychiatric Scandinavica, 97:1–9

775. Walker EA, Katon WJ, Nerass K, Jemelka RP, Massoth D (1992).

Dissociation in women with chronic pelvic pain. American Journal of Psychiatry 149:534–7

776. Walker EA, Gelfand AN, Gellfand MD, Koss MP & Katon WJ (1995). Medical and psychiatric symptoms in female gastroenterology clinic—patients with histories of sexual victimization General Hospital Psychiatry 17:85–92

777. Walker EA, Unutzer J, Rutter C, Gelfand A, Saunders K, Von Korff M, Koss MP, Katon W (1999). Costs of healthcare use by women HMO members with a history of childhood abuse and neglect. Archives of General Psychiatry 56:609–13

778. Walker EA, Gelfand A, Katon WJ, Koss MP, Von Korff M, Bernstein D, Russo J (1999). Adult health status of women with histories of childhood abuse and neglect. Am J Med 107(4):332–9

779. Walker E, DiFornio D (1997). Schizophrenia: A neural diathesis-stress model. Psychological Review 104:667–85

780. Wallen J, Berman K (1992). Possible indicators of childhood sexual abuse for individuals in substance abuse treatment. Journal of Child Sexual Abuse, 1 (3): 63–74

781. Weaver TL, Clum GA (1993). Early family environments and traumatic experiences with borderline personality disorder. Journal of Consulting and Clinical Psychology 61:1068–75

782. Weiss MJ, Wagner SH (1998). What explains the negative consequences of adverse childhood experiences on adult health? Insights from cognitive and neuroscience research. Am J Prev Med 14(4):356–60

783. Westen D, Ludolph P, Misle B, Ruffins S, Block J (1990). Physical and sexual abuse in adolescent girls with borderline personality disorder. Am J Orthopsychiatry 60(1):55–66

784. Wexler B, Lyons L, Lyons H, Mazure C (1997). Physical and sexual abuse during childhood and development of psychiatric illness during adulthood. J. Nerv. Ment. Dis. 185: 522–4

785. Whealin JM, Jackson JL (2002). Childhood unwanted sexual attention and young women's present self-concept. Journal of Interpersonal Violence, 17 (8): 854–871

786. Whitfield BH (1995). Spiritual Awakenings: Insights of the near-death experience and other doorways to our soul. Deerfield Beach, FL: Health Communications

787. Whitfield BH (1998). Final Passage: Sharing the journey as this life ends. Deerfield Beach, FL: Health Communications

788. Whitfield CL (1988). Advances in alcoholism & chemical dependence. American Journal of Medicine 85(4):465

789. Whitfield CL, Anda RF, Dube S, Felitti VJ (2003). Violent childhood experiences and the risk of intimate partner violence in adults: assessment in a large health maintenance organization. Journal of Interpersonal Violence 18(2)166–185

790. Whitfield CL, Silberg J, Fink P (eds) (2001). Exposing misinformation concerning child sexual abuse and adult survivors. Journal of Child Sexual Abuse 9(3–4):1–8, special volume also published separately by Haworth Press, Binghamton, NY, 2002

791. Whitfield CL, Stock WE (1996). Traumatic amnesia in 100 survivors of childhood sexual abuse. Presented at the national conference on trauma & memory (peer-reviewed), Univ. of New Hampshire, July

792. Whitfield CL (1998). Adverse childhood experience and trauma (editorial). American Journal of Preventive Medicine, 14(4):361–364, May

793. Whitfield CL (1991). A Gift to Myself: A personal workbook and guide to healing. Health Communications, Deerfield Beach, FL

794. Whitfield CL (1995). Memory and Abuse: Remembering and healing the wounds of trauma. (p. 238–242) Health Communications, Deerfield Beach FL

795. Whitfield CL (1998). Internal evidence and corroboration of traumatic memories of child sexual abuse with addictive disorders. Sexual Addiction & Compulsivity 5:269–292

796. Whitfield CL (1997). Internal verification and corroboration of traumatic memories. Journal of Child Sexual Abuse 6(3):99–122

796a. Whitfield CL (2001): The false memory defense: using disinformation in and out of court. Journal of Child Sexual Abuse 9(3–4):53–78

797. Whitfield CL (1993). Boundaries and Relationships: Knowing, protecting and enjoying the self. Health Communications, Deerfield Beach, FL

798. Whitfield CL (1995). Memory and Abuse: Remembering and Healing the Effects of Trauma. Health Communications, Deerfield Beach, FL

798a. Whitfield CL (2003). My Recovery Plan Healing from Illness in 3 Stages. Health Communications, Deerfield Beach, FL

799. Widom CS, Shepard RL (1996). Accuracy of adult recollections of childhood

victimization: Part 1. Childhood physical abuse. Psychological Assessment. 8: 412–421

800. Widom CS, Morris S (1997). Accuracy of adult recollections of childhood victimization: Part 2. Childhood sexual abuse. Psychological Assessment, 9: 34–46

801. Widom CS (1999). Posttraumatic stress disorder in abused and neglected children grown up. American Journal of Psychiatry, 156: 1223–1229

802. Widom CS, Ireland TO, Glynn PG. (1995). Alcohol abuse in abused and neglected children followed-up: are they at increased risk? Journal of the Study of Alcohol, 56: 207–217

803. Wiesegger G, Schloegelhofer M, Eder H, Itzlinger U, Leisch F, Bailer U, Hornik K, Jorgl G, Willinger U, Aschauer HN (2002). Bibliotherapy—cognitive-behavioral self help strategies in patients with major depression. Eur Psychiatry May;17 Suppl 1:174–5

804. Wilsnack RW, Wilsnack SC, Krisjainson P, Harris TR (1998). Ten year prediction of women's drinking behavior in a national representative sample. Women's Health: Research on Gender, Behavior and Policy 4(3):199–230

805. Wilsnack SC, Vogeltanz ND, Klassen AD, Harris TR (1997). Childhood sexual abuse and women's substance abuse: national survey findings. Journal of Studies on Alcohol 58:264–71

806. Wilsnack SC, Wonderlich SA, Kristjanson AF, Vogeltanz-Holm ND, Wilsnack RW (2002). Self-reports of forgetting and remembering childhood sexual abuse in a nationally representative sample of US women. Child Abuse Negl 26(2):139–47

807. Wilson JP, Friedman MJ, Lindey JD (2001). Treating Psychological Trauma and PTSD. Guilford, New York

808. Wind TW, Silvern L (1992). Type and extent of child abuse as predictors of adult functioning Juumal of Family Violence, 7. 261–281

809. Winfield I, George LK, Swartz M, Blazer DG (1990). Sexual assault and psychiatric disorders among a community sample of women. Am J Psychiatry 147(3):335–41

810. Windle M, Windle RC, Scheidt DM, Miller GB (1995). Physical and sexual abuse and associated mental disorders among alcoholic in-patients. American Journal of Psychiatry 152: 1322–8 802

811. Windle M, Windle RC (2001). Depressive symptoms and cigarette smoking among middle adolescents: prospective associations and intrapersonal and interpersonal influences. J Consult Clin Psychol. 69(2):215–26

812. Winokur G (1997). All roads lead to depression: clinically homogeneous,

etiologically heterogeneous. J Affect Disord 1997 45(1–2):97–108

813. Wolfsdorf BA, Zlotnick C (2001). Affect management in group therapy for women with posttraumatic stress disorder and histories of childhood sexual abuse. J Clin Psychol 2001 Feb;57(2):169–81

814. Wonderlich S, Wusnack R, Wisnack S, & Harris TR (1996). Childhood sexual abuse and bulimic behavior in a nationally representative sample. American Journal of Public Health, 86, 1082–1086

815. Wonderlich S, Crosby R, Mitchell J, Thompson K, Redlin J, Demuth G, Smyth J (2001). Pathways mediating sexual abuse and eating disturbance in children. Int J Eat Disord 29(3):270–9

816. Wood BL (1987). Children of Alcoholism: The Struggle for Self and Intimacy in Adult life. University Press, NY

817. Wozencraft T, Vagner W, Pellegrin A (1991): Depression and suicidal ideation in sexually abused children. Child Abuse & Neglect 15: 505–511

818. Wozniak J, Crawford MH, Biederman J, Faraone SV, Spencer TJ, Taylor A, Blier HK (1999). Antecedents and complications of trauma in boys with ADHD: findings from a longitudinal study. J Am Acad Child Adolesc Psychiatry 38(1):48–55

819. Wurr JC, Partridge IM (1996). The prevalence of a history of childhood sexual abuse in an acute adult in patient population Child Abuse & Neglect 20:867–72

820. Wurtele SK, Kaplan GM, Keairnes M (1990). Childhood sexual abuse among chronic pain patients. Clin J Pain 6(2):110–3

821. Wyatt GE (1985). The sexual abuse of Afro-American and White American women in childhood. Child Abuse & Neglect, 9:507–519

Y

822. Yama MF, Tovey SL, Forgas BS, Teegarden LA (1992). Joint consequences of parental alcoholism and childhood sexual abuse, and their partial mediation by family environment. Violence & Victimology 7(4):313–25

823. Yama MF, Tovey SL, Fogas BS (1993). Childhood family environment and sexual abuse as predictors of anxiety and depression in adult women. American Journal of Orthopsychiatry. 63: 136–141

824. Young EA, Abelson JL, Curtis GC, Nesse RM (1997). Childhood adversity and vulnerability to mood and anxiety disorders. Depress Anxiety 5(2):66–72

825. Young EB (1990): The role of incest in relapse. Journal of Psychoactive Drugs, 22: 249–258

Z

826. Zanarini MC, Gunderson JG, Marino MF, Schwartz EO, Frankenburg FR (1989). Childhood experiences of borderline patients. Comprehensive Psychiatry 30:18–25

827. Zlotnick C, Ryan CE, Miller IW, Keitner GI (1995). Childhood abuse and recovery from major depression. Child Abuse Negl 19:1513–1516

828. Zlotnick C (1999). Antisocial personality disorder, affect dysregulation and childhood abuse among incarcerated women. J Personal Disord 13(1):90–5

829. Zlotnick C (2001). Mattia J.I.; Zimmerman M. The relationship between posttraumatic stress disorder, childhood trauma and alexithymia in an outpatient sample. Journal of Traumatic Stress, January vol. 14, no. 1, pp. 177–188(12)

830. Zlotnick C, Mattia J, Zimmerman M (2001). Clinical features of survivors of sexual abuse with major depression. Child Abuse Negl 2001 Mar;25(3):357–67

831. Zuravin SJ, Fontanella C (1999). The relationship Between Child Sexual Abuse and Major Depression Among Low-Income Women: A Function of Growing Up Experiences? Child Maltreatment 4:3–12

Note: Some journal titles are abbreviated.

Index

Numbers *in italics* indicate tables and figures.